AMC'S BEST DAY HIKES NEAR
BOSTON

Four-Season Guide to 60 of the Best Trails in Eastern Massachusetts

4th Edition // Michael Tougias • John S. Burk • Alison O'Leary

Appalachian Mountain Club Books // Boston, Massachusetts

AMC is a nonprofit organization, and sales of AMC Books fund our mission of protecting the Northeast outdoors. If you appreciate our efforts and would like to become a member or make a donation to AMC, visit outdoors.org, call 617-523-0626, or contact us at Appalachian Mountain Club, 10 City Square, Boston, MA 02129.

outdoors.org/books-maps

Distributed by National Book Network.

Front cover photograph of Blue Hills Reservation by Paula Champagne © Appalachian Mountain Club
Back cover photograph of Middlesex Fells Reservation by Matthew Grymek © Appalachian Mountain Club
Title page photo of the Blue Hills Reservation Skyline Trail © Michael Tougias
Interior photographs © John S. Burk, except pages 65, 68, 82, 157, 161, 166, 192, 219, 223, 236, 241 © Alison O'Leary, and as otherwise noted
Maps by Ken Dumas © Appalachian Mountain Club
Cover design by Jon Lavalley
Text design by Abigail Coyle

Library of Congress Cataloging-in-Publication Data
Names: Tougias, Mike, 1955- author. | Burk, John S., author. | O'Leary, Alison, author. | Appalachian Mountain Club.
Title: AMCs best day hikes near Boston : four-season guide to 60 of the best trails in Eastern Massachusetts / Michael Tougias, John S. Burk, Alison O'Leary.
Description: Fourth edition. | Boston, Massachusetts : Appalachian Mountain Club Books, 2022. | Includes index. | Summary: "A guide to the best hikes near Boston that can be completed in a single day"-- Provided by publisher.
Identifiers: LCCN 2022016098 (print) | LCCN 2022016099 (ebook) | ISBN 9781628421484 (trade paperback) | ISBN 9781628421491 (epub) | ISBN 9781628421507 (mobi)
Subjects: LCSH: Hiking--Massachusetts--Guidebooks. | Trails--Massachusetts--Guidebooks. | Massachusetts--Guidebooks.
Classification: LCC GV199.42.M4 T68 2022 (print) | LCC GV199.42.M4 (ebook) | DDC 917.4404/4--dc23
LC record available at https://lccn.loc.gov/2022016098
LC ebook record available at https://lccn.loc.gov/2022016099

The paper used in this publication meets the minimum requirements of the American National Standard for Information Sciences-Permanence of Paper for Printed Library Materials, ANSI Z39.48-1984. ∞

Outdoor recreation activities by their very nature are potentially hazardous. This book is not a substitute for good personal judgment and training in outdoor skills. Due to changes in conditions, use of the information in this book is at the sole risk of the user. The authors and the Appalachian Mountain Club assume no liability for accidents happening to, or injuries sustained by, readers who engage in the activities described in this book.

Interior pages and cover are printed on responsibly harvested paper stock certified by The Forest Stewardship Council®, an independent auditor of responsible forestry practices.
Printed in the United States of America, using vegetable-based inks.

5 4 3 2 1   22 23 24 25 26

MIX
Paper from responsible sources
FSC
www.fsc.org   FSC® C005010

Dedicated to my friends Frank Quirk III,
Maureen Quirk, Sharon Fish, and Gard Estes.

—Michael Tougias

To my family for their support and encouragement (and
exploring some of these trails with me), and to the organizations
responsible for the protection of these special places.

—John S. Burk

To all of those who need a daily dose of nature.

—Alison O'Leary

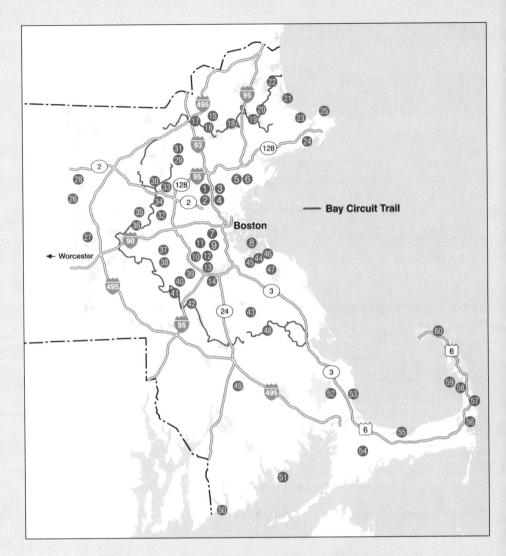

— Bay Circuit Trail

Boston

← Worcester

Icon	Description	Icon	Description
	Difficult brook crossing		Swimming
	Good for kids		Picnic area
	Dog-friendly		Visitor center
	Accessible		Public transit
	Pond, stream, spring, or other water feature		Fee
	Snowshoeing		Fishing
	Cross-country skiing		Horseback riding
	Scenic views		Bicycle trails
	Designated tentsite		

CONTENTS

Locator Map/Key to Icons   iv
At-a-Glance Trip Planner   viii
Preface   xvi
Acknowledgments   xviii
Introduction   xix
How to Use This Book   xx
Trip Planning and Safety   xxi
Leave No Trace   xxiv

1 // BOSTON/INSIDE ROUTES 95 AND 128   1

1 Middlesex Fells: Skyline Trail   3
2 Middlesex Fells: Reservoir Trail   8
3 Middlesex Fells: Rock Circuit Trail   12
4 Middlesex Fells: Cross Fells Trail   16
5 Breakheart Reservation   21
6 Lynn Woods Reservation   25
7 Arnold Arboretum   29
8 Spectacle Island   34
9 Stony Brook Reservation   39
10 Blue Hills Reservation: Observation Tower Loop   44
11 Blue Hills Reservation: Great Blue Hill Green Loop   49
12 Blue Hills Reservation: Ponkapoag Pond   53
13 Blue Hills Reservation: Houghton's Pond Yellow Dot Loop   58
14 Blue Hills Reservation: Skyline Trail   62

2 // NORTH OF BOSTON   69

15 Weir Hill Reservation   71
16 Charles W. Ward Reservation   75
17 Baker's Meadow   80
18 Bald Hill Reservation   84
19 Ipswich River Wildlife Sanctuary   88

20 Bradley Palmer State Park   93
21 Parker River National Wildlife Refuge (Plum Island)   97
22 Old Town Hill   102
23 Crane Beach   106
24 Ravenswood Park   111
25 Halibut Point State Park and Reservation   115

3 // WEST OF BOSTON   119

26 Wachusett Reservoir and Reservation   121
27 Mount Pisgah Conservation Area   126
28 Oxbow National Wildlife Refuge   130
29 Great Brook Farm State Park   134
30 Great Meadows National Wildlife Refuge   138
31 Minute Man National Historical Park: Battle Road Trail   142
32 Walden Pond   146
33 Lincoln Conservation Land   151
34 Nobscot Hill and Tippling Rock   155
35 Callahan State Park   159
36 Sudbury Reservoir   164
37 Broadmoor Wildlife Sanctuary   169
38 Rocky Narrows Reservation and Sherborn Town Forest   173
39 Noanet Woodlands   178
40 Rocky Woods Reservation   182

4 // SOUTH OF BOSTON/CAPE COD   187

41 Moose Hill Wildlife Sanctuary   189
42 Borderland State Park   194
43 Ames Nowell State Park   198
44 Great Esker Park   202
45 World's End Reservation   207
46 Whitney and Thayer Woods   212
47 Massasoit State Park   217
48 Burrage Pond   221
49 North Hill Marsh Wildlife Sanctuary   225
50 Allens Pond Wildlife Sanctuary   229
51 West Island   234
52 Myles Standish State Forest   238
53 Ellisville Harbor State Park   243

54 Lowell Holly Reservation   247
55 Sandy Neck Circuit   251
56 Nickerson State Park   256
57 Fort Hill   260
58 Wellfleet Bay Wildlife Sanctuary   265
59 Great Island   270
60 Cape Cod National Seashore: Pilgrim Heights   275

NATURE AND HISTORY ESSAYS

Introduced Pests: A Threat to Our Eastern Forests   38
An Urban Oasis   48
Endangered Predator: Eastern Timber Rattlesnake   67
The Life and Times of a Bog   79
Massachusetts's Watershed Wilderness   125
Henry David Thoreau: Naturalist, Explorer, and Writer   150
King Philip's War: An Early American Conflict   177
Climate Change in New England   206
Cranberries in New England   216
Great White Sharks Return to Massachusetts   264
The Birth of Cape Cod National Seashore   279

APPENDICES

A: Camping and State Parks   280
B: The Bay Circuit Trail   286

Index   288
About the Authors   293
About AMC in Massachusetts   293
AMC Books Updates   293

AT-A-GLANCE TRIP PLANNER

Trip number	Trip name and location	Difficulty rating	Round-trip distance	Elevation gain	Estimated time
SECTION 1 // BOSTON/INSIDE ROUTES 95 AND 128					
1	Middlesex Fells: Skyline Trail *Stoneham, Medford, and Winchester, MA*	Strenuous	6.8 mi	1,400 ft	5 hrs
2	Middlesex Fells: Reservoir Trail *Stoneham, Medford, and Winchester, MA*	Moderate	5.2 mi	1,000 ft	3 hrs
3	Middlesex Fells: Rock Circuit Trail *Medford, Melrose, and Malden, MA*	Strenuous	4 mi	875 ft	3.5 hrs
4	Middlesex Fells: Cross Fells Trail *Stoneham, Medford, Melrose, and Malden, MA*	Moderate–Strenuous	4.3 mi	865 ft	5 hrs
5	Breakheart Reservation *Saugus, MA*	Moderate	2.7 mi	410 ft	2 hrs
6	Lynn Woods Reservation *Lynn, MA*	Easy–Moderate	3.7 mi	450 ft	2 hrs
7	Arnold Arboretum *Boston, MA*	Easy–Moderate	4.1 mi	230 ft	3 hrs
8	Spectacle Island *Boston, MA*	Easy	3 mi	150 ft	1.25 hrs
9	Stony Brook Reservation *Boston, MA*	Easy	2.6 mi	Minimal	1.5 hrs
10	Blue Hills Reservation: Observation Tower Loop *Canton and Milton, MA*	Moderate	2 mi	400 ft	1.5 hrs
11	Blue Hills Reservation: Great Blue Hill Green Loop *Canton and Milton, MA*	Easy–Moderate	2.8 mi	200 ft	1.5 hrs
12	Blue Hills Reservation: Ponkapoag Pond *Canton and Randolph, MA*	Easy	4 mi	Minimal	2 hrs
13	Blue Hills: Houghton's Pond Yellow Dot Loop *Milton, MA*	Easy	1 mi	Minimal	30 mins
14	Blue Hills Reservation: Skyline Trail *Canton, Milton, and Quincy, MA*	Strenuous	9 mi (full traverse); 2.4 mi (North and South Skyline trails loop)	1,800 ft (full traverse); 700 ft (North and South Skyline Trails loop)	6 hrs (full traverse); 1.75 hrs (North and South Skyline trails loop)

Trip highlights	Trip features
Long-distance circuit, great view of Boston	
Views of three reservoirs	
Views, rugged hills, waterfall	
Rocky hills, diverse forests	
Saugus River, rocky outcroppings	
Hilltop views, rock caves, pond	
Scenic paths, botanical gardens	
Boston views, beaches	
Peaceful forest trails, wetlands	
Observation tower, trailside museum	
Wetlands, forest, trailside museum	
Large scenic pond, bog, views of Blue Hills	
Easy loop, ideal for families	
Long-distance trail, hilltop vistas	

Trip number	Trip name and location	Difficulty rating	Round-trip distance	Elevation gain	Estimated time
SECTION 2 // NORTH OF BOSTON					
15	Weir Hill Reservation *North Andover, MA*	Moderate	2.3 mi	170 ft	1.5 hrs
16	Charles W. Ward Reservation *Andover, MA*	Easy–Moderate	3.6 mi	290 ft	2.5 hrs
17	Baker's Meadow *Andover, MA*	Easy–Moderate	2.5 mi	30 ft	1.5–2 hrs
18	Bald Hill Reservation *Boxford, MA*	Easy–Moderate	2.8 mi	150 ft	2 hrs
19	Ipswich River Wildlife Sanctuary *Topsfield, MA*	Easy–Moderate	3.2 mi	100 ft	2 hrs
20	Bradley Palmer State Park *Hamilton and Topsfield, MA*	Easy	3.3 mi	255 ft	2 hrs
21	Parker River National Wildlife Refuge (Plum Island) *Newburyport, MA*	Easy	1.6 mi	50 ft	1 hr
22	Old Town Hill *Newbury, MA*	Easy–Moderate	2.9 mi	300 ft	1.5 hrs
23	Crane Beach *Ipswich, MA*	Moderate	3 mi	270 ft	2.5 hrs
24	Ravenswood Park *Gloucester, MA*	Easy–Moderate	2.7 mi	360 ft	2 hrs
25	Halibut Point State Park and Reservation *Rockport, MA*	Easy	1.5 mi	Minimal	1 hr
SECTION 3 // WEST OF BOSTON					
26	Wachusett Reservoir and Reservation *West Boylston, MA*	Easy	4.2 mi	225 ft	2.25 hrs
27	Mount Pisgah Conservation Area *Northborough, MA*	Easy	1.75 mi	115 ft	1–1.5 hrs
28	Oxbow National Wildlife Refuge *Harvard, MA*	Easy	1.9 mi	Minimal	1.25 hrs
29	Great Brook Farm State Park *Carlisle, MA*	Easy	2.25 mi; 3 mi with extenstion	Minimal	1.5 hrs; 2 hrs with extension
30	Great Meadows National Wildlife Refuge *Concord, MA*	Easy	1.7 mi	Minimal	1 hr
31	Minute Man National Historical Park: Battle Road Trail *Concord, Lincoln, and Lexington, MA*	Moderate	5 mi	Minimal	3 hrs

Trip highlights	Trip features
Hilltop view, trail along pond shore	
Bog, wetlands, solstice stones	
Wildlife-filled pond, easy-to-follow trails	
Hilltop meadow, historic farm site, wetlands	
Boardwalks, ponds, small island, rockery	
Former estate, well-maintained trails	
Barrier beach, renowned for birding	
Views from hilltop meadow, tidal marshes and river	
Dunes, white-sand beach, Castle Neck estuary	
Rare magnolia swamp, boardwalk	
Rocky shoreline, historic quarry, views to Maine	
Shore views, excellent birding and wildlife	
Scenic vistas, streams, good for kids	
Nashua River and associated wetlands	
Scenic pond, historic mill and mill sites	
Concord River floodplain, abundant wildlife	
Historic sites; farm, field, and wetland views	

Trip number	Trip name and location	Difficulty rating	Round-trip distance	Elevation gain	Estimated time
32	Walden Pond *Concord, MA*	Easy	3 mi	270 ft	1.5 hrs
33	Lincoln Conservation Land *Lincoln, MA*	Moderate	3 mi	50 ft	1.5 hrs
34	Nobscot Hill and Tippling Rock *Sudbury and Framingham, MA*	Moderate	4 mi	515 ft	2.25 hrs
35	Callahan State Park *Framingham, MA*	Moderate	2.75 mi	230 ft	2 hrs
36	Sudbury Reservoir *Southborough and Framingham, MA*	Easy	4 mi	75 ft	2 hrs
37	Broadmoor Wildlife Sanctuary *Natick and Sherborn, MA*	Moderate	3 mi	50 ft	1.5–2 hrs
38	Rocky Narrows Reservation and Sherborn Town Forest *Sherborn, MA*	Moderate	2.7 mi	165 ft	1.5 hrs
39	Noanet Woodlands *Dover, MA*	Moderate	3.5 mi	230 ft	1.75 hrs
40	Rocky Woods Reservation *Medfield, MA*	Easy–Moderate	3.5 mi (southern section); 3.1 mi (northern section)	180 ft (southern section); 360 ft (northern section)	1.5 hrs (southern section); 1.75 hrs (northern section)

SECTION 4 // SOUTH OF BOSTON/CAPE COD

Trip number	Trip name and location	Difficulty rating	Round-trip distance	Elevation gain	Estimated time
41	Moose Hill Wildlife Sanctuary *Sharon, MA*	Moderate	2.5 mi (The Bluffs); 1.75 mi (Ovenbird/ Kettle trails)	130 ft (The Bluffs); 50 ft (Ovenbird/ Kettle trails)	1.5–2 hrs (The Bluffs); 1 hr (Ovenbird/ Kettle trails)
42	Borderland State Park *North Easton, MA*	Moderate	3.5 mi	50 ft	1.75 hrs
43	Ames Nowell State Park *Abington, MA*	Easy	2 mi	Minimal	1 hr
44	Great Esker Park *Weymouth, MA*	Easy	1.5 mi	285 ft	1 hr
45	World's End Reservation *Hingham, MA*	Moderate	4.5 mi	300 ft	3 hrs
46	Whitney and Thayer Woods *Hingham and Cohasset, MA*	Easy	3 mi	200 ft	1.75 hrs
47	Massasoit State Park *East Taunton, MA*	Moderate	4 mi	Minimal	2.5 hrs
48	Burrage Pond *Hanson and Halifax, MA*	Easy	3 mi	90 ft	2 hrs

Trip highlights	Trip features
Pond views, Thoreau cabin site	
Forested hill, Sudbury River floodplain	
Highest point on Bay Circuit Trail, outstanding views	
Traditional New England mix of carriage roads and trails	
Gentle walk along historic reservoir	
Boardwalks along wetlands, glacial drumlins	
Rugged hillsides, highlight of Charles River Valley	
Historic millponds, hilltop vista	
Scenic vistas, ponds, rock canyon	
Hilltop overlook, meadows, wildlife	
Close-up views of ponds, meadows	
Variety of wildlife and terrain	
Unique geological ridge, river and marsh views	
Scenic views, coastal peninsula	
Rhododendron and laurel groves, glacial boulders	
Glacial topography, waterfowl, historic sites	
Views of open cranberry bog	

Trip number	Trip name and location	Difficulty rating	Round-trip distance	Elevation gain	Estimated time
49	North Hill Marsh Wildlife Sanctuary *Duxbury, MA*	Moderate	3.3 mi	110 ft	2 hrs
50	Allens Pond Wildlife Sanctuary *Dartmouth, MA*	Easy–Moderate	5.9 mi	130 ft	3.25 hrs
51	West Island *Fairhaven, MA*	Easy	1.75 mi	Minimal	1–1.5 hrs
52	Myles Standish State Forest *Plymouth and Carver, MA*	Moderate–Strenuous	3 mi (East Head Reservoir Trail); 4.5 mi (Bentley Loop); 7.5 mi (combined loop)	50 ft	2–4 hrs
53	Ellisville Harbor State Park *Plymouth, MA*	Easy	2 mi	75 ft	1.5 hrs
54	Lowell Holly Reservation *Mashpee and Sandwich, MA*	Easy–Moderate	3.1 mi	100 ft	1.5 hrs
55	Sandy Neck Circuit *Barnstable, MA*	Moderate	4.7 mi	Minimal	2–3 hrs
56	Nickerson State Park *Brewster, MA*	Easy–Moderate	2.9 mi	50 ft	1.75 hrs
57	Fort Hill *Eastham, MA*	Easy	2 mi	50 ft	1 hr
58	Wellfleet Bay Wildlife Sanctuary *South Wellfleet, MA*	Easy	2.3 mi	50 ft	1.5 hrs
59	Great Island *Wellfleet, MA*	Moderate	4 mi	120 ft	2.5 hrs
60	Cape Cod National Seashore: Pilgrim Heights *Truro, MA*	Easy	1.3 mi	115 ft	1 hr

Trip highlights	Trip features
Large pond and marshes, cranberry bog	🚶 🐕 🔍 ⛷️
Coastal views, diverse habitats, outstanding birding	🚶 ♿ 💧 🔍 ❄️ ⛺
Oceanfront hike, horizon views	🚶 🐕
Pitch-pine and scrub oak woods, kettle ponds	🚶 🐕 💧 🔍 ⛷️ 🐎 🚲
Rocky beach, harbor seal colony, salt marsh	🚶 🐕 💧 ❄️ 🏊 ⛺
Beech and American holly groves, ponds	🚶 🐕 💧 🔍 ⛷️ ❄️ 🏊 ⛺ 🎣
Barrier beach, dunes, large salt marsh	🐕 💧 🔍 ⛷️ ❄️ 🏊 $
Large kettle pond, beaches, vista	🚶 🐕 💧 🔍 ⛷️ ❄️ ⛺ 🏊 ⛺ 🚻 $ 🛶 🚲
Scenic coastal views, meadows, red maple swamp	🚶 💧 🔍 ⛷️ ❄️ ⛺ 🚌
Tidal flats, salt marsh, wildlife, family trails	🚶 ♿ 💧 🔍 ❄️ ⛺ 🚻 $
Tall dunes, pine woods, marsh, historic site	🔍 ❄️ 🏊 ⛺ 🚌
Overlooks, historic sites, great for families	🚶 💧 🔍 ❄️ ⛺ 🚌 🚲

PREFACE

Hiking and visiting natural places can "wash your spirit clean," according to the naturalist John Muir.

Despite high population density and development, eastern Massachusetts is home to a surprisingly extensive and diverse array of conservation lands and trails that offer opportunities to explore tidal flats and salt marshes bordering scenic ocean beaches; to enjoy challenging full-day hikes in the rugged Middlesex Fells and Blue Hills; and to stroll through deep woods and around lakes and ponds visited by moose, black bears, fishers, and common loons.

Many of the preserves lie inside the I-95/Route 128 corridor, including several within Boston's city limits, while others offer solitude in less traveled locales. Although humans have made changes to the natural topography—such as leveling hills near Boston, creating cranberry bogs, and damming the natural flow of rivers—the wildlife has adapted and, where sufficient habitat remains, flourished.

For this fourth edition, we have added new hikes at Old Town Hill in Newbury, Baker's Meadow in Andover, Callahan State Park and Sudbury Reservoir on the Bay Circuit Trail in Framingham, and Allens Pond Wildlife Sanctuary and West Island on the southeast coast. We have also revisited and updated 54 hikes from the previous edition. Our goal is to inspire people to get out and explore while making it as easy as possible to do so with updated information on trail routes, descriptions, and driving directions. Along with descriptions of the plants and bird and animal species hikers may encounter, we added historical tidbits where possible to heighten a visitor's appreciation of the people who shaped the land, either by helping create trails or by other work. Two examples: the bridges, buildings, and stone tower in the Blue Hills that were created by the Civilian Conservation Corps in the 1930s and the cranberry bogs of southeastern Massachusetts.

Complementing the hike descriptions are essays on the region's natural and human history, along with two appendices, one detailing regional campgrounds and state parks and the other describing the Bay Circuit Trail. Sixteen trips in the guide fall along the Bay Circuit Trail, a 231-mile trail that links nearly 60 communities in eastern Massachusetts. The route offers countless recreational opportunities and serves as a crucial conservation corridor.

It's particularly heartwarming to meet local residents and speak to caretakers of the properties highlighted in this book because they tend to be fiercely protective and proud of these lands, pitching in to clean up after storms, volunteering to show newcomers around, and sharing wildlife sightings. We encourage readers to likewise embrace natural areas and to treat them with care.

While exploring these trails, we have been fortunate to enjoy many memorable sights, such as snowy owls and other rare birds in the marshes and dunes of Plum Island, colorful spring blooms at the Arnold Arboretum, fall foliage from hilltops on the Bay Circuit Trail, and vivid sunsets over the tidal flats of Wellfleet Bay Wildlife Sanctuary and Great Island. We hope that readers will discover similar scenes while visiting this diverse group of natural areas.

ACKNOWLEDGMENTS

The three of us have been exploring special outdoor places in Massachusetts for many years. Although it is easy to take the region's numerous conserved lands for granted, we would like to acknowledge the many people past and present who have made efforts to protect open space for future generations. Today more and more people are realizing the benefits of protecting wild places, and the work goes on.

Many individuals and organizations were helpful in preparing the material for this and the previous editions. Thanks to the Appalachian Mountain Club, Arnold Arboretum of Harvard University, Barnstable Marine and Environmental Affairs Division, Bay Circuit Alliance, Boston Harbor Islands National Recreation Area, Cape Cod National Seashore, Essex County Greenbelt Association, the town of Lincoln, Lynn Woods Reservation, Mass Audubon, Massachusetts Department of Conservation and Recreation, Minute Man National Historical Park, Sherborn Forest and Trail Association, Sudbury Valley Trustees, The Nature Conservancy, The Trustees of Reservations, and the U.S. Fish and Wildlife Service. Special thanks to Michael Arnott, Patti Austin, Holly Berube, Kevin Block, Maggi Brown, Nina Coleman, Nathan Combs, the Crane Beach Reservation staff, David Davis, Jeremy Dick, Winslow Dresser, Debbie Ebersold, Mike Francis, Aaron Gouveia, Dan Gove, Michele Grzenda, Beth Gula, David McKinnon, Stacy Miller, Sue Moynihan, Mike Nelson, Jennifer Norwood, Leslie Obleschuck, Michael P. O'Connor, Kathryn Parent, Matt Poole and the Parker River National Wildlife Refuge staff, Mary-Ellen Schloss, Dan Small, Kristen Sykes, and Julie Warsowe for providing feedback and updates about specific places.

Michael Tougias would like to thank everyone who helped with this book over the past twenty years. This guidebook grew out of two books in AMC Books' earlier Nature Walk series: *Nature Walks in Eastern Massachusetts* and *More Nature Walks in Eastern Massachusetts*.

John Burk and Alison O'Leary would like to thank AMC's senior books editor, Tim Mudie, and AMC's senior production manager, Abigail Coyle. Additional thanks go to the members of the AMC Books staff who worked on the first three editions of this book.

INTRODUCTION

Finding a trail or woodsy reserve that feels like your own is sublime: you get to know its rhythms of growth and bloom, the way the trees bend when the wind kicks up, where to avoid rock heads poking out of the pathway, and the exact spot where you begin to hear the gurgling of the stream meeting the brook.

This comforting familiarity is only surpassed by the subtle surprises during everyday visits, such as the songs of migrating birds, the discovery of new animal prints in the snow or mud, or the red or yellow hue of a leaf contrasted against an old gray stone wall.

Each path and property has its own character and history, natural inhabitants, and visitors. Knowing a handful of them evokes a feeling of riches; they are a quiver of cures for daily stress and soothing to ponder when we are away from them.

Discovering new places is also enchanting. Wonder and excitement accompany every bend in the path and view through the canopy. Tall, stalwart trees stand as sentinels to the passing of time, sunlight, and storms. Our minds wander to the people who lived here in centuries past, toiling on unforgiving land or walking through the same woods. Brooks and ponds reflect light, and the currents carry our worries away. We return home feeling refreshed and exhilarated, as if we've made a new friend.

As eastern Massachusetts grows and becomes more densely populated, it is more important than ever to seek out natural spaces for a break from the city environment. We hope this book introduces readers to peaceful areas near them, as well as to opportunities for exploring others.

More than 100 organizations in Massachusetts are committed to land conservation. The ubiquity of protected land here is a testament to the values most people hold in common: the health of individuals and the health of the ecosystem. We thank these organizations every time we visit a preserve or share a recommended hiking route.

The 60 hikes in this book are among the best we know of in this part of the state that we call home. We challenge readers to step out of their usual routines and use this guide to explore unfamiliar places—we're certain the result will be positive. Enjoy!

—from the authors, John Burk, Alison O'Leary, and Michael Tougias

HOW TO USE THIS BOOK

With 60 hikes to choose from, you may wonder how to decide where to go. The locator map at the front of this book will help you narrow down the trips by location, and the at-a-glance trip planner that follows the table of contents will provide more information to guide you toward a decision.

Once you settle on a destination and turn to a trip in this guide, you will find a series of icons that indicate recommended or permitted activities, fees for parking or admittance to a property, potential hazards, and features such as water and scenic vistas.

Information on the basics follows: location, rating, distance, elevation gain, estimated time, and maps. The ratings are based on the authors' perception and are estimates of what the average hiker will experience. You may find the hikes to be easier or more difficult than stated. The estimated time is also based on the authors' perception. Consider your own pace when planning a trip.

The elevation gain is calculated using measurements and information from U.S. Geological Survey (USGS) topographic maps, landowner maps, and Google Earth. Information is included about the relevant USGS maps, as well as where you can find trail maps. The boldface summary provides a brief overview or highlights of what you will see on your hike.

The directions explain how to reach the trailhead by car and, for some trips, by public transportation. GPS coordinates for parking areas are also included. When you enter the coordinates into your device, it will provide driving directions. Whether or not you own a GPS device, it is wise to consult an atlas before leaving home.

Under "Trail Description" in each trip, you will find instructions on where to hike, the trails on which to hike, and where to turn. You will also learn about the natural and human history along your hike, as well as information about flora, fauna, and any landmarks and objects you may encounter.

The trail maps that accompany each trip will help guide you along your hike, but it would be wise to take an official trail map with you. They are often—but not always—available online, at the trailhead, or at the visitor center, when there is one.

In each trip, a section titled "More Information" provides details about the locations of restrooms, access times and fees, a property's rules and regulations, and contact information for the place where you will be hiking.

Each trip ends with a section called "Nearby," which includes information about restaurants, shops, or other points of interest near the trailhead.

TRIP PLANNING AND SAFETY

Although elevations in and around Boston are relatively low compared with other regions of New England, and the hikes detailed in this guide aren't particularly dangerous, you should still be prepared. Some of the walks traverse moderately rugged terrain along rocky hills, while others lead to beaches, ponds, and fields where you'll have extended periods of exposure to sun and to areas where walking is slow in soft sand. Many reservations in eastern Massachusetts have complex trail networks based on old cart and carriage roads, some of which are unmarked. Allow extra time in case you get lost.

You will be more likely to have an enjoyable, safe hike if you plan ahead and take proper precautions. Before heading out, consider the following:

Select a hike that everyone in your group is comfortable taking. Match the hike to the abilities of the people in the group. If anyone is uncomfortable with the weather or is tired, turn around and complete the hike another day.

Plan to be back at the trailhead before dark. Before beginning your hike, determine a turnaround time even if you have not reached your intended destination.

Check the weather. If you are planning a ridge or a summit hike, start early so that you will be off the exposed area before the afternoon hours, when thunderstorms most often strike, especially in summer. An average of twenty thunderstorms occur in the region annually. The weather in eastern Massachusetts is highly variable. Hikers at coastal locations should be prepared for wind year-round, especially during winter, when windchill is a concern. Compared with inland locations, the climate is generally cooler along the immediate coast during warm months and milder in winter. Significant storms—including heavy winter snowfalls, spring rainstorms, and tropical storms in late summer and fall—may cause flooding, potentially dangerous ocean tides, and other hazards. When exploring beaches or other areas along the coast, be sure to check tide tables in advance and to keep an eye on the water at all times.

Bring a pack with the following items:

- Water: Two quarts per person is usually adequate, depending on the weather and the length of the trip.
- Food: Even if you are planning a one-hour hike, bring some high-energy snacks, such as nuts, dried fruit, or snack bars; pack a lunch for longer trips.
- Map and compass: Be sure you know how to use them; a handheld GPS device may also be helpful, but it is not always reliable.
- Headlamp or flashlight, with spare batteries.
- Extra clothing: Rain gear, wool sweater or fleece, hat, and mittens.

- Sunscreen.
- First-aid kit, including adhesive bandages, gauze, nonprescription painkillers, and moleskin.
- Pocketknife or multitool.
- Waterproof matches and a lighter.
- Trash bag.
- Toilet paper.
- Whistle.
- Insect repellent.
- Sunglasses.
- Cell phone: Be aware that cell phone service is unreliable in rural areas; if you are receiving a signal, use the phone only for emergencies to avoid disturbing the backcountry experience for other hikers.
- Binoculars (optional).
- Camera (optional).

Wear appropriate footwear and clothing. Wool or synthetic hiking socks will keep your feet dry and help prevent blisters. Comfortable, waterproof hiking boots will provide ankle support and good traction. Avoid wearing cotton clothing, which absorbs sweat and rain and contributes to an unpleasant hiking experience. Polypropylene, fleece, silk, and wool all wick away moisture from your body and keep you warm in wet or cold conditions. To help avoid bug bites, you may want to wear long pants and a long-sleeved shirt.

When you are ahead of the rest of your hiking group, wait at all trail junctions until the others catch up. This avoids confusion and keeps people from getting separated or lost.

If you see downed wood that appears to be purposely covering a trail, it probably means the trail is closed due to overuse or hazardous conditions. Don't cross it.

If a trail is muddy, walk through the mud or on rocks, never on tree roots or plants. Waterproof boots will keep your feet comfortable. Staying in the center of the trail will keep it from eroding into a wide hiking highway.

Leave your itinerary and the time you expect to return with someone you trust. If you see a logbook at a trailhead, be sure to sign in when you arrive and to sign out when you finish your hike.

After you complete your hike, check for deer ticks, which can carry dangerous Lyme disease.

Poison ivy is always a threat when hiking. To identify the plant, look for clusters of three leaves that shine in the sun but are dull in the shade. If you do come into contact with poison ivy, wash the affected area with soap as soon as possible.

Wear blaze-orange items in hunting season. In Massachusetts, the peak hunting season for deer and game birds generally runs from mid-October to the end of December, with shotguns permitted from late November to early or mid-December. Yearly schedules are available at mass.gov and a fishing and hunting guide published by the Massachusetts Division of Fisheries and Wildlife, which is available for free at town halls, stores, and other public areas.

Biting insects are present during warm months, particularly in the vicinity of wetlands. They can be a minor or a significant nuisance, depending on seasonal and daily conditions. One serious concern is the eastern equine encephalitis virus (commonly referred to as EEE), a rare but potentially fatal disease that can be transmitted to humans by infected mosquitoes. Southeastern Massachusetts's many swamps provide ideal mosquito habitats; the threat is generally greatest in the evening hours, when mosquitoes are most active.

A variety of options exist for dealing with bugs, ranging from sprays that include the active ingredient diethyl-meta-toluamide (commonly known as DEET) to more skin-friendly products. Head nets, which often cost less than repellents, are useful during especially buggy conditions.

Remember, hiking should be fun. If you are uncomfortable with the weather or are tired, turn back and make the complete hike another day. Don't create a situation where you risk yourself or your companions. And try not to walk alone. Be sure someone knows your intended route and expected return time. Always sign in at a trailhead register if one is available.

The unexpected can occur. Weather can change, trail markings can become obscured, you can fall, and you can get lost. But you are more likely to avoid serious danger if you have anticipated the unexpected.

LEAVE NO TRACE

 The Appalachian Mountain Club is a national educational partner of Leave No Trace, a nonprofit organization dedicated to promoting and inspiring responsible outdoor recreation through education, research, and partnerships. The Leave No Trace program seeks to develop wildland ethics—ways in which people think and act in the outdoors to minimize their impact on the areas they visit and to protect our natural resources for future enjoyment. Leave No Trace unites four federal land management agencies— the U.S. Forest Service, the National Park Service, the Bureau of Land Management, and the U.S. Fish and Wildlife Service—with manufacturers, outdoor retailers, user groups, educators, organizations such as AMC, and individuals.

The Leave No Trace ethic is guided by these seven principles:

1. *Plan Ahead and Prepare.* Know the terrain and any regulations applicable to the area you're planning to visit, and be prepared for extreme weather or other emergencies. This will enhance your enjoyment and ensure that you've chosen an appropriate destination. Small groups have less impact on resources and the experiences of other backcountry visitors.

2. *Travel and Camp on Durable Surfaces.* Travel and camp on established trails and campsites, rock, gravel, dry grasses, or snow. Good campsites are found, not made. Camp at least 200 feet from lakes and streams, and focus activities on areas where vegetation is absent. In pristine areas, disperse use to prevent the creation of campsites and trails.

3. *Dispose of Waste Properly.* Pack it in, pack it out. Inspect your camp for trash or food scraps. Deposit solid human waste in cat holes dug 6 to 8 inches deep, at least 200 feet from water, camps, and trails. Pack out toilet paper and hygiene products. To wash yourself or your dishes, carry water 200 feet from streams or lakes and use small amounts of biodegradable soap. Scatter strained dishwater.

4. *Leave What You Find.* Cultural or historic artifacts, as well as natural objects such as plants and rocks, should be left as found.

5. *Minimize Campfire Impacts.* Cook on a stove. Use established fire rings, fire pans, or mound fires. If you build a campfire, keep it small and use dead sticks found on the ground.

6. *Respect Wildlife.* Observe wildlife from a distance. Feeding animals alters their natural behavior. Protect wildlife from your food by storing rations and trash securely.

7. *Be Considerate of Other Visitors.* Be courteous, respect the quality of other visitors' backcountry experiences, and let nature's sounds prevail.

AMC is a national provider of the Leave No Trace Master Educator course. AMC offers this five-day course, designed especially for outdoor professionals and land managers, as well as an introductory two-day Leave No Trace Trainer course, at locations throughout the Northeast.

For Leave No Trace information and materials, contact the Leave No Trace Center for Outdoor Ethics, P.O. Box 997, Boulder, CO 80306. Phone: 800-332-4100 or 303-442-8222; fax: 303-442-8217; web: lnt.org. For information on the AMC Leave No Trace Master Educator training course schedule, see outdoors.org/get-involved/center-for-outdoor-learning-and-leadership.

1 // BOSTON/INSIDE ROUTES 95 AND 128

Boston and its inner suburbs might seem to be unlikely places to find nature preserves and hiking trails. Yet amid the development of New England's largest metropolitan area, a surprising array of areas offers recreational opportunities and provides crucial habitat for flora and fauna.

Boston's landscape has changed substantially over the past 400 years. The first European settlers arrived in 1623, and by the 1630s, Boston Harbor was regarded as an ideal location for ships that brought goods to and from England. To accommodate rapid population growth during the nineteenth century, many of the city's largest hills were excavated, and the dirt was used to fill coves and marshy areas.

In response to the increasing urbanization, metropolitan planners, including the renowned landscape architect Frederick Law Olmsted, designed a chain of parks collectively known as the Emerald Necklace because they form a strand of green "gems" that extends from Boston Common west and south to Franklin Park. These urban sanctuaries are home to roughly 50 distinct historical sites. One of the highlights is the Arnold Arboretum in Jamaica Plain, where beautifully designed paths wind past extensive botanical collections from around the world and lead to hilltop vistas. East of the arboretum is Jamaica Pond, the largest pond in Boston and home to a popular recreational trail.

A short distance southwest of downtown Boston is the quieter and wilder Stony Brook Reservation, which encompasses a rocky, forested valley and wetlands between the Roxbury and Hyde Park neighborhoods.

Just outside of Boston, expansive preserves offer hiking over terrain that ranges from gentle to rugged. The largest is the popular 7,000-acre Blue Hills Reservation, located a mere 10 miles south of the city. A chain of 22 forested low hills includes the 635-foot Great Blue Hill, home to a historical stone tower with panoramic views and to the nation's oldest continuously operating weather observatory. Several ponds and wetlands lie within the reservation, including Ponkapoag Pond, where a side trail leads into a bog.

Facing page: The Boston skyline as seen from Spectacle Island, the highest point in Boston Harbor (see Trip 8).

1

To the north, the Middlesex Fells, Lynn Woods, and Breakheart reservations combine to protect roughly 6,000 acres along the corridors of Routes 95 and 128. Low hills, rocky outcroppings, ponds, and wetlands characterize all three reservations. At the Middlesex Fells, a cluster of hills composed of igneous and sedimentary rock offers scenic views, uncommon botanical communities, and hiking trails ranging from easy to challenging.

The Boston Harbor Islands are a short distance offshore from the city's waterfront. These islands have a long and diverse history: they were used by American Indians in pre-Colonial times and were later home to coastal defense forts, factories, hospitals, and other municipal buildings. Thirty-four of the islands are now protected from development as part of a partnership between national and state parks. Several of the protected islands are open to the public for recreation, including Spectacle Island, which was a barren landfill until the late 1990s. Now revegetated with a variety of carefully selected trees and shrubs and home to scenic swimming beaches, picnic areas, and walking trails, the island boasts striking views as the highest point in the harbor.

1   MIDDLESEX FELLS: SKYLINE TRAIL

This hike, which loops the western side of the Fells, includes steep ascents and offers a great view of Boston from the Wright's Tower area.

Features

Location Stoneham, Medford, and Winchester, MA

Rating Strenuous

Distance 6.8-mile loop

Elevation Gain 1,400 feet

Estimated Time 5 hours

Maps USGS Boston North; Massachusetts Department of Conservation and Recreation: mass.gov/eea/docs/dcr/parks/trails/fells.pdf; Friends of the Middlesex Fells Reservation: fells.org

GPS coordinates 42° 25.854′ N, 71° 06.469′ W

Contact Massachusetts Department of Conservation and Recreation: mass.gov/locations/middlesex-fells-reservation, 617-727-1199, ext. 406

DIRECTIONS

From I-93, take Exit 24 to MA 28, travel around Roosevelt Circle to South Border Road, and proceed to the Bellevue Pond parking area on the right.

By public transportation, take the MBTA Orange Line to Wellington Station and then the number 100 bus to Roosevelt Circle Rotary. From there, walk south to the rotary and follow South Border Road (on the right) less than 0.25 mile to Bellevue Pond.

TRAIL DESCRIPTION

This popular loop trail is in the western section of the Middlesex Fells Reservation. Marked with white blazes, it makes a long circuit that mostly follows the low hills ringing the three Winchester reservoirs. In places, it joins several of the reservation's other popular routes, including Cross Fells Trail and Reservoir Trail. Although Skyline Trail is rated as a strenuous outing due to the distance and rolling terrain, the steep sections are fairly brief. For an easier walk that also loops around the reservoirs, see Trip 2.

The counterclockwise circuit begins at Bellevue Pond, which has a parking area off South Border Road in Medford. The loop may also be reached at other locations along South Border Road, including any of the parking pull-offs and the Long Pond parking lot.

From the Bellevue Pond parking area, follow dirt Quarry Road north along the eastern shores of the pond. At the pond's northern tip, white-blazed Skyline Trail bears right off Quarry Road to ascend Pine Hill.

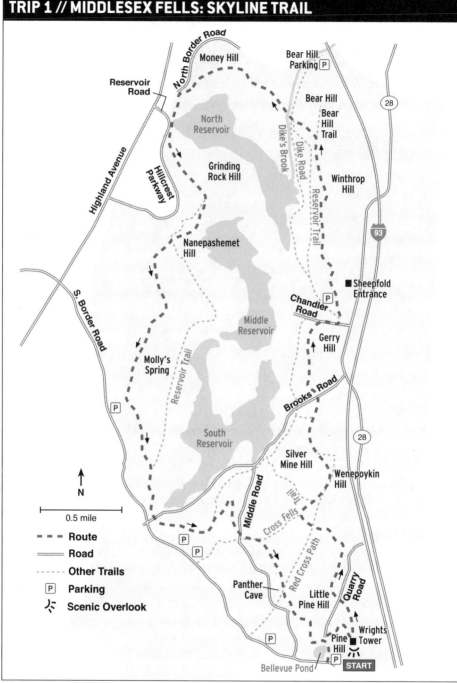

A hiker takes in the view from Middlesex Fells' Skyline Trail. Landmarks, such as the Prudential Tower and gold dome of the Massachusetts State House, can be seen from this vantage point. *Photo by Christina Xu, Creative Commons on Flickr.*

At the top of Pine Hill at the 0.5-mile mark, enjoy commanding views of Boston, its harbor, the Blue Hills, and busy Interstate 93 below. Atop the hill is Wright's Tower, which was built during the 1930s in memory of Elizur Wright, a businessman who worked hard to preserve the Middlesex Fells in the late nineteenth century. The tower is open weekends Memorial Day through mid-October, staff and weather dependent. From the tower, the trail continues north along a rocky ridge before turning west to drop into the valley between Pine Hill and Little Pine Hill, where it again crosses Quarry Road. Follow the path as it winds over the top of 211-foot Little Pine Hill, climbs over another hill, turns sharply left (west), and then traverses Red Cross Path.

Near the summit of Wenepoykin Hill, Skyline Trail turns to the right (northeast) and joins blue-blazed Cross Fells Trail for a short distance to the summit. Continue to follow Skyline Trail to the north as it traverses several hills, including Silver Mine Hill. Skyline Trail then rejoins Cross Fells Trail for a short distance as it descends to cross dirt Brooks Road. Skyline Trail continues north over Gerry Hill and then descends to Chandler Road (also dirt) along the Winchester Reservoir fence, where it briefly follows orange-blazed Reservoir Trail. In spring, listen for the calls of migratory songbirds, such as American redstarts and scarlet tanagers, and check the trail edge for the tracks of white-tailed deer and raccoons. Turn right at Chandler Road and follow both trails east toward the reservation's Sheepfold entrance.

After a few hundred feet, the combined Reservoir and Skyline trails cut across the access road and through the lower lot. They ascend a small hill, turn right, and then turn left, adjacent to the old Soap Box Derby track. At a slight reroute at the southern base of Winthrop Hill, go right and then left up the 291-foot hill, where there is a fine view of North Reservoir. From here, Skyline Trail continues north along a ridge toward Bear Hill. About 0.2 mile from the summit of Winthrop Hill, you reach a junction where Skyline Trail turns sharply to the left and continues down the slope of the hill. You have the option here of detouring straight ahead onto short Bear Hill Trail, which makes a quick climb to Bear Hill's 317-foot summit. After the detour, return to Skyline Trail, and descend.

At the base of the descent, Skyline Trail crosses dirt Dike Road through an overgrown meadow and a pine grove and then continues over the fairly level, wooded Money Hill. On the western slope of Money Hill, Reservoir and Skyline trails meet again and descend, crossing dirt North Border Road into a ravine north of the North Reservoir dam.

Walk over a small wooden bridge that crosses a brook formed by outflow from the reservoir and then follow Reservoir and Skyline trails, which climb the western slope of the ravine. A short distance to the south is the old municipal firehouse, near the Winchester–Stoneham town line. (Access to the reservoirs and shoreline is restricted.) The combined trails pass close by residences near Reservoir Road along the reservation's northwest boundary and then reach Hillcrest Parkway, a paved town road that offers parking and trail access. In winter, this is an excellent place to see winter ducks, such as buffleheads and mergansers, often by the dozen.

Walk along the left-hand side of the road for a short distance and then follow the trails back into the woods on the left. After crossing a dirt service road, the trails diverge at a junction, where Reservoir Trail exits to the right. Stay straight here and follow Skyline Trail over a pair of low hills. Skyline Trail then crosses Reservoir Trail and climbs steeply to the top of 295-foot Nanepashemet Hill, where there are limited views.

From Nanepashemet Hill, continue on Skyline Trail, which leads south over rolling terrain, crossing a series of hills and dirt roads near the reservation's western boundary. As the trail approaches the southern tip of South Reservoir, it once again merges with Reservoir Trail, which comes in from the left. Follow the combined trails as they bend south and then east around the corner of the reservoir near South Border Road, which offers parking and trail access. The trails wind up a hill and then split again. Bear right and follow white-blazed Skyline Trail, which ascends another hill and ridge before dropping down to cross dirt Middle Road.

At a junction a short distance from Middle Road, Skyline Trail briefly follows blue-blazed Cross Fells Trail. Cross Fells Trail is a one-way path that connects many of the Middlesex Fells Reservation's trails; it is described in Trip 4. At the next junction, Skyline Trail turns right and heads toward a rocky outcropping known as Panther Cave. Although panthers, more commonly known as mountain lions, are now officially considered extirpated from the Northeast, they and eastern timber wolves were once the region's top predators. Frequent rumors fuel lively debates, but the last confirmed sighting of a mountain lion in Massachusetts was in 1858, in the western part of the state; since then, there has been one confirmed report of scat in 1997 and another of tracks in 2011.

The trail passes near the cave and then descends to traverse Red Cross Path and Straight Gully Brook. You have one last climb to make, as the trail winds up the southwestern slopes of Little Pine Hill and then closes the loop at the northern tip of Bellevue Pond. In early spring, the path around Bellevue Pond is a reliable place to find native plants, such as the trout lily, named for having mottled brown markings akin to a brook trout. Turn right and walk back to the parking area.

DID YOU KNOW?

A herd of more than 25 sheep once grazed the Sheepfold. The Fells' popularity increased greatly with the opening of a trolley line that ran through the Fells from 1910 to the 1950s.

MORE INFORMATION

The reservation is open year-round, dawn to dusk; no fee. Dogs are allowed but must be leashed outside the 5.5-acre Sheepfold off-leash area. Trail maps are available in boxes at parking areas, at the Botume House Visitor Center, 4 Woodland Road, Stoneham, MA 02180, and through the Friends of the Middlesex Fells Reservation.

NEARBY

Historical sites in Medford include the Amelia Earhart residence at 76 Brooks Street, the Jonathan Wade House, and the site of Fannie Farmer's home at the intersection of Paris and Salem streets. Medford Square offers numerous places to eat.

2   MIDDLESEX FELLS: RESERVOIR TRAIL

This pleasant circuit around the three Winchester reservoirs offers an easier alternative to the reservation's more rugged trails.

Features

Location Stoneham, Medford, and Winchester, MA

Rating Moderate

Distance 5.2-mile loop

Elevation Gain 1,000 feet

Estimated Time 3 hours

Maps USGS Boston North; Massachusetts Department of Conservation and Recreation: mass.gov/eea/docs/dcr/parks/trails/fells.pdf, Friends of the Middlesex Fells Reservation: fells.org

GPS coordinates 42° 27.153′ N, 71° 06.349′ W

Contact Massachusetts Department of Conservation and Recreation: mass.gov/locations/middlesex-fells-reservation, 617-727-1199, ext. 406

DIRECTIONS

From I-93, take Exit 24 to MA 28 north and follow it 2.2 miles to the Sheepfold entrance. Turn left and continue to the parking lot.

By public transportation, from Wellington Station on the MBTA Orange Line, take the number 100 bus to Fellsway West, opposite Elm Street. From there, walk north along MA 28 1.2 miles to the Sheepfold entrance.

TRAIL DESCRIPTION

Reservoir Trail makes a long but mostly easy circuit around the Winchester reservoirs, which were created from 1874 to 1880 by the impoundment of brooks and other water sources in the watershed. Reservoir Trail can be reached from several locations. It is described here starting from the reservation's Sheepfold entrance on the east side of the reservoirs. Public access to the reservoirs is restricted, and violators are subject to a fine.

From the entrance, follow the orange-blazed trail along the fence near the southern and western edges of the Sheepfold picnic/off-leash dog area. The trail soon leaves the fence, crosses an old paved Soap Box Derby track, and enters the woods on an old bridle path. It leaves the path and follows the valley below the slopes of Winthrop Hill, crossing white-blazed Skyline Trail before merging with green-blazed Mountain Bike Trail just below the crest of Bear Hill. Then it descends to meet dirt Dike Road at its intersection with North Border Road.

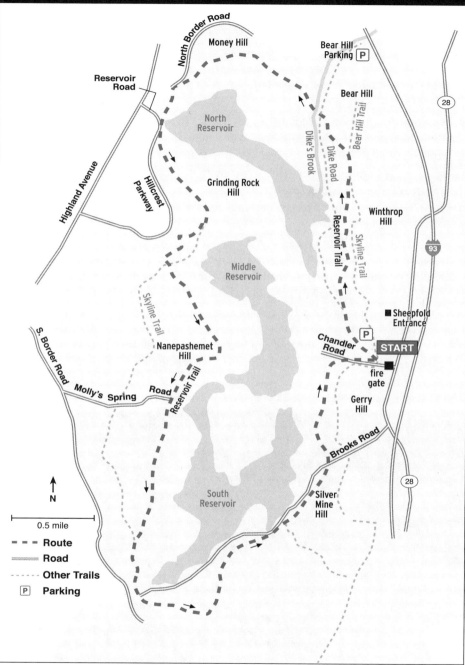

North Border Road

Money Hill

Bear Hill Parking 🅿

Reservoir Road

Bear Hill

28

North Reservoir

Highland Avenue

Hillcrest Parkway

Grinding Rock Hill

Dike's Brook

Dike Road

Bear Hill Trail

Reservoir Trail

Winthrop Hill

Skyline Trail

Middle Reservoir

Skyline Trail

Nanepashemet Hill

Sheepfold Entrance

🅿

START

Chandler Road

fire gate

S. Border Road

Molly's Spring Road

Reservoir Trail

Gerry Hill

Brooks Road

28

N

0.5 mile

South Reservoir

Silver Mine Hill

- - - Route

Road

Other Trails

🅿 **Parking**

Continue to follow the orange blazes along North Border Road until the trail leaves the road before gate 19 to follow the shoreline of North Reservoir. Pass through an old meadow that is now overgrown and has reverted to forest. Like many areas of New England, much of the Middlesex Fells was cleared for agriculture during Colonial times. Near gate 18, Reservoir, Skyline, and Mountain Bike trails converge and follow the same route, going close by residences near Reservoir Road along the reservation's northwest boundary and then reaching Hillcrest Parkway, a paved town road that offers parking and trail access.

Walk along the edge of the road for a short distance; then bear left back into the woods and continue south along an old bridle path. After crossing a dirt service road, Reservoir Trail and Skyline Trail split again; bear to the right at the junction and follow orange-blazed Reservoir Trail to the southwest. (Skyline Trail continues straight.) The path skirts a marshy area and crosses a brook. Turn left at another junction and follow the trail through the woods to the southeast, toward Middle and South reservoirs. You'll walk through portions of three towns within a matter of minutes, traversing the boundaries of Winchester, Stoneham, and Medford.

You'll soon reach a bluff that rises above the causeway between Middle and South reservoirs, offering fine views of both reservoirs through the trees. The trail continues to the south, descends into a ravine, and then reaches dirt Molly Spring Road. At this point, you are a little more than halfway through the circuit; the road is 2.9 miles from the Sheepfold parking area, and you have 2.3 more miles to go. Keep an eye out for barred owls in this area, especially in winter, when they're most easily seen roosting on a sunny day.

From Molly Spring Road, the trail continues south and follows rolling terrain along the eastern slopes of two low hills. After crossing another dirt road, reach another junction

A bridge crosses peaceful Dike's Brook. This trip offers an alternative to the Fells' more strenuous hikes.

with Skyline Trail, which enters from the right near the South Reservoir standpipe. The combined Reservoir, Mountain Bike, and Skyline trails then turn to the left (east) to curve around the southern arm of South Reservoir and West Dam. The trails almost reach South Border Road at gate 12 (no parking allowed) before going over a hill to a bridle path. They go straight and then bend left (north) off one bridle path and onto another, where they separate. Skyline Trail turns to the right (east) up a hill, while Reservoir Trail continues straight ahead to the north.

As Reservoir Trail winds through the woods along the shore of South Reservoir, it leaves the road and heads northeast, parallel to nearby dirt East Dam Road. The route descends into a ravine adjacent to small East Dam and then ascends the other side and continues to parallel the municipal road. After going north over the west shoulder of Silver Mine Hill, the trail passes close to the sealed shaft of a silver mine. Watch for concrete posts marking an old fence that once circled the mine shaft. Reservoir Trail continues north and then reaches dirt Chandler Road. Turn right here and follow Chandler Road to the east. Skyline Trail soon comes in from the right. Follow both trails left at the next junction and then walk back to the Sheepfold parking lot.

DID YOU KNOW?

The Friends of the Middlesex Fells Reservation is a stewardship and advocacy organization that shares knowledge and enjoyment of the park through a variety of programs, including hikes for various ages, educational programs on botany, and scavenger hunts. To learn more, visit fells.org.

MORE INFORMATION

The reservation is open year-round, dawn to dusk; no fee. Dogs must be leashed except at the designated area at Sheepfold. Trail maps are available in boxes at parking areas, at the Botume House Visitor Center at 4 Woodland Road, Stoneham, MA 02180, and through the Friends of the Middlesex Fells Reservation.

NEARBY

The Griffin Museum of Photography at 67 Shore Road in Winchester features exhibits and holds lectures and programs related to photography. Restaurants in Winchester are along and off Main Street (MA 38).

MIDDLESEX FELLS: ROCK CIRCUIT TRAIL

This rugged and rocky route offers some of the best views in the reservation, including those from Boojum Rock, the MIT Observatory site, White Rock, and Melrose Rock.

Features

Location Medford, Melrose, and Malden, MA

Rating Strenuous

Distance 4-mile loop

Elevation Gain 875 feet

Estimated Time 3.5 hours

Maps USGS Boston North; Massachusetts Department of Conservation and Recreation: mass.gov/eea/docs/dcr/parks/trails/fells.pdf; Friends of the Middlesex Fells Reservation: fells.org

GPS coordinates 42° 26.668′ N, 71° 05.678′ W

Contact Massachusetts Department of Conservation and Recreation: mass.gov/locations/middlesex-fells-reservation, 617-727-1199, ext. 406

DIRECTIONS

From I-93, take Exit 33 to MA 28 north, which is also Fellsway West. At the first traffic circle, take the first exit to stay on MA 28/Fellsway West. At Elm Street, turn right and drive 0.6 mile to a rotary. At the rotary, take the second exit for Woodland Road. Turn left into the Flynn Rink parking lot.

By public transportation, take the MBTA Orange Line to Wellington Station and then take the number 99 bus to the Flynn Rink parking lot.

TRAIL DESCRIPTION

Rock Circuit Trail is a moderately challenging route that leads to some of the best views in the Middlesex Fells. It passes several low, rocky ridges and hilltops that offer fine vantages of Boston and the neighborhoods surrounding the reservation. Living up to its name, it is very rocky, with rewarding but rugged hiking over rolling terrain, although the last segment follows a series of old paths and roads over much easier terrain. (You may meet other hikers completing this loop as preparation for long-distance outings in the White and Green mountains.) It is not well suited to families with young children. While the route is well marked with white blazes, there are many junctions with other trails. If you don't see white blazes for a few minutes, backtrack to Rock Circuit Trail.

TRIP 3 // MIDDLESEX FELLS: ROCK CIRCUIT TRAIL

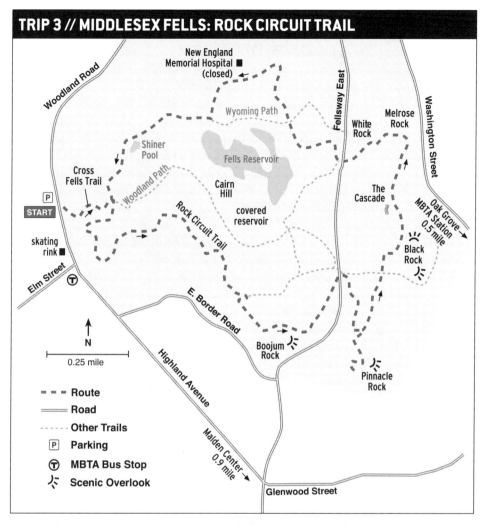

From the ice-skating rink parking lot, carefully cross Woodland Road to enter the woods through the green park gate and follow the combined Woodland Path and Cross Fells Trail to a junction where the Rock Circuit Trail loop begins. Turn right here, off Cross Fells Trail, and follow the white blazes up the hill to a ridge, where there are views across the reservation's forests to sections of Medford. This is the first of many hills and ridges on this outing. None of them are especially high or steep, but the terrain is rugged in places. The trail then descends from this ridge and drops into a valley between the hills.

Follow Rock Circuit Trail past a small seasonal brook and then left across a bridle path. The trail climbs southeast up a ridge, soon turning to the right (south) and dropping into another valley. At this point, it begins a long, gentle climb up to 275-foot Boojum Rock, which rises out of the reservation's southeast corner. Along this stretch, where the Massachusetts Institute of Technology built an observatory in 1899, several open rock ledges offer fine views of the greater Boston area. Bring binoculars or a camera with a telephoto lens for close-up views of the various landmarks.

From the low vegetation atop these ridges, you may hear a mockingbird imitating other birds. Mockingbirds often repeat each call three times before moving on to the next song in their repertoires. The imitations aren't limited to bird calls—mockingbirds also mimic car alarms and ringing telephones. In spring, look for colorful migratory songbirds, such as scarlet tanagers and a variety of woodland warblers.

From Boojum Rock, the trail drops sharply and heads east to cross a bridle path before reaching paved Fellsway East. Carefully cross this busy road and follow the white-blazed trail as it winds to 250-foot Pinnacle Rock, with excellent views. From Pinnacle Rock, backtrack a short distance to the East Path trail junction and then follow Rock Circuit Trail north. This portion of the route follows a rough ridge along the reservation's east boundary. You'll soon reach Black Rock, where there is fine scenery to the east and north across the neighborhoods adjacent to the reservation. This open, rocky hilltop is a good spot to stop for lunch.

From Black Rock, continue to follow the trail north, along the crest of the ridge. Pass the Cascade, a seasonal waterfall where Shilly Shally Brook tumbles to the valley below, and reach Melrose Rock, where there is more scenery to enjoy. Rock Circuit Trail turns to the west and crosses 256-foot White Rock, the last of the overlooks along the route.

From White Rock, carefully follow the white blazes across an old cart path and then left through the woods back toward Fellsway East. Cross the road (carefully) and continue to follow Rock Circuit Trail west through the woods, near the north and east shores of the Fells Reservoir (no views of the water). Here, the walking becomes easier and faster, a welcome break after the extended stretches along the narrow, rocky ridges. The trail crosses Wyoming Path and leads through the forest to a low ridge east of the now-closed New England Memorial Hospital, where it meets the southern terminus of Virginia Woods Trail.

Bear left here and follow Rock Circuit Trail as it leaves the ridge, heads west through a shady pine grove, and traverses a series of cart paths. Although there are many junctions, the main route is well marked and easy to follow. After passing the northwest corner of a small pond called Shiner Pool, complete the Rock Circuit loop at the junction with Cross Fells Trail. Backtrack the short distance to Woodland Road and the parking area.

DID YOU KNOW?

Spot Pond, the largest body of water in the Fells, is just west of I-93 and North, Middle, and South reservoirs (see Trip 4 map for more details). The area near Spot Pond Brook (east of the boating center on Spot Pond) was the site of a mill and manufacturing center called Haywardville from the mid-1700s to the late 1800s. Rubber items were the primary products during the latter phase of manufacturing, but the surrounding towns took away rights to water access, forcing the plants to close. The state took over Haywardville in 1894 when the parkland was planned and removed the buildings. Rangers at the Botume House Visitor Center may offer tours of the historical area.

Rock Circuit Trail offers some great views of Boston and the surrounding towns. A strenuous outing, this trip can be used as training for tackling hikes in the White and Green mountains.

MORE INFORMATION

The reservation is open year-round, dawn to dusk; no fee. Dogs must be leashed except at the designated area at Sheepfold. Trail maps are available in boxes at parking areas, at the Botume House Visitor Center at 4 Woodland Road, Stoneham, MA 02180, or through the Friends of the Middlesex Fells Reservation.

NEARBY

Boating in Boston at Spot Pond rents a variety of watercraft and offers lessons for beginners; see boatinginboston.com for information. Flynn Rink, an ice-skating rink operated by Friends of the Flynn Rink for the Department of Conservation and Recreation, is open from middle or late August to middle or late June. For more information, call 781-396-8500. Many restaurants can be found in Malden, Medford, and Melrose.

MIDDLESEX FELLS: CROSS FELLS TRAIL

Blue-blazed Cross Fells Trail serves as a handy connector between the eastern and western sections of the reservation, touching every major route.

Features

Location Stoneham, Medford, Melrose, and Malden, MA

Rating Moderate to Strenuous

Distance 4.3 miles one way

Elevation Gain 865 feet

Estimated Time 5 hours

Maps USGS Boston North; Massachusetts Department of Conservation and Recreation: mass.gov/eea/docs/dcr/parks/trails/fells.pdf; Friends of the Middlesex Fells Reservation: fells.org

GPS coordinates 42° 26.614' N, 71° 04.439' W

Contact Massachusetts Department of Conservation and Recreation: mass.gov/locations/middlesex-fells-reservation, 617-727-1199, ext. 406

DIRECTIONS

From I-93, take Exit 24 or 25 to MA 28/Fellsway West. Follow MA 28/Fellsway West for 0.5 mile and then turn right onto Elm Street. At the rotary, take the first exit to continue north on MA 28/Fellsway West toward Lawrence; then keep right to stay on Fellsway West. In 0.5 mile, turn right onto Elm Street, and 0.5 mile later take the second exit from the rotary for Woodland Road. After a mile on Woodland Road, keep right to turn onto Ravine Road and then turn right onto Fellsway East. Stay left to take Washington Street. On Washington Street, pass Goodyear Avenue at 0.8 mile. This is where the trail begins, but parking is not available at the trailhead. Continue past Goodyear Avenue on Washington Street to the parking area near the Oak Grove MBTA station and walk 0.5 mile back to Goodyear Avenue to start the hike.

By public transportation, take the MBTA Orange Line to Oak Grove Station and walk 0.5 mile down Washington Street to Goodyear Avenue. Turn left and walk to the trailhead at the end of the road.

TRAIL DESCRIPTION

Cross Fells Trail is a 4.3-mile, one-way connecting path that traverses the heart of the Middlesex Fells Reservation. It passes many junctions with the reservation's other routes, including Skyline Trail, and is often used by hikers to create long circuits. Along the way are views of diverse forest communities, including uncommon pitch-pine groves along the

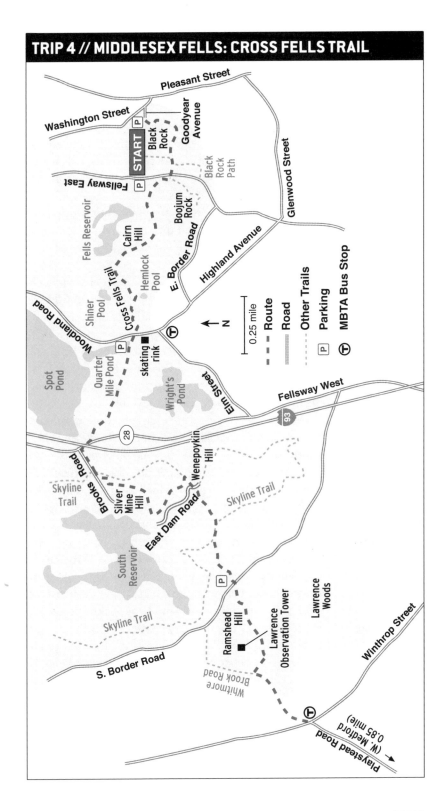

rocky hilltops. A variety of birds, mammals, reptiles, and amphibians live within the various habitats. You can also make short detours off the route to explore hilltops, such as Boojum Rock. Cross Fells Trail is well marked throughout with dark-blue blazes and is easy to follow despite the numerous intersections.

Although we describe here the full one-way trip from Goodyear Avenue to Winthrop Street in Medford, you have the option of walking portions of it in segments or combining it with other trails. You can backtrack from your endpoint to the parking areas, use two cars, or arrange for transportation where the trail crosses public roads, which are detailed below. The route follows rolling, periodically rocky terrain with multiple short ascents and descents over the reservation's hills.

From Goodyear Avenue, follow the trail as it bears left to East Path (Rock Circuit Trail leaves to the right just beyond the entrance) and then turn right onto Fells Path. The trail rises, crosses Rock Circuit Trail, and then follows more cart paths for a short distance before reaching Fellsway East, a paved town road.

Carefully cross this active road and follow the blue blazes to the right at a junction where Rock Circuit Trail diverges and goes left, up the hill to Boojum Rock. (This site offers excellent views south and east across the reservation's woodlands to Boston and the surrounding area from Boojum Rock, and hikers have the option of making a short detour here.) At the junction, Cross Fells Trail bends to the left and winds up a hill adjacent to Boojum Rock. This point is 1.0 mile from Woodland Road and Flynn Rink's parking lot (see Trip 3). Follow the trail across a partially open hilltop, through a grove of pitch pines, along a wire fence south of Fells Reservoir, and across the next hilltop.

Pitch pines are hardy trees that thrive in marginal growing conditions most other species can't tolerate. In addition to rocky hilltops, such as those in the Middlesex Fells, they are found in areas with sandy, acidic soils, such as Cape Cod and other parts of southeastern Massachusetts. Pitch pines are distinguished from other pine trees by their ball-shaped needle bundles and thick, plated bark. They can grow as high as 55 feet, although on these windy hilltops they generally have a lower, more twisted profile.

At a four-way junction at Hemlock Pool, continue straight, along the pool's north edge, and then merge onto Woodland Path. Keep an eye out for fishers, which are large weasels most frequently spotted in this area, and the great blue herons that await their next meal in Hemlock Pool. After turning right on a cart road, Cross Fells Trail again meets Rock Circuit Trail, just west of Woodland Road. Follow the blue blazes for a short distance to the road, cross it (watch for traffic), and continue to the Flynn Rink parking lot.

From the back edge of the parking lot, Cross Fells Trail passes the southern end of Quarter Mile Pond and heads west over the hills. At 0.3 mile past the ice rink, you'll reach a junction where another trail exits left and continues south to near Wright's Pond. Continue on Cross Fells Trail west as it winds through the woods and descends to Fellsway West (MA 28). When the trail reaches the road, turn right onto the I-93 underpass, picking up the trail again on the other side.

From Fellsway West, Cross Fells Trail follows dirt Brooks Road to a junction with green-blazed Mountain Bike Trail and white-blazed Skyline Trail, a popular long-distance circuit detailed in Trip 1. Turn left here and follow the combined Cross Fells and Skyline trails left (south) up a low hill. Soon Cross Fells Trail leaves to the right (west) to follow a ridge above

Brooks Road. Continue on blue-blazed Cross Fells Trail, which bends to the left (south) and picks up a series of bridle paths before turning left (east) into the woods to rejoin Skyline Trail on the summit of Wenepoykin Hill, which features a partial view of Boston. You may spot a white-tailed deer in this fairly quiet section of the reservation, even this close to the city.

From Wenepoykin Hill, Cross Fells Trail crosses dirt East Dam Road, continues south downhill to a brook, and rejoins another section of Skyline Trail. The two trails continue west until Cross Fells Trail turns to the left (southwest) to pick up a group of bridle paths and then reaches paved South Border Road.

Carefully cross the road and then reenter the woods and begin a short, easy climb up Ramshead Hill. The remains of the former Lawrence Observation Tower are visible at the summit. Descend the hill and follow a series of old bridle paths to the reservation's Whitmore Brook entrance on Winthrop Street in Medford, across from Playstead Road (the end of the MBTA Sullivan Square–West Medford bus line). The entrance is 4.3 miles from the Goodyear Avenue trailhead and is the endpoint of this one-way trip. If you're backtracking to the Goodyear Avenue trailhead, retrace your steps, making sure to follow the blue blazes at the intersections.

DID YOU KNOW?

In this context, the English word *fell* comes from the Old Norse word *fjall*, meaning hilly, rocky terrain. Both sedimentary and igneous rock can be found at the Fells.

Portions of Middlesex Fells Reservation are great for families. Use a topographic trail map to plan any outings for small children, as the elevation can rise steeply in a short distance. *Photo by Matthew Grymek/ AMC Photo Contest.*

NEARBY

The 26-acre Stone Zoo, at 149 Pond Street in Stoneham, includes species from a wide variety of locales, such as the North Woods in Canada, the southwestern United States, Africa, and the Himalaya highlands. Numerous restaurants are in Stoneham on Main Street (MA 28).

MORE INFORMATION

The reservation is open year-round, dawn to dusk; no fee. Dogs are allowed but must be leashed outside the 5.5-acre Sheepfold off-leash area. Trail maps are available in boxes at parking areas and at the Botume House Visitor Center at 4 Woodland Road, Stoneham, MA 02180, or through the Friends of the Middlesex Fells Reservation. Mountain biking is popular here as well; the New England Mountain Bike Association (nemba.org) is active in trail maintenance and advocacy.

5 BREAKHEART RESERVATION

This hike leads to a variety of features, including the Saugus River and its associated wetlands, an outcropping, rocky hills, and ponds.

Features 🐕 💧 📍 ⛷ 🎿 ✳ ⬆ 🚌

Location Saugus, MA

Rating Moderate

Distance 2.7 miles

Elevation Gain 410 feet

Estimated Time 2 hours

Maps USGS Boston North, USGS Lynn; Friends of Breakheart Reservation: saugus.org/FOBR

GPS coordinates 42° 29.008′ N, 71° 01.664′ W

Contact Friends of Breakheart Reservation: saugus.org/FOBR; Massachusetts Department of Conservation and Recreation: mass.gov/locations/breakheart-reservation, 781-233-0834

DIRECTIONS
From I-95, take Exit 63 for US 1 south. After passing Salem Street, continue 2.4 miles and take the Lynn Fells Parkway exit. Turn right onto Forest Street and continue to the parking areas adjacent to the visitor center and Kasabuski Rink.

By public transportation, take the MBTA number 429 bus to Saugus Plaza. Staying on Forest Street, cross Lynn Fells Parkway and walk about 0.5 mile, past the skating rink, to the trailhead.

TRAIL DESCRIPTION
Breakheart Reservation encompasses more than 700 acres of forests, wetlands, and rocky hills along the south banks of the Saugus River. It offers recreational opportunities, wildlife habitats, and travel corridors in the midst of a heavily developed area. In Colonial times, the reservation was common land used by residents of the present-day towns of Saugus and Wakefield, and farms and mills were established throughout the vicinity. In the late nineteenth century, two local residents purchased the land, made it a private game preserve, and created Pearce and Silver lakes. In 1935, the state bought the property and established Breakheart Reservation.

This hike explores a variety of features in the eastern and central portions of the reservation. Because it follows rolling terrain and several rocky stretches, it is rated as moderately difficult, although none of the climbs is especially long or steep.

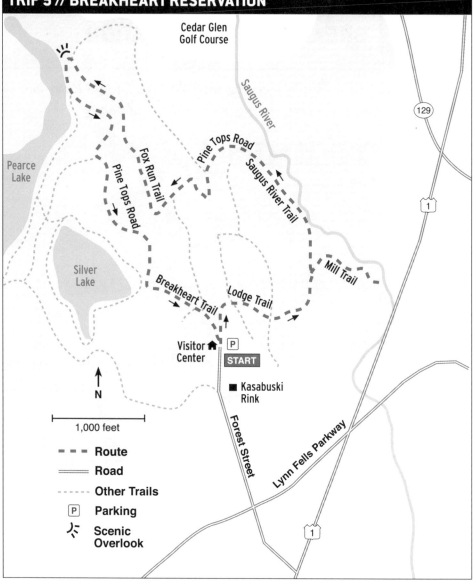

From the parking area and visitor center, walk around the gate to the right of the building onto paved Pine Tops Road and then quickly turn left at a marked junction onto Saugus River Trail. This rocky dirt path, marked with yellow blazes, leads east toward the river, crossing red-blazed Lodge Trail. Saugus River Trail narrows through a young hardwood forest and then passes an apartment building on the right and curves left through mature woodlands.

At a junction, blue-blazed Mill Site Trail forks to the right. This short side path curves right and then bears left as it approaches a viewpoint at an old mill site along the riverbank. Several tall pines grow out of a thin layer of soil atop the mill's large stone wall. Walk quietly here while you approach the river, as a variety of wildlife is present. One wading bird

From the Breakheart visitor center, follow Pine Tops Road to Saugus River Trail.

to watch for is the black-crowned night heron, which is most often found along the coast but occasionally nests in marshy inland areas near woodlots. These birds can often be seen perched on trees across the peninsula where Mill Site Trail ends. This heron's two most distinctive traits are its black head patch and its hunting activity at night, when it quietly stalks wetlands.

Return to the junction and continue to the right on Saugus River Trail. The route leads northwest along the edge of the wetlands that border the river, which is part of the water supply for the town of Lynn. The trail then passes through a field of rocks and boulders, with a large rock ledge visible on the hillside to the left. Here, the walking briefly becomes slower and more difficult; children should use caution in this section. Tiny blue and jewel-wing damselflies perch on the ferns and shrubs bordering the trail. Check muddy areas for tracks and signs of raccoons, mink, river otters, and white-tailed deer.

Beyond the rocky section, the trail continues over easy ground through low vegetation and a pine grove along the riverbank.

Continue to Saugus River Link on the left and follow it to Pine Tops Road. Turn left on Pine Tops Road. After about a minute, take Fox Run Link (half-green, half-white blazes) on the right to Fox Run Trail (green blazes). Continue straight to a beautiful rock wall; the trail goes left around it and then to the top.

Fox Run Trail descends through a large hemlock grove, where many trees have been infested and killed by hemlock woolly adelgids (see "Introduced Pests: A Threat to Our Eastern Forests" on page 38). It then makes a quick, moderately steep climb to an open hilltop, where there's an interesting view of Eagle Rock and Pearce Lake across the valley below. The trail steeply descends the rock—use caution here, as pine needles can be slippery—and ends at Pine Tops Road, at the swimming beach on the northeast shore of Pearce Lake. (Swimming is allowed at the lake from Memorial Day to Labor Day when lifeguards are present.) Pearce and Silver lakes and their associated marshes are home to bass, pickerel, painted and snapping turtles, double-crested cormorants, and hawks.

From Pearce Lake, follow Pine Tops Road south. The paved path, popular with dog walkers and joggers, follows gently rolling terrain through the center of the reservation. About a half-mile from the lake, you'll reach a four-way intersection at Silver Lake and continue to the left here, on an unnamed fire road.

Follow the orange blazes on the fire road and turn right to ascend Breakheart Hill, one of six rocky hills within the reservation that exceed 200 feet. The route then descends to join the lower portion of Fox Run Trail near the reservation entrance. Bear right and make the short walk to the visitor center and parking area.

DID YOU KNOW?

The reservation's paved trails—Forest Street, Pine Tops Road, Elm Road, and Hemlock Road—were built during the 1930s and were added to the National Register of Historic Places in 2003.

NEARBY

Saugus Iron Works National Historic Site at 244 Central Street offers guided tours of the seventeenth-century Iron Works House and industrial site. Restaurants are on US 1 (Newburyport Turnpike).

MORE INFORMATION

Trails are open from dawn to dusk. Swimming is allowed at Pearce Lake from Memorial Day to Labor Day when lifeguards are on duty.

LYNN WOODS RESERVATION

Easy fire road trails lead to overlooks atop low, rolling hills and to the famous Dungeon Rock.

Features

Location Lynn, MA

Rating Easy to Moderate

Distance 3.7-mile loop

Elevation Gain 450 feet

Estimated Time 2 hours

Maps USGS Boston North, USGS Lynn; Friends of Lynn Woods: lynnwoods.org; City of Lynn: lynnma.gov/cityhall_documents/maps/misc_maps/Lynn_Woods_2020.pdf

GPS coordinates 42° 29.588′ N, 70° 58.639′ W

Contact Friends of Lynn Woods: lynnwoodsranger@aol.com, 781-477-7123

DIRECTIONS

Take I-95 to Exit 63 for MA 129 east in Lynn. Follow it through a well-marked rotary and turn right onto Great Woods Road. Continue 0.3 mile to the park entrance and large parking area at the road's end, at a baseball field.

By public transportation, take the number 436 bus from the Central Square–Lynn Station on the MBTA Commuter Rail to the Great Woods Road stop.

TRAIL DESCRIPTION

At 2,200 acres, Lynn Woods Reservation is one of the largest municipal forest parks in the United States. Located northwest of central Lynn, near the city's boundary with Saugus and Lynnfield, it is home to a variety of features. Low, rolling hills with views to Boston rise above a series of swamps and wetlands, such as the narrow Walden Pond (not to be confused with the famous Walden Pond in Concord, see Trip 32), which bisects the reservation.

This hike begins at the reservation's east entrance on Great Woods Road and makes a loop that visits overlooks atop Mount Gilead and Burrill Hill, atop Dungeon and Union rocks, and on the shores of Walden Pond. The main fire roads are blazed orange, and other trails are blazed green.

From the back side of the parking area, walk around the green gate to the left onto Great Woods Road, which is an unpaved extension of the entrance road. On your right are short side paths that quickly lead to the southwest corner of Walden Pond. This narrow, L-shaped

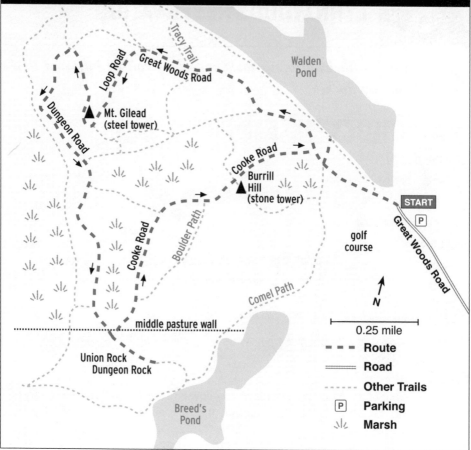

pond offers attractive scenery along its shores. You can visit the pond at either the start or the finish of the walk, as the hike returns via this section of the trail.

Great Woods Road continues to the northwest, rising gently past a rocky brook before leveling at a cluster of glacial boulders. In late spring or early summer, listen for the distinctive *pee-a-wee* call of the eastern wood peewee, one of many migratory songbirds that call this forest home. Another familiar sound is the flutelike call of the hermit thrush. More than 100 other species of birds have been documented here, and according to one ranger, large pileated woodpeckers are among the more recent arrivals. You may hear their loud hammering on dead trees from a long distance away.

At a Y junction where Cooke Road—the return leg of this hike—branches to the left, continue straight on Great Woods Road. Walden Pond will be visible through the trees to the right. Tall oaks line the trail, along with clusters of eastern hemlocks, many of which are infested with deadly hemlock woolly adelgids, visible as white spots underneath branches where the needles meet the wood. (See "Introduced Pests: A Threat to Our Eastern Forests" on page 38.)

At 0.8 mile from the trailhead, Great Woods Road passes a marked junction with Tracy Trail on the right and then reaches another Y junction at the site of an old foundation. Bear left here onto Loop Road, following signs to the summit of Mount Gilead. An easy 0.3-mile ascent leads to the 272-foot summit, where an old steel fire tower rises high above a small clearing. Although the tower cannot be climbed, rock ledges a short distance beyond it offer a fine view south across the reservation's forests to the Boston skyline and the ocean. This sunlit, open area is an ideal spot for a picnic or a rest break. In summer, watch for crickets hopping in the grass and dragonflies, such as lancet clubtails, circling on hunting rounds.

From the summit, Loop Road winds past more rock ledges. Note the shorter vegetation

Stone Tower, a 48-foot-tall fieldstone structure atop Lynn Woods' Burrill Hill, was created as a fire tower in 1936 under the Works Progress Administration.

here, even at the hilltop's relatively modest elevation. After a few minutes of easy walking, the trail reaches a four-way junction with a fire road. Go left. (Another trail goes straight.) The fire road briefly follows a contour below the summit and then descends to meet Dungeon Road at Junction C5-3.

Turn left onto Dungeon Road, which leads south along the east side of Mount Gilead, passing rocky outcroppings and two junctions with other trails on the left. A grove of hemlocks partially shades the sunlit road, which rises easily along rolling terrain. An opening in the woods on the left behind a rest bench indicates Long Swamp, one of several swamps and wetlands that lie within the bounds of the reservation. It's a location for potentially sighting some of the park's elusive residents, including mink, fishers, and beavers. Barred owls may be heard calling during quiet times, especially dawn and dusk.

Shortly after Dungeon Road curves to the left and passes more trail junctions on the right, it meets Cooke Road (also known as Burrill Hill Road) at Junction C7-1. Although this hike continues left on Cooke Road, you can make a short detour straight on Dungeon Road past the middle pasture wall to visit nearby Dungeon and Union rocks. Side paths on the right lead to both of these interesting geological features. Dungeon Rock is an especially colorful part of Lynn Woods' history, as pirates are believed to have stashed treasure in the vicinity. During the mid-seventeenth century, an earthquake closed the rock cave. In subsequent years, one treasure hunter spent a considerable amount of effort reopening the cave in an unsuccessful attempt to locate the loot. Within Dungeon Rock is a 174-foot-deep tunnel open to tours during certain hours; contact the park for more information.

After exploring the rocks, backtrack to the junction and turn right onto Cooke Road. This pleasant path leads north through the woods above the east side of Long Swamp. After passing a junction with a side path that descends into the valley on the left, the road curves to the right and gradually rises to the large stone tower atop 285-foot Burrill Hill. You can climb a portion of the tower for views south toward Boston.

Complete the circuit by following Cooke Road as it descends at a moderate grade to its end at the junction with Great Woods Road, next to Walden Pond. Turn right and walk back to the reservation entrance.

DID YOU KNOW?

The Penny Bridge on the northwest side of Tomlin's Swamp got its name from the stone bridge built there for early settlers. Each crosser paid a penny to use the bridge until the cost of construction was repaid.

NEARBY

Lynn Museum and Historical Society at 590 Washington Street features exhibits dedicated to the town's seafaring, manufacturing, and commercial histories. Restaurants are nearby in Wyoma Square at the intersection of Parkland Avenue and Lynnfield Street.

MORE INFORMATION

The reservation is open to blackberry and blueberry picking, mushroom hunting, hiking, mountain biking, and horseback riding; bikes are allowed only on official, blazed trails; horses are allowed only on fire roads. Dogs are allowed but must be leashed. Camping, fishing, and motorized vehicles are prohibited. Picnics are allowed, but grills, stoves, and fires are not permitted. To find out when the stone tower or Dungeon Rock are open to the public, check with Friends of Lynn Woods on Facebook.

7 ARNOLD ARBORETUM

Paved roads and footpaths pass botanical collections, leading to scenic hilltops with long views of downtown Boston and the Blue Hills.

Features

Location Boston, MA (Jamaica Plain)

Rating Easy to Moderate

Distance 4.1-mile loop

Elevation Gain 230 feet, including both hills

Estimated Time 3 hours

Maps USGS Boston South; Arnold Arboretum: arboretum.harvard.edu/explorer (landscape maps and interactive map)

GPS coordinates 42° 18.461' N, 71° 07.203' W

Contact Arnold Arboretum: arboretum.harvard.edu, 617-524-1718

DIRECTIONS

The Arnold Arboretum of Harvard University is at 125 Arborway (MA 203), near Centre Street and Murray Circle. From I-95 (reached by I-90), take Exit 36 and follow MA 9 (East Worcester Street) east toward Brookline–Boston. After 2.9 miles, bear slightly right at Florence Street. Turn right onto Hammond Pond Parkway, continue to the rotary, and then take the third exit onto Newton Street. Follow Newton Street to Pond Street and turn right onto Arborway. At the rotary, continue to follow Arborway to the Arboretum on the right. This hike begins at the main entrance at the Arborway gate; on-street parking is limited, but there are municipal parking lots a couple of blocks away on Burroughs Place.

By public transportation, take the MBTA Orange Line to Forest Hills Station and exit through the Arnold Arboretum door. Continue west on Arborway (toward MA 1) to the gate. Or take the number 39 bus to Custer Street in Jamaica Plain and proceed west on Custer Street three blocks to the Arboretum.

TRAIL DESCRIPTION

Renowned for its beautifully landscaped grounds and historical botanical collections, Arnold Arboretum is a highlight of the Emerald Necklace, a 7-mile chain of urban parks totaling more than 1,000 acres that extends from Boston Common west and south through the city to Franklin Park.

Spread throughout the Arboretum's 265 acres are more than 15,000 trees, shrubs, and vines, representing some 4,500 species from around the world. The Arboretum was founded in 1872 and named for James Arnold, who donated funds to begin the project.

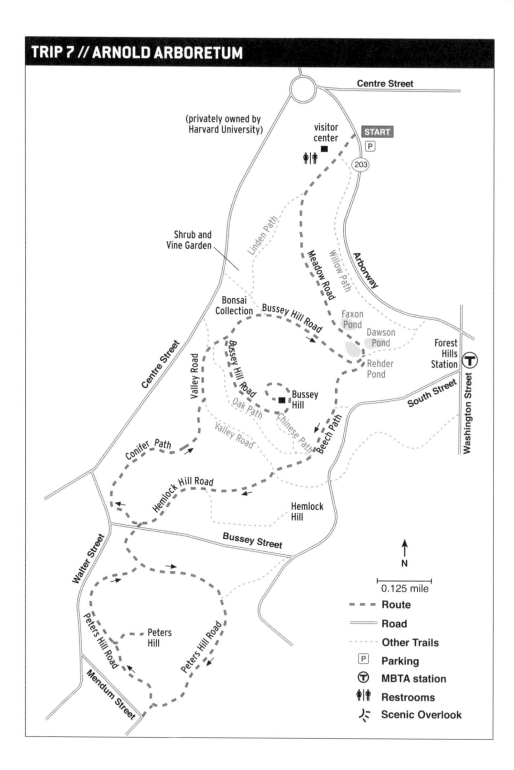

Centre Street

(privately owned by Harvard University)

visitor center

START

P

203

Shrub and Vine Garden

Linden Path

Meadow Road

Willow Path

Arborway

Bonsai Collection

Bussey Hill Road

Faxon Pond

Dawson Pond

Forest Hills Station

Centre Street

Valley Road

Bussey Hill Road

Rehder Pond

Bussey Hill

Oak Path

Chinese Path

Beech Path

South Street

Washington Street

Valley Road

Conifer Path

Hemlock Hill Road

Hemlock Hill

Walter Street

Bussey Street

N

0.125 mile

- - - Route
=== Road
···· Other Trails
P Parking
T MBTA station
Restrooms
Scenic Overlook

Peters Hill Road

Peters Hill

Peters Hill Road

Mendum Street

Since 1882 it has been run under a cooperative agreement between Harvard University, which manages the grounds and directs education and research, and the city of Boston, which is responsible for security and infrastructure. An arboretum is a living museum—a place where trees and other woody plants are grown and cultivated for scientific research, education, and aesthetics.

This hike, which combines paved roads and two gravel paths, passes most of the Arboretum's diverse botanical collections and leads to a pair of sweeping vistas on 240-foot Peters Hill and 200-foot Bussey Hill. The walking is easy, and detailed maps are posted at major junctions. In addition to the paths described in this hike, self-guided trails also allow visitors to explore and enjoy the collections. The Arboretum's website and printed maps include information about the species present and the best times to view them.

The route begins at the main gate on Arborway. On your right is the Hunnewell Building, where the Arboretum's visitor center and a large diorama of the grounds are located. Research scientists based here travel around the world to study trees and plants. From the building, head south on wide, paved Meadow Road.

On the left are shadbushes, blueberries, and azaleas; on your right are dogwoods, golden rain trees, and redbuds. The grounds were designed by the legendary landscape architect Frederick Law Olmsted and by the Arboretum's first director, Charles Sprague Sargent, to highlight both scenic and scientific aspects. Along the way, you'll see tags on the plantings featuring information about the species, their original location, and the year they were planted.

After an easy half-mile of walking, you'll arrive at a junction near three small ponds and the Bradley Rosaceous Collection. Here, the main road bears to the right and continues toward Bussey Hill and the lilac collection. (It is the return leg of the loop described here; those looking for a shorter outing can follow it to the Bussey Hill overlook.) This hike continues straight on Beech Path, a narrow, gravel quarter-mile trail that leads through the forsythia collection along the base of the hill.

Shortly after passing a giant beech tree on the right, Beech Path ends at the junction of paved Valley Road and Hemlock Hill Road; at this point, you've walked 0.75 mile. Continue straight on Hemlock Hill Road, passing groves of rhododendrons and mountain laurels. This is one of the Arboretum's better wildlife-viewing areas, as it is home to Bussey Brook and clearings adjacent to the planted trees that offer habitat diversity. A familiar resident of the grounds is the eastern cottontail rabbit, the most common rabbit throughout North America due to its prolific reproductive rate. (Under ideal circumstances, it is estimated that a single pair could be responsible for producing as many as 350,000 offspring within five years, although in the wild, usually only a few offspring survive each year.) Cottontails are an important source of food for predators, such as coyotes and foxes.

Up the slope to your left along the road are the evergreen groves for which Hemlock Hill is named. The eastern hemlock trees have been devastated by the spread of the hemlock woolly adelgid (HWA) in recent decades, and the dead trees are being replaced by pioneer species, such as black birch, as well as experimental plantings of Asian hemlocks. The Arboretum is especially susceptible to HWA infestation due to its mild climate and its location along the coastal Atlantic flyway; transient birds are largely responsible for the spread of HWA, typically a forest pest. The hill has been used for research yielding data on how to

The Arnold Arboretum is a highlight of Boston's Emerald Necklace. With more than 15,000 trees, shrubs, and vines on 265 acres, the Arboretum is a must-see for any botanical garden enthusiast. The summit of Peters Hill offers a striking vew of Boston's skyline.

protect individual trees. (Read more in "Introduced Pests: A Threat to Our Eastern Forests" on page 38.)

After walking for about a quarter-mile along Hemlock Hill Road, you'll arrive at the Bussey Street gate. Carefully cross the street and continue straight into the Peters Hill area. The road soon forks into a loop of slightly less than a mile. Bear left (this is Peters Hill Road) and follow the curving path as it rises gently past colorful crab apples, hawthorns, and a grove of cypresses planted in a wet area. Turn right near the Mendum Street gate to reach a short side path on the right that leads to the 240-foot summit of Peters Hill, which affords long views across the grounds to the Boston skyline. Look carefully for the low gold dome of the State House amid the tall buildings, to the right of the Prudential Tower. This scenic clearing also presents opportunities for bird-watchers; tree swallows and bluebirds use the nest boxes.

After enjoying the scenery, return to Peters Hill Road, follow it right as it descends to complete the loop, and then backtrack to Bussey Street. After recrossing the street, bear left away from Hemlock Hill and then quickly right onto narrow Conifer Path, which begins near the Walter Street gate and offers a pleasant, shady stroll beneath a variety of pines, spruces, larches, junipers, and other evergreens. At the end of the path, go left on paved Valley Road and follow it for a short distance to the junction with Bussey Hill Road. Turn right and follow the road as it curves uphill at an easy grade to the partially open top of Bussey Hill, with a view south to the Blue Hills Reservation.

From the overlook, backtrack along Bussey Hill Road and continue to follow it as it curves right and descends to the lilac collection. This area is especially scenic and popular in early and mid-May, when the lilacs are in peak bloom; the Arboretum hosts a popular lilac festival annually in early May. Shortly beyond the lilacs, the road returns to the junction with Meadow Road at the three ponds. Turn left and retrace your steps to the visitor center.

DID YOU KNOW?

Arnold Arboretum is North America's oldest arboretum that has been open to the public since its inception; others are older but started as private estates or cemeteries.

MORE INFORMATION

The grounds are open from sunrise to sunset year-round. Contact the Arboretum for access to the Hunnewell Visitor Center (usual hours are weekdays from 10 A.M. to 5 P.M.; closed Wednesdays; visitors should check beforehand, as the center's hours could vary due to the COVID-19 pandemic).

8   SPECTACLE ISLAND

Once a landfill, Spectacle Island now offers amazing views of Boston and the coast from the highest point in Boston Harbor.

Features

Location Boston, MA

Rating Easy

Distance 3-mile loop

Elevation Gain 150 feet

Estimated Time 1.25 hours

Maps USGS Boston North; Boston Harbor Islands National and State Park: bostonharborislands.org/spectacle-island

GPS coordinates 42° 21.598′ N, 71° 02.977′ W

Contact Boston Harbor Islands: bostonharborislands.org

DIRECTIONS

The main ferry departure point is Long Wharf in Boston; another ferry leaves from Hingham Shipyard but does not go directly to Spectacle Island. It is best to use public transit to get to Long Wharf, but if driving from the north, follow I-93 to Exit 17 (Government Center). Take the right fork and then stay left. At the traffic light, turn onto Atlantic Avenue. Parking facilities are available at the Boston Harbor Garage, near the New England Aquarium.

By public transportation, take the MBTA Blue Line to Aquarium Station.

Ferry service is provided by Boston Harbor Cruises, which is on Long Wharf. Ferry tickets ($24.95 for adults and $17.95 for children) may be purchased in advance online (bostonharborislands.org/ferry-tickets), reserved by phone (617-227-4321), and reserved or purchased in person at the wharf.

TRAIL DESCRIPTION

The Boston Harbor Islands are a group of 34 islands rich in history, natural resources, and scenic views. From the American Revolution through World War II, Boston Harbor was an important coastal defense site, and old forts and gun batteries are still visible today on some of the islands. The islands have hosted a wide variety of other institutions, including factories, hospitals, and fishing villages. Today, they are protected by a partnership that includes the National Park Service and the Massachusetts Department of Conservation and Recreation.

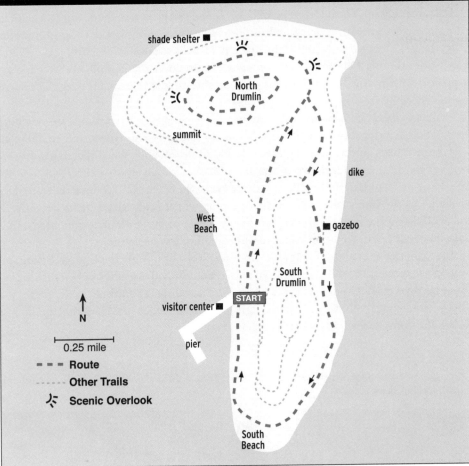

This hike explores Spectacle Island, which has been revitalized after being used as a landfill for many years. The island comprises two glacial drumlins (low, rolling hills): North Drumlin and South Drumlin. North Drumlin is the highest point in the harbor at 155 feet. This route climbs North Drumlin and then follows a portion of the island's perimeter trail (1.8 miles long and ADA accessible) as it loops back to the pier. The walking is easy along well-maintained gravel paths, with a gradual, gentle ascent to the top of North Drumlin. Interpretive signs along the route detail the island's natural and cultural history, and a brochure is available at the visitor center.

As you depart the ferry at the island's boat dock, the visitor center is at the end of the pier to your right. Be sure to check out the exhibits and photographs. Rangers are available to answer questions about trails, history, flora and fauna, and planning your visit. The trail begins to the left of the visitor center, adjacent to West Beach and the perimeter trail. It leads uphill at a gradual grade, with views of Boston across the harbor to the left and of the mostly open hillside to the right, and soon reaches a marked junction for the trails to North and South drumlins. Continue straight on the main trail, following signs for North Drumlin, and pass a crossover path at the next intersection that leads right toward a gazebo.

The route rises up North Drumlin, offering a good perspective of the island's vegetation. The picturesque grasslands, trees, and shrubs visible today are a marked contrast from the past: the island served as a landfill for the city of Boston until 1959. During the 1990s, earth from the Big Dig project was brought over to cover the landfill, and it was then replanted with nearly 30,000 varieties of trees, shrubs, and grasses, creating the present parklike setting.

Thanks to its varied habitats and open areas, the island is an interesting bird-watching destination. Species such as bobolinks, Savannah sparrows, fish crows, and swallows all may be seen here. Bird variety is greatest during spring and fall, when shorebirds, hawks, and songbirds are migrating along the coast. Raccoons, coyotes, turkeys, and deer are present as well. Some of the wildflowers that grow in the openings and along the trail edges include Queen Anne's lace and bird's-foot trefoil, which is identified by its pea-shaped, yellow flowers. The flowers' nectar nourishes a variety of butterflies, including red admirals, monarchs, pearl crescents, cabbage whites, and yellow mustards.

The main trail curves to the left as it winds up North Drumlin. The Boston skyline and waterfront come back into view, and you'll see a continuous stream of planes taking off from nearby Logan Airport, which lies across the harbor on a peninsula to the right. At a fork where a gravel path descends to the right, continue to follow the main trail uphill. Just below the summit, the trail forks into a short loop.

Spectacle Island, one of the 34 Boston Harbor Islands, features two glacial drumlins (low, rolling hills) with beautiful ocean views.

The 155-foot summit of North Drumlin is the highest point in Boston Harbor, and the panoramic vistas are striking. Most visitors are drawn to the buildings of downtown Boston, which is just 4.5 miles west of the island, but be sure to scan the surroundings for views of the Blue Hills, Dorchester Bay, the other islands in Boston Harbor, and the open ocean.

After enjoying the scenery, retrace your steps downhill, back to the interpretive sign that details the revegetation project. At the next junction, bear left and follow the path to the gazebo. From the gazebo, the interpretive trail continues south above the island's eastern shores. (The perimeter trail is visible below, on the left.) At a marked junction, a side path offers a short detour to South Drumlin. Although the views are not quite as sweeping as those from the north, this overlook is worth a visit if you have time.

From the marked junction, the interpretive trail descends to join the perimeter trail. Bear to the right where the paths meet and continue on a pleasant, easy walk along the base of South Drumlin, with planted evergreens and shrubs along the hill on the right. As the trail approaches South Beach at the island's southern tip, it curves right, and Boston comes back into view across the water. You'll soon see the visitor center and pier in the distance to the right. Complete the loop by following the route along the fence back to the visitor center.

DID YOU KNOW?

On nearby Little Brewster Island is 89-foot Boston Light. Built on the rocky island in 1716, it's the oldest working lighthouse in the country. It was automated in 1996.

NEARBY

Visitors to Spectacle Island easily can combine their trip with a stop at Georges Island to tour historic Fort Warren or with a visit to one of the other islands. Ferry schedules and maps are available at the terminals. Waterside cafes are on Spectacle and Georges islands.

MORE INFORMATION

The island is open year-round, although the ferry operates only from mid-May to Columbus Day. Visitor centers and concessions with snacks and light meals are at Spectacle and Georges islands. A carry-in, carry-out policy is enforced on all the Boston Harbor Islands. Short ranger-led programs are available near the pier in summer; contact the Massachusetts Department of Conservation and Recreation for the weekly schedule.

INTRODUCED PESTS: A THREAT TO OUR EASTERN FORESTS

While walking along the trails through hemlock groves at conservation areas in Massachusetts, you may notice that many of the trees are dead or dying. This is due to infestation by the hemlock woolly adelgid (HWA), a tiny, aphidlike insect that poses a substantial threat to eastern hemlock trees throughout the forests of eastern North America.

HWA, which is native to Asia, was introduced to North America during the 1950s in Virginia and has gradually spread through the forests of the Northeast and South. The insects are carried by wind and by animals, such as deer, squirrels, and birds. HWA became established in southern New England during the 1980s. It has caused extensive eastern hemlock mortality in coastal areas and river valleys in Connecticut, Massachusetts, and Rhode Island but has been slower to affect cooler, higher elevations.

Although the adelgids themselves are less than one-sixteenth of an inch in size, evidence of infestation is easy to observe, as their puffy white egg masses are often obvious at the base of hemlock needles. Adelgids kill their hosts by feeding on tissues and starches that are essential to the trees' survival. Once infested, a tree can die in four to ten years or even faster in milder southern regions, such as the Great Smoky Mountains.

Because eastern hemlock is a "climax" forest species that takes a long time to recover once disturbed (as opposed to a "pioneer" species, such as white pine or black birch, which responds well to disruption), HWA is of considerable concern. Research into control measures is ongoing. Options for treating individual trees include injecting chemicals into the roots and spraying entire trees with repellent oils. In larger forest groves, adelgid predators, such as ladybugs, have been introduced.

HWA is just one of many introduced pests and diseases that have affected North America's forests. The American chestnut, once one of the Northeast's most significant species from both ecological and economic perspectives, was all but eliminated by a blight in the early twentieth century. An outbreak of Asian long-horned beetles in the greater Worcester area in 2008 resulted in removal of 35,000 trees and the establishment of a 110-square-mile quarantine zone. This insect poses a serious threat to many important hardwood species, including maples, birches, and poplars. A smaller outbreak near the Arnold Arboretum in 2010 was eradicated. In recent years, the emerald ash borer, which has killed hundreds of millions of ash trees across North America since being introduced in the Midwest in 2002, has rapidly spread across Massachusetts. Researchers are working to document and contain these and other threats to New England's forests.

STONY BROOK RESERVATION

This easy walk explores forests, rocky outcroppings, wetlands, and a scenic pond—all within Boston's city limits.

Features

Location Boston, MA (near West Roxbury and Hyde Park)

Rating Easy

Distance 2.6-mile loop

Elevation Gain Minimal

Estimated Time 1.5 hours

Maps USGS Boston South; Massachusetts Department of Conservation and Recreation: mass.gov/doc/stony-brook-reservation-trail-map/download

GPS coordinates 42° 15.512′ N, 71° 08.154′ W

Contact Massachusetts Department of Conservation and Recreation: mass.gov/locations/stony-brook-reservation, 617-727-5290

DIRECTIONS

From I-95, take Exit 32 for MA 135 toward Needham/Natick. At the exit, turn right on West Street toward Dedham. The road becomes Common Street and then, in the center of Dedham, becomes High Street (still going straight, under a highway overpass). Turn slightly right after the overpass to stay on High Street. After crossing Milton Street, High Street becomes Sawmill Lane as it crosses a bridge. It becomes Dedham Boulevard and then Dedham Parkway. At Dedham Parkway's intersection with Turtle Pond Parkway and Enneking Parkway, go left onto Enneking Parkway and proceed 0.5 mile to the parking lot, which might be difficult to see.

By public transportation, take the MBTA Commuter Rail to Hyde Park Station. Walk 0.3 mile northwest on Gordon Avenue, turn left onto Enneking Parkway, and walk 0.4 mile to the parking lot. You also can take the MBTA number 40 bus from Forest Hills Station to the intersection of Turtle Pond Parkway and Enneking Parkway. From there, walk 0.2 mile east to the parking lot.

TRAIL DESCRIPTION

Stony Brook Reservation is a 613-acre oasis of forests, wetlands, rocky outcroppings, and glacial drumlins nestled between Boston's West Roxbury and Hyde Park neighborhoods, constituting the largest open space within city limits. In spite of the reservation's urban location, you may enjoy a surprising degree of solitude. This hike makes a hairpin-shaped

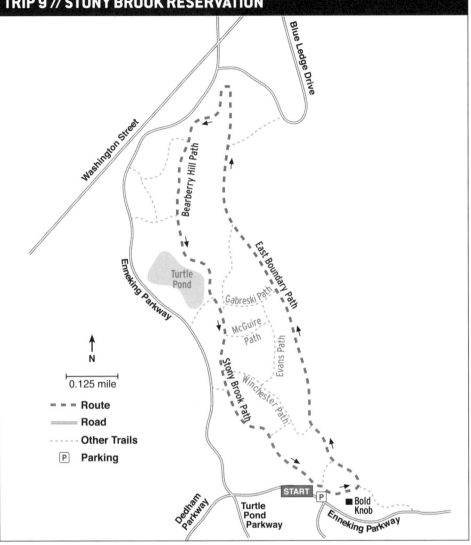

loop through the area on the east side of Enneking Parkway, combining two of the paved recreational paths with footpaths and old cart roads.

From the parking lot, walk past the light-green gate and turn right on the paved recreational trail. This blue-blazed route soon passes through a field of boulders as it skirts a rocky outcropping known as Bold Knob. (An unmarked side path here leads right to the reservation boundary.) The trail continues to the north, passing a wetland in the woods to the right. At a junction at marker 210, Winchester Path leaves left and connects to a series of short woodland paths. Stay right, on East Boundary Path, as it continues along the recreational trail, which crosses a rocky seasonal brook and then follows a fence along the edge of the George Wright Golf Course.

Stony Brook Reservation boasts 613 acres of forest, the largest open space within Boston's city limits.

Areas where different habitats meet, such as the border of the forest and the golf course clearings, are beneficial for wildlife because the "edge effect" allows opportunities both for foraging and protection. Scan these locations carefully for glimpses of coyotes, foxes, white-tailed deer, eastern cottontail rabbits, and wild turkeys. All these species thrive in mixed habitats, and their populations have increased rapidly throughout New England as the region has become reforested and fewer of the animals are hunted.

The reservation is also home to a variety of birdlife. Recent surveys and bird counts by local groups indicate that at least 70 species are present at various times of the year. These expansive woodlands in the heart of a heavily developed area offer crucial habitat for migratory songbirds, which are most visible in midspring and early summer. Three of the most conspicuous are black-throated green warblers, red-eyed vireos, and ovenbirds.

At marker 240, paved Stony Brook Path enters from the left. This hike continues straight along East Boundary Path, which passes through a large wetland. Animals here include mink and raccoons, both of which frequent the reservation's waterbodies. Raccoons are much more tolerant of humans; in fact, they often are found in urban and suburban neighborhoods. Waterfowl in this wetland include great blue herons and green herons; black, mallard, and wood ducks; and double-crested cormorants.

East Boundary Path soon reaches its end at the reservation's boundary, near Enneking Parkway and Blue Ledge Drive. Just before the trail reaches gate 29, turn left on a narrow footpath at marker 250, which is 1.2 miles from the trailhead. The path winds beneath tall pines and oaks; crosses a rocky, partially open area; and slopes downhill to bear left again, near Enneking Parkway. From here, Bearberry Hill Path follows a wide old cart road along the base of Bearberry Hill, a 246-foot drumlin that rises to your left. The hill is one of the higher points of the reservation, which features topography ranging from 15 feet above sea level to 338 feet (Bellevue Hill). Bearberry is an evergreen shrub with tiny, bell-shaped white flowers that bloom in May and June. It thrives in sandy and exposed rocky habitats.

Continue straight through the next junction and then bear left at marker 238 on a short side path that arcs to the north shore of Turtle Pond. Here, a wooden fishing platform offers pleasant views and is an ideal spot for a break. Sunfish and perch are among the inhabitants of the pond.

From the pond, begin the last leg of the hike by following Bearberry Hill Path past large, rocky outcroppings, staying straight at junction 232 (this is Turtle Pond Path) and turning left at junction 230. When Turtle Pond Trail ends at the next junction, turn right onto paved, blue-blazed Stony Brook Path and follow it south toward the reservation's entrance, passing junctions with several short forest footpaths and more rocky outcroppings.

Stony Brook Path continues to the southeast. After 20 to 30 minutes of easy walking from Turtle Pond, you'll reach marker 202, adjacent to the parking lot. The green gate and parking area will be on your right.

DID YOU KNOW?

At 338 feet, Bellevue Hill is the highest point in the city of Boston.

NEARBY

The southern tip of Stony Brook Reservation is home to a recreational area that includes tennis courts, baseball and soccer fields, picnic areas, an ice rink, and a swimming pool. Local restaurants are on Hyde Park Avenue and on River Street in Cleary Square.

MORE INFORMATION

The reservation is open year-round, dawn to dusk. Dogs are allowed but must be leashed.

10 BLUE HILLS RESERVATION: OBSERVATION TOWER LOOP

A hike to the Blue Hills Reservation's observation tower takes you through a variety of woodland terrain, with an outstanding view at the top.

Features

Location Canton and Milton, MA

Rating Moderate

Distance 2-mile loop

Elevation Gain 400 feet

Estimated Time 1.5 hours

Maps USGS Norwood; Massachusetts Department of Conservation and Recreation: mass.gov/eea/docs/dcr/parks/trails/blue-hills-trail-map-2016.pdf

GPS coordinates 42° 13.016′ N, 71° 07.165′ W

Contact Massachusetts Department of Conservation and Recreation: mass.gov/locations/blue-hills-reservation, 617-698-1802; Mass Audubon: massaudubon.org, 508-255-3421; Friends of the Blue Hills: friendsofthebluehills.org

DIRECTIONS

From I-93, take Exit 2B and follow MA 138 north 1.0 mile to the parking lot on the right, adjacent to Blue Hills Trailside Museum.

By public transportation, take the MBTA Red Line to Ashmont Station and then ride the high-speed trolley line to Mattapan. From there, take the number 716 bus to Blue Hills Trailside Museum.

TRAIL DESCRIPTION

The 635-foot summit of Great Blue Hill is the highest point in the Blue Hills chain. The observation tower at the top of the hill offers sweeping vistas to Boston and beyond. Great Blue Hill lies at the western end of the Blue Hills Reservation. At its base is Blue Hills Trailside Museum, operated by Mass Audubon. The trails here are popular on weekends, so plan accordingly. If you are hiking with young children, you might want to go only partway up the hill or to reverse the walk and go up the gentler incline first. Another option is to walk up paved Summit Road, which is closed to public vehicles (see trail map).

Begin your hike from the trailhead in the parking lot just to the right of Blue Hills Trailside Museum (as you face it from the street). Watch for a signboard; red dots on trees mark the trail. This is the most direct route to the summit, and it rises steeply in some places. On your right are the open slopes of the Blue Hills Ski Area.

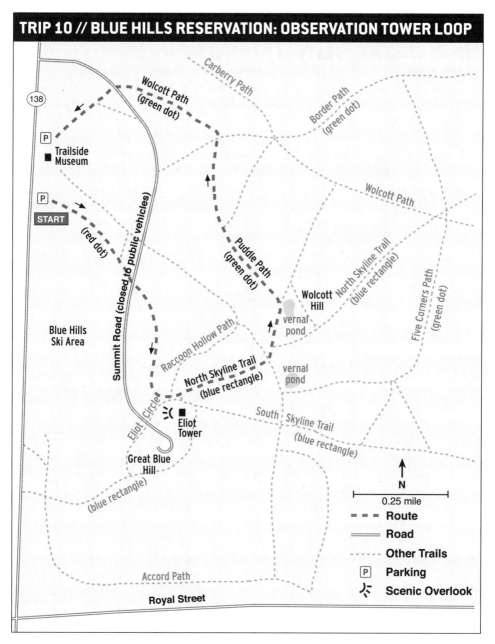

About 15 minutes into the hike, cross a narrow trail and then paved Summit Road. Proceed through an area of red pines. You can distinguish them from the more common white pines because their needles are thicker and a bit longer, and their bark is lighter, with a rusty hue. This portion of the trail has exposed granite ledges, and children will love the challenge of "mountain climbing." It's a great place to introduce kids to mountainous hikes without taxing their endurance. Be sure to stop every now and then after the first few minutes of climbing, both to catch your breath and to glance back and admire the view of the

Boston skyline over your shoulder. The birches growing in this rocky soil are mostly of the gray variety, which are among the first trees to colonize an area of poor soil or land where fire has destroyed a more mature forest.

Continue to follow the red dots to the summit's stone observation tower 0.6 mile from the trailhead. Eliot Tower is named for Charles Eliot, a famed landscape architect and lover of open spaces. Two picnic benches sit beneath the shelter of the tower structure. Lowbush blueberries grow in sunny spots. In fall, their scarlet leaves contrast nicely with the gray bedrock.

The summit of Great Blue Hill offers sweeping vistas of Boston and the ocean beyond, but the trees and hilltops in the foreground also may capture your attention. From this vantage point, you can see interesting patterns of tree species, particularly in fall, when the rust-colored oaks dominate, with patches of hemlock and white pine scattered about the hills.

The summit also provides a good site for watching hawks during their spring and fall migrations. Early September is usually the best time for a successful hawk watch. Plan for a day when the wind is out of the north or west, which helps propel the hawks (mostly the broad-winged type) on their southerly journeys.

Although the most direct route back to the parking area is via another section of the red-dotted trail, called Raccoon Hollow Path, you may want a more gradual descent in a northwesterly direction. For that option, follow North Skyline Trail (marked on a granite post), which begins near the back of Eliot Tower. The trail is marked by blue rectangles, but be aware that South Skyline Trail is also marked by blue rectangles. As you descend North Skyline Trail, the partial views of the surrounding hills will give you an appreciation for just how large the reservation is. (*Caution*: The footing can be a bit tricky due to many small rocks and the trail's steepness.)

At the intersection near the base of the hill, take the second left onto Puddle Path, which is marked by both blue rectangles and green dots. (Do not take the first hard left onto the unmarked trail going uphill.) In 30 feet, the blue rectangle trail goes right; stay straight on Puddle Path, following the green dots. In a couple of minutes, you will come to a fork in the trail. Go left, continuing to follow the green dots.

Puddle Path is a wide trail passing through an area of handsome beech trees. Even in the dead of winter, the lower branches are covered with paper-thin tan leaves, which do not fall off until new growth begins in spring. Follow Puddle Path straight past an unmarked trail on the right. Turn left here onto wide Wolcott Path, ignoring the narrow trail on the left just before the T intersection. Wolcott Path crosses the northern end of Summit Road and soon arrives at the north parking lot and the museum. Walk through the museum to return to your starting point at the south lot.

The otter exhibit outside Blue Hills Trailside Museum is a must-see because the animals are elusive in the wild. Spend some time here, as the otter puts on quite a show, diving beneath the water and rolling on the surface. Next to the otter pen are areas for injured wildlife, which may include deer, turkeys, hawks, and owls. Inside the museum are interpretive exhibits, such as a wigwam, and live animals, including a timber rattlesnake, a copperhead, and a snapping turtle.

Plan future visits to travel the trails to the east of Great Blue Hill. Consider making it an all-day hike with a friend, leaving one car at the opposite end of the reservation. Skyline

Trail is approximately 9 miles long, and some hikers use this as a training ground to get in shape before climbing the White Mountains of New Hampshire.

DID YOU KNOW?

Founded in 1885, Blue Hill Meteorological Observatory is the source of the longest continuously recorded weather data in North America. Many pioneering weather discoveries have been made here, and it is an important resource in ongoing studies of climate change.

NEARBY

The Neponset River Reservation protects a large, natural estuary with extensive tidal marshes at its mouth and a complex of freshwater wetlands. Over the past century, the state has acquired 750 acres of this watershed. Several access points exist to the reservation, including Pope John Paul II Park on Gallivan Boulevard near its intersection with I-93 in Boston. A second entrance is on Hallett Street.

MORE INFORMATION

The Blue Hills Reservation is open year-round, dawn to dusk; no fee. Dogs are allowed but must be leashed. Guided hikes and special programs are offered by the Friends of the Blue Hills. Trailside Museum is open Wednesday through Sunday, 9 A.M. to 4 P.M.; there is an admission fee. Norman Smith Environmental Education Center on Chickatawbut Hill offers workshops and programs for organized groups by reservation only through Mass Audubon.

Eliot Tower provides sweeping views of Boston and the ocean beyond.

AN URBAN OASIS

Blue Hills Reservation is a large oasis of forested land just a few miles from downtown Boston. Of the 22 hills within the chain, the highest is 635-foot Great Blue Hill, followed by 517-foot Chickatawbut Hill—both in the northern section of the reservation. In addition to the low, wooded hills, the reservation encompasses a stretch of the Neponset River; the adjoining wetlands of Fowl Meadow; Ponkapoag Pond, Houghton's Pond, and several smaller ponds; and the Quincy Quarries Historic Site, now a popular rock-climbing destination.

People have been living in the Blue Hills for more than 10,000 years. The native people who lived here chose the area due to its close proximity to the ocean and to the Neponset River, as well as for its high vantage points and the presence of quarry materials (brown volcanic rock, or hornfels) for making tools.

The Blue Hills received their present name from European explorers, who described the hills as having a bluish tint when observed from boats on the ocean. The colonists who subsequently settled in the area cleared much of the land for agriculture, built houses and barns, and cut the forests on the hills. In 1825, a large-scale quarry was established that produced granite for buildings, monuments, and fortifications across the nation. Today, sixteen individual sites within the reservation are listed on the National Register of Historic Places.

The windswept summit of Great Blue Hill is home to the Blue Hill Meteorological Observatory, founded in 1885 by the meteorologist Abbott Lawrence Rotch as a private scientific center for weather-related experiments. The observatory is the oldest continuously operated weather station in the United States and retains long-term data especially important to climate change studies. It is now operated as the Blue Hill Weather Observatory and Science Center.

In 1893, the Metropolitan Parks Commission purchased the Blue Hills land to establish one of the first state parks in Massachusetts. Today, the extensive woodlands offer habitat and travel corridors for large animals, such as white-tailed deer, red foxes, eastern coyotes, and raccoons. The reservation is also home to many smaller creatures, including butterflies, dragonflies, salamanders, and both migratory and year-round birds.

11 BLUE HILLS RESERVATION: GREAT BLUE HILL GREEN LOOP

This loop meanders through the Great Blue Hill section of the reservation, following the cols between the hills without ascending any summits.

Features

Location Canton and Milton, MA

Rating Easy to Moderate

Distance 2.8-mile loop

Elevation Gain 200 feet

Estimated Time 1.5 hours

Maps USGS Norwood; Massachusetts Department of Conservation and Recreation: mass.gov/eea/docs/dcr/parks/trails/blue-hills-trail-map-2016.pdf

GPS coordinates 42° 13.016′ N, 71° 07.165′ W

Contact Massachusetts Department of Conservation and Recreation: mass.gov/locations/blue-hills-reservation, 617-698-1802; Mass Audubon: massaudubon.org, 508-255-3421; Friends of the Blue Hills: friendsofthebluehills.org

DIRECTIONS

From I-93, take Exit 2B and follow MA 138 north 1.0 mile to the parking lot on the right, adjacent to Blue Hills Trailside Museum.

By public transportation, take the MBTA Red Line to Ashmont and then ride the high-speed trolley line to Mattapan. From there, take the number 716 bus to Blue Hills Trailside Museum.

TRAIL DESCRIPTION

Green Loop offers a pleasant, fairly easy walk for hikers who wish to explore the western portion of the Blue Hills Reservation without climbing any of the hills. The route begins at the north parking lot next to Blue Hills Trailside Museum, at the base of Great Blue Hill, and follows a series of trails that wind through the reservation's extensive forests and past wetlands and rocky outcroppings. From the trailhead at the parking lot, follow the green blazes northeast. The trail crosses the paved access road that leads to Great Blue Hill's summit and then joins Wolcott Path, continuing beneath white pines, oaks, and maples. A field is visible through the trees to the left.

At junction 1085, the loop proper begins. Here, Puddle Path—the return route—comes in from the right. Continue straight on Wolcott Path for a few hundred feet to marker 1100 and then turn left onto Border Path. Smooth, easy Border Path leads northeast through the

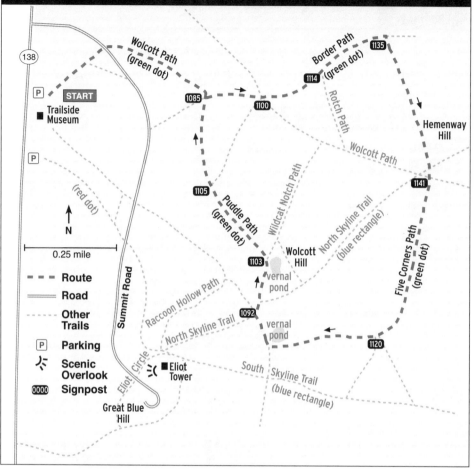

woods and crosses Balster Brook at the outlet of a wetland. Stay straight at a fork at marker 1114 when Rotch Path branches to the right. The trail slopes downhill to another stream crossing.

This is a relatively quiet corner of the reservation and a good place to watch for a variety of wildlife. The Blue Hills wetlands are home to seven species of turtles. The most common are painted turtles, which are often observed basking on logs, rocks, and aquatic vegetation during warm months. Also present are much larger snapping turtles, which, as the name implies, have a powerful bite. Less common species include spotted, box, musk, Blanding's, and wood turtles. Visit in the early morning or evening, and you may glimpse a white-tailed deer or a red fox.

At a four-way junction (marker 1135), turn right off Border Path and follow the green-blazed trail, which continues southwest through the col between Wolcott Hill on your right and Hemenway Hill on the left. Walk 0.4 mile from Border Path to reach a six-way junction of the reservation's trails, including North Skyline Trail (which leads to the summits of nearby Great Blue Hill and Wolcott Hill to the west and Hancock Hill to the east), at marker 1141. A map is posted at this intersection. Green Loop continues straight here on Five Corners Path and leads south for 0.3 mile along the base of Wolcott Hill, which rises to the west.

At marker 1120, turn right and begin an easy climb past a series of glacial boulders on the south slopes of Wolcott Hill. These rocks were deposited by melting glaciers at the end of the most recent ice age, more than 10,000 years ago. The antenna atop Great Blue Hill comes into view a short distance west of Wolcott Hill.

The trail bears right at a junction near a small wetland and then right again at nearby marker 1092 to head north on Wildcat Notch Path, which leads through the narrow valley between the eastern slopes of Great Blue Hill and the west side of Wolcott Hill. After passing another small pond, where birds such as robins, blue jays, and tufted titmice drink and bathe, bear left at marker 1103 onto Puddle Path. Puddle Path continues straight (left) at marker 1105 and slopes gently downhill to close the loop where it meets Wolcott Path. Turn left here and retrace your steps to the Blue Hills Trailside Museum parking lot, following the green blazes.

DID YOU KNOW?

Six native species of turtle are threatened or endangered, including the box turtle, the bog turtle, and the red-bellied cooter. They've lost habitat to development and are often struck by cars when trying to cross roads.

An otter grooms in the outdoor exhibit at the Blue Hills Trailside Museum. River otters' thick fur traps a layer of air next to the skin—insulation that allows the otter to swim in winter.

NEARBY

The Forbes House Museum, a National Historic Landmark property on Adams Street in Milton, preserves the home of Captain Robert Bennet Forbes, a member of one of the prominent local families involved in maritime sailing and trading during the nineteenth century. It is open for tours by reservation on Friday and Saturday; visit forbeshousemuseum.org for information. Restaurants are along Adams Street in Milton and on Hancock Street in the center of Quincy.

MORE INFORMATION

Blue Hills Reservation is open year-round, dawn to dusk; no fee. Dogs are allowed but must be leashed. Trail information and maps (maps $3) are available at Blue Hills Trailside Museum or online (maps free) at mass.gov/dcr. Guided hikes and special programs are offered by the Friends of the Blue Hills.

Mass Audubon operates two educational facilities within the reservation. Blue Hills Trailside Museum is open to the public Wednesday through Sunday, 9 A.M. to 4 P.M.; there is an admission fee. Mass Audubon's Norman Smith Environmental Education Center on Chickatawbut Hill offers workshops and programs for organized groups by reservation only.

12 BLUE HILLS RESERVATION: PONKAPOAG POND

A short hike to a quaking bog via Maple Avenue gives you a chance to see rare plant species; the pond loop offers a longer outing.

Features

Location Canton and Randolph, MA

Rating Easy

Distance 4-mile loop

Elevation Gain Minimal

Estimated Time 2 hours

Maps USGS Norwood; Massachusetts Department of Conservation and Recreation: mass.gov/eea/docs/dcr/parks/trails/blue-hills-trail-map-2016.pdf

GPS coordinates 42° 11.514′ N, 71° 06.997′ W

Contact Massachusetts Department of Conservation and Recreation: mass.gov/locations/blue-hills-reservation, 617-698-1802; Mass Audubon: massaudubon.org, 508-255-3421; Friends of the Blue Hills: friendsofthebluehills.org; Appalachian Mountain Club: ponkapoagcamp.org, 781-961-7007

DIRECTIONS

From I-93 take Exit 2A for Washington Street in Canton. Turn left just before the first set of lights into the Ponkapoag Golf Course parking lot. Follow the signs to the reservation.

By public transportation, take the MBTA Red Line to Ashmont and then ride the high-speed trolley line to Mattapan. From there, take the number 716 bus to the Ponkapoag Golf Course.

TRAIL DESCRIPTION

Due to its location near I-93, Ponkapoag Pond is a popular weekend destination for hiking and cross-country skiing. On most weekdays, however, the area is usually free of people, even after work hours. The main trail loops the 200-acre pond and a regionally uncommon Atlantic white cedar swamp on the property's northwest side. The pond attracts all sorts of wildlife, including ospreys and great blue herons. Dogs are not allowed on the boardwalk leading into the quaking bog.

From the golf course parking lot on the right side of the buildings, look for a paved road that passes through the fairways (no cars allowed). The entrance to this road is lined with a row of stately sugar maples. Appropriately enough, the road is called Maple Avenue. Walk down Maple Avenue, through the golf course, and to the edge of Ponkapoag Pond. The

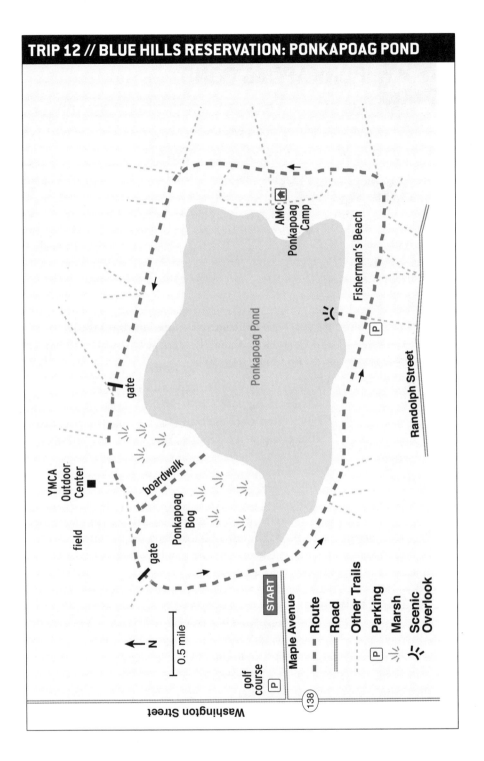

Sunset over Ponkapoag Pond, a popular hiking destination in the Blue Hills. *Photo by Cynthia Sexton/AMC Photo Contest.*

paved road ends here, and a wide, well-maintained dirt trail circles the pond. Go left to reach the quaking bog in about 0.5 mile—a good ramble if you are with young children. The floating boardwalk leading into the bog begins opposite a field and some cabins operated by the YMCA.

The following directions are for a complete circuit of the pond. At the end of Maple Avenue, go right onto the dirt road. The trail hugs the edge of the pond, offering plenty of opportunities to reach the shoreline. A little more than 0.5 mile down the trail is an open area with an attractive view of the Blue Hills across the water. The road opposite the beach leads to a parking lot at Randolph Street. This entrance is known as Fisherman's Beach. Cartop boats can be carried down the path and launched here. (The entrance off Randolph Street is next to Temple Beth David, across the street from Westdale Road.)

The first mile of the pond trail has rich, moist soil. Trees commonly associated with more northern forests—yellow birch, hemlock, maple, beech—grow above the ferns. Although the trees are quite large, most of them are probably less than 100 years old. As in much of Massachusetts, settlers here cleared the old forests for pastures and farmland, using the wood for lumber and fuel.

Along the trail, look for skunk cabbage, one of the first harbingers of spring. It has large, cabbage-like leaves and sometimes grows right through late-season snow. Its odor is quite similar to a skunk's. During the summer months, the smell of skunk cabbage is replaced by the pleasant fragrance of sweet pepperbush. You can identify this plant by the narrow green leaves and clusters of tiny white flowers growing in dense, slender spikes at the ends of its branches. It can reach a height of 10 feet.

Great blue herons frequent the pond, thanks to the abundance of warmwater fish. Both herons and human anglers try their skill at catching largemouth bass and pickerel, but herons tend to hunt for prey smaller than 5 inches. Anglers on the shore have the best chance of catching fish in spring, when the fish are seeking warm, shallow water for spawning and feeding. Ospreys occasionally stop at the pond, so if you're visiting during their spring or fall migration, be sure to bring binoculars. The sight of an osprey diving from the sky to snatch a fish with its talons is one you will never forget. Red-winged blackbirds also descend upon the pond; in springtime, the red-shouldered males arrive first in huge flocks and explore the entire shoreline as they wait for the females. Mosquitoes also inhabit the reservation, so come prepared.

As the trail passes around the back of the pond, green-dot markers attached to trees help guide you. A group of cottages on the left is managed by the Appalachian Mountain Club; to stay on the trail, keep to the right at all junctions leading toward the cabins. (Feel free to take a detour for a closer look, however. AMC's Ponkapoag Camp features twenty cabins and a limited number of seasonal tentsites for those who wish to extend their hike to an overnight stay. Visit outdoors.org for more information and to request a reservation.) At the third trail junction, go down a small hill where a map is posted. Soon the trail intersects with another; go left, following the green-dot markers. Finally, turn left again at a gate. You are now on the north side of the pond. The YMCA Outdoor Center is a little farther down the trail. The boardwalk to the bog is opposite the field.

The bog has been designated a National Environmental Study Area due to its uncommon ecosystem. A beautiful stand of Atlantic white cedar grows here, along with the unusual pitcher plant. Because the nutrients in the bog soil are limited, pitcher plants and other carnivorous plants, such as the sundew, obtain their nourishment from insects. While many people are familiar with the Venus flytrap (indigenous to the southeastern United States), which captures its prey by snapping shut over them, the bog plants of the Northeast use a different method of entrapment. The pitcher plant attracts insects onto its leaves with its scent and colorful veins. Once the insect touches down, it has a hard time escaping. Tiny hairs in the plant point downward, trapping the insect and drowning it in the liquid at the bottom of the pitcher, after which the plant's enzymes digest the insect. To identify the plant, usually 1 to 2 feet tall, look for its pitcher-shaped, reddish-green leaves. In summer, it will have a large, solitary, purplish-red flower on a leafless stalk.

The boardwalk starts out in a dense jungle of swamp maples and other trees before it reaches the white cedars, finally penetrating the more open area of the bog, which is dominated by leatherleaf. In summer, you will see the pink flowers (about a half-inch wide) of sheep laurel. The sheep laurel grows between 1 and 3 feet tall and looks similar to the more common mountain laurel. It thrives in bog areas and is expanding its range at Ponkapoag as the bog expands. Each year, the water becomes shallower as vegetation closes its ring around the pond. No underground streams and few springs exist to replenish and oxygenate the water. Sphagnum moss flourishes in the stagnant water of the bog, and as it dies, it fills in the pond.

Once you finish exploring the bog, retrace your steps along the boardwalk to the main trail by the YMCA Outdoor Center and go left. Walk about 0.5 mile down the main trail to reach the golf course and then Maple Avenue, which leads to the parking area.

DID YOU KNOW?

According to a history of Canton, *Ponkapoag* was an interpretation of an American Indian word meaning "sweet water." It was also the name given to the 6,000-acre reservation that colonists set aside in 1657 for American Indians displaced from their homes near the Neponset River.

NEARBY

Mass Audubon's Museum of American Bird Art, at 963 Washington Street in Canton, houses collections of natural history photography and art and offers related programs and exhibitions. The grounds are also home to the Mildred Morse Allen Wildlife Sanctuary, where 2 miles of trails explore forests, a red maple swamp, and meadows. Restaurants are in Canton on Washington Street and along MA 27.

MORE INFORMATION

The Blue Hills Reservation is open year-round, dawn to dusk; no fee. Restrooms are available at the Houghton's Pond Visitor Center year-round and at the Houghton's Pond bathhouse during summer. Dogs are allowed but must be leashed. Guided hikes and special programs are offered through the Friends of the Blue Hills. Blue Hills Trailside Museum is open Wednesday through Sunday, 9 A.M. to 4 P.M.; there is an admission fee. Mass Audubon's Norman Smith Environmental Education Center at Chickatawbut Hill offers workshops and programs for organized groups by reservation only.

AMC's Ponkapoag Camp, on the eastern shore of Ponkapoag Pond, rents cabins and tentsites for overnights. Reservations are required.

13

BLUE HILLS RESERVATION: HOUGHTON'S POND YELLOW DOT LOOP

This easy 1-mile pond loop is a popular walk for families with small children.

Features

Location Milton, MA

Rating Easy

Distance 1-mile loop

Elevation Gain Minimal

Estimated Time 30 minutes

Maps USGS Norwood, Massachusetts Department of Conservation and Recreation: mass.gov/eea/docs/dcr/parks/trails/blue-hills-trail-map-2016.pdf

GPS coordinates 42° 12.579′ N, 71° 05.826′ W

Contact Massachusetts Department of Conservation and Recreation: mass.gov/locations/blue-hills-reservation, 617-698-1802; Mass Audubon: massaudubon.org, 508-255-3421; Friends of the Blue Hills: friendsofthebluehills.org

DIRECTIONS

Take I-93 to Exit 3 (Houghton's Pond). At the end of Blue Hill River Road, turn right onto Hillside Street and follow it 0.3 mile to the parking lot on your right.

By public transportation, take the MBTA Red Line to Ashmont and then ride the high-speed trolley line to Mattapan. From there, take the number 716 bus to the intersection of Washington Street and Royall Street. Walk 1.2 miles east on Blue Hill River Road, which will turn into Hillside Street along the way.

TRAIL DESCRIPTION

One of the attractions of the Blue Hills Reservation is its wide variety of hiking trails, with options ranging from challenging full-day traverses to shorter, less strenuous strolls through quiet woodlands and around scenic ponds. One of the reservation's most popular destinations is Houghton's Pond, a small pond nestled at the base of the southern slopes of the Blue Hills chain. It is a short distance east of Great Blue Hill and north of the much larger Ponkapoag Pond.

The loop trail encircling Houghton's Pond is especially good for families with young children. It is just long enough to feel like a real outing, and there are continuous views across the water to hold kids' attention. Although the trail intersects with a number of other footpaths and dirt roads (closed to vehicles), it is easy to follow, well marked with yellow dots. The trail is 1.0 mile long and can be completed in half an hour or less.

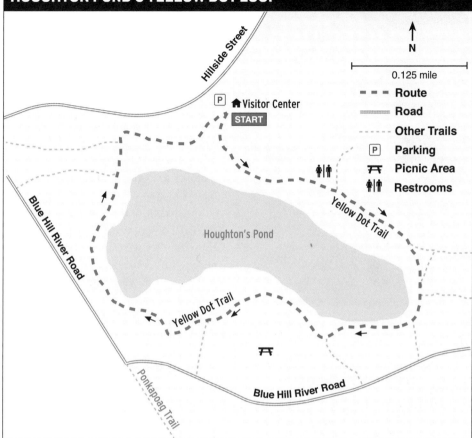

For a warm-up to the actual outing, visit the Marigold Marsh boardwalk that connects the playground to the beach. It includes interpretive signage that allows caregivers to introduce young ones to wetland plant, insect, and animal species as well as helping to develop observation skills.

The trail begins at the main parking lot for the Houghton's Pond swimming area, off Hillside Street. Follow the path to the left, which leads east past the swimming beach on the pond's north shore, bearing right just after the bathhouse. A dirt road branches to the left and leads north toward Bugbee Path and Skyline Trail just east of Houghton Hill.

The trail turns to the right to run along the pond's narrow eastern tip, where it briefly follows a dirt service road before continuing west along the south shore, passing a picnic area. Great Blue Hill, the highest point in the Blue Hills Reservation, rises across the water to the west, and pine trees line the shore.

This trail is a great place to introduce children to some of the common wildlife people often take for granted. One of the most familiar creatures in these woodlands is the eastern chipmunk, which is most active during summer and fall, gathering food to store for the colder winter months. The chipmunks' metabolism slows during winter, and they go into

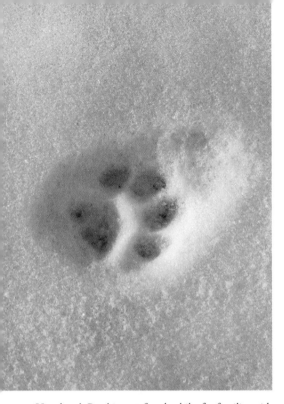

Houghton's Pond is a perfect day hike for families with dogs and young children. In summer, it's a popular swimming destination. Watch for animal tracks in winter.

a torpor-like state in which they are mostly asleep, waking up periodically to feed on the food they have cached in storage areas. Chipmunks' varied diet includes fruits, nuts, seeds, insects, small rodents, and even snakes. In turn, they are an important prey species for predators such as coyotes, foxes, and bobcats.

One of the birds you may see on the pond is the double-crested cormorant, which is easily distinguished by its long, thin neck and black color. Although cormorants are now a familiar sight along New England's coast, they were largely eliminated from the region as recently as the early twentieth century. In Massachusetts, they were absent from the early nineteenth century until the 1940s, when breeding pairs were noted in the Boston area. Many commercial fishers once considered cormorants a threat to their livelihood—not for the volume of fish they ate but because they often broke up schools of fish at key fishing areas, diving and jumping into the water on their hunting rounds. Thanks to their adaptability, cormorants have strongly rebounded and are now seen even on some inland lakes.

Spring is an excellent time to watch for migratory waterfowl and songbirds. Due to the reservation's proximity to the coast and its concentration of forest in a heavily developed area, it is an important stopover point for birds flying long distances. Some of the colorful songbirds you may see or hear include pine warblers, scarlet tanagers, chestnut-sided warblers, and American redstarts.

The pond is a popular fishing spot, and as you walk along the south shore, you'll probably pass several anglers. Fishing enthusiasts who frequent the site report that the south shore is a good place to catch trout, especially after the pond has been stocked. Other species include sunfish, perch, bass, pickerel, and carp. Fishing is allowed from the shore only, and a license is required.

The trail curves to the right around the pond's southwest corner, near Blue Hill River Road, where there are good views across the water to the east. From there, the trail crosses the pond's outlet and leads north past a field. After passing through a small swampy area at the pond's northwest tip, near Hillside Street, complete the outing with a short walk east past a pavilion to the entrance and parking area.

DID YOU KNOW

Many features of the Blue Hills, including Eliot Tower, trails, and bridges, were constructed by the Civilian Conservation Corps in the mid-1930s. The workers, mostly veterans of World War I who had trouble finding employment during the Depression, lived in a rustic camp off MA 28 in Randolph. The site is marked by interpretive signs and a granite memorial bench.

NEARBY

Convenience stores, a restaurant, and gas stations can be found on MA 138 near the intersection of Blue Hill River Road.

MORE INFORMATION

The Blue Hills Reservation is open year-round, dawn to dusk; no fee. Dogs are allowed but must be leashed. Guided hikes and special programs are offered through the Friends of the Blue Hills. Trail information and maps (maps $3) are available at Blue Hills Trailside Museum, one of two educational facilities operated by Mass Audubon within the reservation, or online (maps free) at mass.gov/dcr. The museum is open Wednesday through Sunday, 9 A.M. to 4 P.M.; there is an admission fee. Mass Audubon's Norman Smith Environmental Education Center at Chickatawbut Hill offers workshops and programs for organized groups by reservation only.

14 BLUE HILLS RESERVATION: SKYLINE TRAIL

This trail is the longest in the Blue Hills, extending from Fowl Meadow in Canton east to Shea Rink on Willard Street in Quincy.

Features

Location Canton, Milton, and Quincy, MA

Rating Strenuous

Distance 9-mile loop, full trip; 2.4-mile loop, North and South Skyline trails loop

Elevation Gain Approximately 1,800 feet for full trip; approximately 700 feet cumulative for North and South Skyline trails loop

Estimated Time 6 hours for full trip; 1.75 hours for North and South Skyline trails loop

Maps USGS Norwood; Massachusetts Department of Conservation and Recreation: mass.gov/eea/docs/dcr/parks/trails/blue-hills-trail-map-2016.pdf

GPS coordinates 42° 12.579' N, 71° 05.826' W

Contact Massachusetts Department of Conservation and Recreation: mass.gov/locations/blue-hills-reservation, 617-698-1802; Mass Audubon: massaudubon.org, 508-255-3421; Friends of the Blue Hills: friendsofthebluehills.org; Appalachian Mountain Club: ponkapoagcamp.org, 781-961-7007

DIRECTIONS

Take I-93 to Exit 3 (Houghton's Pond). At the end of Blue Hill River Road, turn right onto Hillside Street and follow it 0.3 mile to the parking lot at Houghton's Pond, 840 Hillside Street, Milton, on the right.

By public transportation, take the MBTA Red Line to Ashmont and then ride the high-speed trolley line to Mattapan. From there, take the number 716 bus to the intersection of Washington Street and Royall Street. Walk 1.5 miles east on Blue Hill River Road, which will turn into Hillside Street along the way.

TRAIL DESCRIPTION

For those wanting a true long-distance hiking experience within a few miles of downtown Boston, Skyline Trail makes a 9-mile east–west trip through the Blue Hills Reservation, traversing most of the major hills along the way. For much of its length, it is a one-way route, but from the summit of Great Blue Hill to Hillside Road, it splits into two branches: North Skyline Trail and South Skyline Trail.

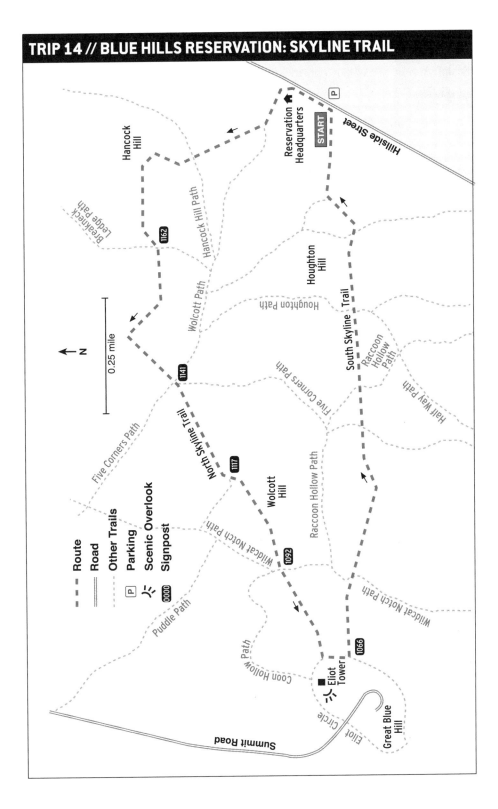

Skyline Trail can be reached from any of the following streets: MA 138, at a parking lot on the west side, about 0.5 mile south of Mass Audubon's Blue Hills Trailside Museum; Randolph Avenue (MA 28), where the closest parking is about 0.25 mile south of the trail crossing; and Willard Street, at the trail terminus at Shea Rink. You can also park at Blue Hills Trailside Museum and follow Red Trail to the summit of Great Blue Hill and then pick up either North Skyline Trail or South Skyline Trail there. Choose your route based on whether you can get a car pickup at some point on the trail, whether you have the time and energy for backtracking (one option is to follow some of the easier trails on the way out or back), or whether you need to return to your car.

For those wanting a shorter sampling that doesn't require backtracking or spotting cars at trailheads, the loop hike described here starts at 695 Hillside Street. It combines the north and south branches of Skyline Trail to create a circuit that includes the summit of Great Blue Hill, the reservation's highest point.

Starting at the trailhead at 695 Hillside Street, follow blue-blazed North Skyline Trail, which makes a 0.25-mile beeline to the top of 506-foot Hancock Hill to the northwest. Fine views are available from a ledge on the right, just below the summit. From the hilltop, continue to follow the blue blazes. The trail descends to the west over rocky ground and crosses Breakneck Ledge Path at marker 1162. It then turns to the southwest as it descends a shoulder of Hemenway Hill.

At a six-way intersection at marker 1141, North Skyline Trail crosses Five Corners Path and Wolcott Path. A map is posted at this intersection. Continue to follow the blue blazes straight. The trail climbs out of the hollow and follows the ridge of Wolcott Hill. Stay straight at marker 1117, where a short side path descends to Wildcat Notch in the valley between Great Blue and Wolcott hills. Wolcott Hill's 465-foot summit is just ahead.

From Wolcott Hill, follow the blue blazes as North Skyline Trail descends to Wildcat Notch; it crosses Wildcat Notch Path at marker 1092 and then begins a rocky ascent up the northeast slopes of Great Blue Hill. A steep but short climb leads to the top of the hill near Eliot Tower and a stone bridge. Excellent views can be seen from the tower.

The return leg of this loop is on South Skyline Trail, which begins approximately 200 yards south of the stone bridge, at marker 1066. This trail, also well marked with blue blazes, leads due east as it descends the eastern slopes of Great Blue Hill. Ledges along the way offer pleasant vistas to the south and east across the reservation. The trail leads along a steep, rocky descent over Shadow Cliff and briefly parallels a seasonal brook before crossing it at two large boulders. Continue to follow the blue blazes straight (east) at a junction with the southern portion of Five Corners Path.

After crossing Houghton Path, South Skyline Trail leads up the western slopes of Houghton Hill and crosses the top of the hill just south of the summit. From here, complete the walk by descending the steep eastern slopes of Houghton Hill. The trail reaches Hillside Street approximately 200 yards south of the trailhead for North Skyline Trail. Turn right to return to the Houghton's Pond parking lot.

DID YOU KNOW?

The Boston skyline is visible to the north on clear days. The tallest building in the city is the 790-foot, 60-story, glass-covered 200 Clarendon (formerly the John Hancock Tower);

As Skyline Trail traverses the Blue Hills, hikers encounter many challenging, rugged hills.

the second-tallest building is a few blocks east, the 749-foot Prudential Tower. They are west of the cluster of buildings in downtown Boston, separated from them by the open spaces of Boston Common and the Public Garden.

NEARBY

The Adams National Historical Park, on 135 Adams Street in Quincy, is home to the birthplaces of presidents John Adams and John Quincy Adams, as well as the Stone Library, which has nearly 15,000 historical volumes. The United States Naval Shipbuilding Museum, on 549 South Street, Pier 3, in Quincy, includes exhibits onboard the USS *Salem*, the world's only preserved heavy cruiser. Many restaurants are along Hancock Street in Quincy.

MORE INFORMATION

The Blue Hills Reservation is open year-round, dawn to dusk; no fee. Dogs are allowed but must be leashed. Trail information and maps are available (maps $3) at Blue Hills Trailside Museum or online (maps free) at mass.gov/dcr. Guided hikes and special programs are offered through the Friends of the Blue Hills.

Mass Audubon operates two educational facilities within the reservation. Blue Hills Trailside Museum on MA 138, 0.5 mile north of I-93, is open Wednesday through Sunday, 9 A.M. to 4 P.M.; there is an admission fee. Mass Audubon's Norman Smith Environmental Education Center at Chickatawbut Hill offers workshops and programs for organized groups by reservation only.

AMC's Ponkapoag Camp, on the eastern shore of Ponkapoag Pond, has cabins and seasonal tentsites available for overnights. Reservations are required.

ENDANGERED PREDATOR: EASTERN TIMBER RATTLESNAKE

Eastern timber rattlesnakes are believed to have been widespread throughout eastern Massachusetts and the rest of New England during pre-Colonial times. Today, however, rattlesnakes inhabit only a handful of sites in Massachusetts, making them an endangered species protected by law. "Rattlers" are identified by a triangular head and a rattle-like feature at the end of the tail that makes a buzzing sound when vibrated. Body color ranges from yellow-brown to almost black, with dark V-shaped bands across the back.

Because other dangerous creatures, such as mountain lions and wolves, have long been extirpated from New England, people are often surprised to find that poisonous rattlesnakes and copperheads still exist in the region. While both species have been decimated by habitat loss, hunting, and gathering by collectors, isolated populations remain in Massachusetts, Connecticut, Vermont, and New Hampshire. In Massachusetts, they are present in the Blue Hills, in the southern Berkshire Hills, and in Hampden County. A 2016 proposal by state wildlife officials to reintroduce rattlesnakes to an island in Quabbin Reservoir triggered considerable debate in central Massachusetts because some local residents strongly objected to the project.

Ideal rattlesnake habitat includes isolated, south-facing hillsides; ridges; and rocky outcroppings that are surrounded by dense forest. This combination provides protected den sites as well as access to prey, such as mice, voles, shrews, rabbits, squirrels, chipmunks, and other small animals and birds. Rattlers are active from midspring until temperatures drop in fall; they hibernate during winter. They usually bask during daytime and hunt at night, although they are more active during the day in cooler weather.

Because rattlesnakes and copperheads inhabit secluded areas and are able to hear approaching footsteps from a long distance away, hikers will rarely encounter them by chance on the trail. In the unlikely event you come across one while hiking, stop and back away slowly. In very rare instances, threatened poisonous snakes can deliver bites that, though not fatal, can cause physical damage. If you are bitten, remain calm and as still as possible to avoid spreading the venom. If you must move, limit the motion of the bitten limb and seek medical assistance as soon as possible.

Some nonvenomous Massachusetts snakes are often mistakenly believed to be poisonous because of their behavior, appearance, or size. Milk snakes, which have a body size and color pattern similar to that of copperheads, often shake their tails like rattlesnakes as a threatening gesture. Northern water snakes, which are relatively large, are regularly seen in wetlands.

The region north of Boston extending to the New Hampshire border includes the North Shore and adjacent inland communities. The topography is relatively gentle, with no significant summits. However, several low hills and drumlins (large mounds of debris left by retreating glaciers) offer sweeping vistas, such as Ward Hill in Andover, where a hilltop meadow features views to Boston and the Blue Hills. On nearby Weir Hill in North Andover, visitors can see Wachusett Mountain, Mount Monadnock, and the Wapack Mountains.

Unlike in southeastern Massachusetts, where harsh soils support extensive woodlands of pitch pine and scrub oak, the forests north of Boston are predominantly of the oak-hickory type characteristic of much of southern New England. A few scattered groves of pitch pine and scrub oak grow along the North Shore, the largest of which is at Crane Beach.

Although suburbanization extending from Boston has led to development pressure, many of the inland communities have retained their rural character. At Bradley Palmer State Park in Hamilton and Topsfield and at Bald Hill in Boxford, trails wind through old farm fields and past building sites that offer a glimpse into the region's past, when much of the land was cleared for agriculture. The nearby Ipswich River Wildlife Sanctuary encompasses a cluster of wetlands along Ipswich River, a short distance from the river's mouth. Baker's Meadow Reservation is part of an expansive network of protected land in Andover.

Along the North Shore, several coastal preserves compose a variety of natural communities, some of which are uncommon. At the tip of Cape Ann—a small promontory that juts along the northern tip of Massachusetts Bay—is Halibut Point, home to rocky bluffs similar to those found in coastal Down East Maine. The point offers excellent tide pool habitat and is a good place to spot wintering seabirds and to enjoy views along the coast north to Mount Agamenticus (Maine). A rare magnolia swamp and rocky outcroppings are at nearby Ravenswood Park in Gloucester.

A short distance north of Cape Ann is Castle Neck, a narrow slice of white-sand beach and dunes that extends between Castle Neck River and the Atlantic Ocean. Endangered piping plovers and other shorebirds nest on Crane Beach.

Facing page: Watch for wading birds in the reeds along the shore of Baker's Meadow, a shallow pond with many boardwalks and a spillway.

Offshore from Newburyport near the New Hampshire border lies Plum Island, a 7-mile-long barrier island at the mouth of the Parker and Merrimack rivers. The bulk of the island lies within Parker River National Wildlife Refuge, and its location and varied natural habitats make it one of the finest bird-watching locations along the eastern seaboard. During migration periods, it serves as a crucial rest area for great numbers of shorebirds, wading birds, songbirds, and raptors. Nearby Old Town Hill, which rises above tidal marshes on the Little and Parker rivers, offers more diverse habitats and scenic coastal views. These properties lie within the 25,000-acre Great Marsh, New England's largest salt marsh ecosystem.

15 WEIR HILL RESERVATION

This peaceful walk leads to scenic views along the shores of Lake Cochichewick and from a meadow at the top of Weir Hill.

Features

Location North Andover, MA

Rating Moderate

Distance 2.3-mile loop

Elevation Gain 170 feet

Estimated Time 1.5 hours

Maps USGS South Groveland; The Trustees of Reservations: thetrustees.org/wp-content/uploads/2020/07/Weir-Hill-Trail-Map.pdf

GPS coordinates 42° 41.839′ N, 71° 06.654′ W

Contact The Trustees of Reservations: thetrustees.org/place/weir-hill, 978-682-3580

DIRECTIONS

From I-495, take Exit 100A (formerly Exit 42A) and follow MA 114 east for 1.0 mile into North Andover. Turn left onto MA 133 east and continue 0.2 mile. At the traffic light, continue straight on Andover Street for 0.8 mile. At the traffic circle, continue straight on Great Pond Road and then turn left onto Stevens Street. Continue 0.8 mile to the entrance and parking on the right.

TRAIL DESCRIPTION

Weir Hill Reservation combines the best of woodlands, fields, and water. Attractions include views from a hilltop and from the shores of beautiful Lake Cochichewick, a water supply reservoir. In 1715, settlers divided Weir Hill, establishing a series of farms along its slopes. The hill was cleared and used for sheep pastures. Although the forests have grown back, legacies of the property's agricultural past include miles of stone walls and scattered red cedar trees, which grew out of the abandoned fields. Several clearings are maintained throughout the reservation, including an upland meadow with long views west to the mountains of central New England.

The trail network includes three color-blazed routes and several unmarked paths. This hike mostly follows Yellow Loop, a yellow-blazed circuit that combines several short, named trails. From the parking area, follow Yellow Loop (named Stevens Trail here) northeast along a wide treadway for a few hundred feet to a three-way intersection at the start of the circuit. Turn right onto Yellow Loop (the return part of the loop is on the left) and begin a steady climb beneath large oaks. At 0.3 mile enter an upland meadow with

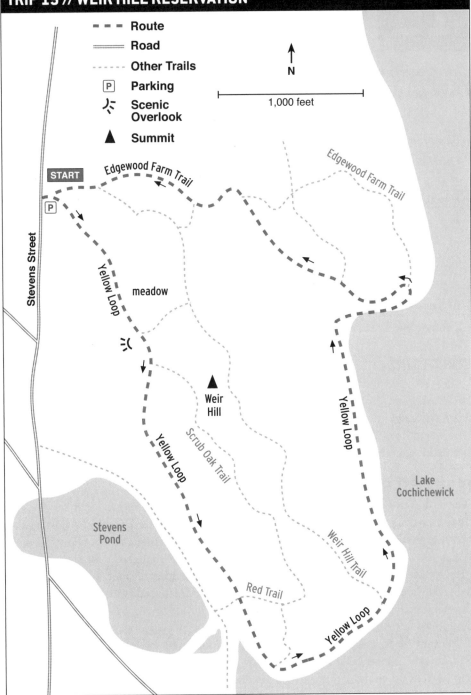

TRIP 15 // WEIR HILL RESERVATION

- - - Route
── Road
······ Other Trails
P Parking
Scenic Overlook
▲ Summit

N

1,000 feet

START
P

Stevens Street

Edgewood Farm Trail

Edgewood Farm Trail

meadow

Yellow Loop

Weir Hill

Scrub Oak Trail

Yellow Loop

Lake Cochichewick

Stevens Pond

Weir Hill Trail

Red Trail

Yellow Loop

Yellow Loop

The top of Weir Hill delivers an idyllic view of New England countryside.

magnificent views across the Merrimack River valley to the west, including Wachusett Mountain, the Wapack Mountain ridge, and New Hampshire's Mount Monadnock on the horizon. The hill is a glacial drumlin that rises 300 feet above the surrounding countryside. Weir Hill, a few hundred yards to the south, is roughly the same size.

After leaving the meadow, continue on Yellow Loop/Stevens Trail down the south side of the drumlin. Pass the upper junction with Red Trail (also named Scrub Oak Trail), a 0.5-mile route that rejoins Yellow Loop near the shore of Lake Cochichewick. At 0.5 mile from the meadow vista, a strip of land separates Stevens Pond from Lake Cochichewick's southern arm and a stone arch bridge.

To stay on Yellow Loop/Stevens Trail, bear left and head away from the strip of land between the bodies of water. At 0.9 mile, reach the lower junction with Red Trail, where Stevens Trail ends. Bear left to continue on Yellow Loop, which now briefly follows Alewife Trail. This peaceful segment by the banks of the lake is especially appealing in spring, when the shadbush blooms with white flowers.

One of the notable features of this reservation is the difference in tree species between its east and west sides. The west tends to be warmer and drier, while the east stays cooler, with more moisture from the lake. You will notice a combination of oak and pitch pine growing in the western section, while in the eastern section are maple, beech, aspen, white pine, white birch, and shagbark hickory. The fruit of these trees, especially hickory and beech, provides food for a variety of animals that live on the reservation, including ruffed grouse, opossum, and raccoon.

Continue on Yellow Loop (now Cochichewick Trail) north along Lake Cochichewick's western shore. After curving right to follow a small promontory, the trail intersects with an unnamed wide dirt road near an old foundation on the shoreline at 1.6 miles. Go left (temporarily leaving Yellow Loop) and follow this road as it angles back, gradually climbing uphill and away from the water. You will pass an impressive stand of large white birch on your right.

Like many parts of New England, the land around Weir Hill at one time was open meadow, allowing sheep and cattle to graze. The settlers of North Andover began clearing the virgin forests in the seventeenth century. Their axes and saws were busy throughout the state, and today only small, scattered stands of old-growth timber remain, including groves in the Berkshire Hills and on Wachusett Mountain.

Stay left where the dirt road forks about 600 feet ahead. Just before the road reaches the reservation boundary, turn left to rejoin Yellow Loop (now Edgewood Farm Trail), which passes over a wooden footbridge and beneath tall pines. Shortly after passing the junction with blue-blazed Weir Hill Trail on the left, reach the end of Yellow Loop. Bear right at the intersection and backtrack to the parking area.

DID YOU KNOW?

Weir Hill Reservation got its name from the fish weirs American Indians once constructed in nearby Cochichewick Brook. The weir, usually a woven fence, would trap migrating fish on their way to the lake.

NEARBY

The North Andover Historical Society preserves several old buildings on the village common, including Parson Barnard House, Carriage Barn, the Granary, Stevens Mills Depot, Hay Scales, and Johnson Cottage. Visit the society's website, northandoverhistoricalsociety.org, for more information. Restaurants are near the reservation on Chickering Road (MA 133/125).

MORE INFORMATION

The reservation is open daily, sunrise to sunset; no fee. Dogs are allowed but must be leashed.

16 CHARLES W. WARD RESERVATION

Follow a short nature trail for close-up views of a quaking bog, a fascinating place with rare and unusual plant life. Then explore the Solstice Stones and enjoy the abundant wildlife and long scenic views on Holt Hill.

Features 🐕 ♿ 🌑 📍 ⛷ ❄ 💲

Location Andover, MA

Rating Easy to Moderate

Distance 3.6 miles round trip

Elevation Gain 290 feet

Estimated Time 2.5 hours

Maps USGS South Groveland; The Trustees of Reservations: thetrustees.org/wp-content/uploads/2022/02/ward-reservation-trail-map.pdf

GPS coordinates 42° 38.438' N, 71° 06.721' W

Contact The Trustees of Reservations: thetrustees.org/place/charles-w-ward-reservation, 978-682-3580

DIRECTIONS
From I-93, take Exit 35 (formerly Exit 41) to MA 125 north and follow it for 5.0 miles. Turn right onto Prospect Road and follow it 0.4 mile to the parking area on the right.

From I-495, take Exit 100A (formerly Exit 42A) to MA 114 east and follow it for 1.2 miles to the junction with MA 125. Continue straight on MA 114/MA 125 for 0.5 mile and then turn right onto MA 125 south (Andover Bypass Street). Follow it for 1.6 miles and then turn left onto Prospect Road. Drive 0.3 mile to the parking lot on the right.

TRAIL DESCRIPTION
Ward Reservation offers diverse attractions, featuring a bog with regionally rare plants and northern tree species, fantastic vistas, and miles of woodland trails. The reservation is on the Bay Circuit Trail (BCT), and its well-signed trail network includes several color-blazed loops that combine named trails. This trip includes portions of Yellow Trail, Red Trail, and the BCT. It leads to the bog, to Holt Hill (the highest point in Essex County), and through a mosaic of woodlands and wetlands in the reservation's northern section.

The first segment of the hike follows portions of Yellow, Bog, and Red trails, which overlap in places. From the parking area, follow Yellow Trail and Bog Trail past a grassy area and a private residence on the left. Be on the lookout for low-growing club mosses, poison ivy (with its three green leaves that shine in the sun), and ghost pipe in the woods. Pass a

TRIP 16 // CHARLES W. WARD RESERVATION

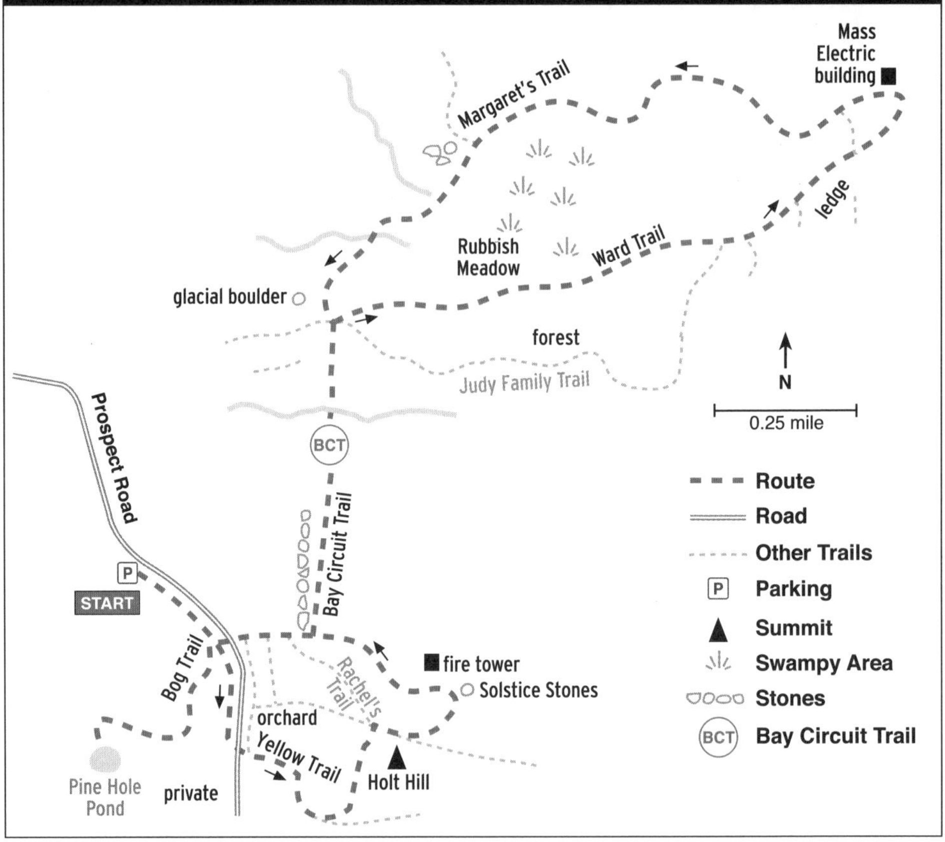
Mass
Electric
building
Margaret's Trail
Rubbish
Meadow
Ward Trail
ledge
glacial boulder
forest
Judy Family Trail
N
0.25 mile
Prospect Road
BCT
Bay Circuit Trail
Route
Road
Other Trails
Parking
Summit
Swampy Area
Stones
Bay Circuit Trail
P
START
Bog Trail
Rachel's Trail
fire tower
Solstice Stones
orchard
Yellow Trail
Holt Hill
Pine Hole
Pond
private

wet area on the right and turn right at a T intersection to make a short out-and-back walk to the bog on Bog Trail.

As soon as you begin walking on the boardwalk, you will smell dank earth, spruce, and hemlock. The boardwalk rests on a mat of vegetation, below which is at least 19 feet of muck (as measured during the boardwalk's construction). Look for cattail; cotton grass, a member of the sedge family that has a cottony tuft in late summer; and highbush blueberries, which prefer the acidic soil of the bog. Ringed by dark cedars, the bog is particularly appealing in fall, when the golden grasses along its edge frame the black water. In a little more than a quarter-mile, the boardwalk ends at Pine Hill Pond.

Return to Yellow Trail and turn right to resume the Yellow Trail loop, which bends left and leads up to Prospect Road. After crossing Prospect Road, turn right at the intersection with Rachel's Trail (Red Loop) near an apple orchard. If you are here in the early morning or evening, watch for white-tailed deer, particularly when fruit is on the trees.

Follow Yellow Trail east to the intersection with the white-blazed Bay Circuit Trail. Turn left and follow combined Yellow Trail and the BCT along a wide treadway that rises easily, turns to the right, and enters the fields just below the summit of Holt Hill. Look for bluebirds, bobolinks, kestrels (small hawks that primarily hunt insects), and other birds that prefer open meadows. To your left, you will see a radio tower.

Continue through the meadow to the Solstice Stones and Holt Hill's 420-foot summit at 0.9 mile. The Solstice Stones were assembled at the direction of the property's former owner, Mabel Ward, during the early twentieth century. They are laid out like a compass, with the largest stones indicating the four primary points. (The north stone is marked.) The narrow stone in the northeast quadrant points in the direction of the sunrise on the summer solstice, the longest day of the year, which is usually June 21. The expansive southerly views from Holt Hill include the Boston skyline and Great Blue Hill in Milton.

After enjoying the scenery, walk toward the radio tower and follow Yellow Trail downhill along the paved access road about a quarter-mile. Turn right at a signed intersection, following the white-blazed BCT and the upper portion of Red Trail. (To return to the parking area and bypass the northern section, go straight.) Continue north along a stone wall, indicating that this area was once pasture. Large white pines now grow here, and farther along the route more oaks and maples appear. The trail gradually goes downhill; after a little more than a quarter-mile, it crosses wooden boards over a tiny stream.

Check the forest floor for ghost pipe, a flowering plant that lacks the green pigment chlorophyll and is unable to manufacture its own food by photosynthesis. With the aid of a fungus that connects it to the roots of a nearby tree, ghost pipe collects its nutrients from the host tree. Ghost pipe grows 4 to 10 inches tall, and its nodding white or pink flowers are similar in shape to a pipe, hence the name.

At a four-way intersection on the other side of the stream at 1.5 miles, continue to follow Red Trail by taking the second right onto Ward Trail. (Leave the Bay Circuit Trail, which

The Solstice Stones are laid out like a compass, with a narrow stone in the northeast quadrant pointing toward the sunrise on the summer solstice, the longest day of the year. Boston's skyline rises to the south. *Photo by spablab, Creative Commons on Flickr.*

continues left.) About a quarter-mile from the junction, you will pass wetlands on the left. This is the unappealingly named Rubbish Meadow. (Wetlands, especially swamps, were historically regarded as undesirable, savage, or waste places, hence the name.) Watch for tree swallows, easily identified by their dark blue backs and their white bellies. These swallows, each about 5 inches long, are very social birds and can provide hours of viewing pleasure as they dip and wheel in the sky, chasing one another or catching insects.

Pass a granite ledge on the right and then continue through an area of small white pines that crowd the trail, creating a tunnel effect. Deer often use this trail on their nocturnal rounds. Look for their heart-shaped hoofprints in the ground.

At a four-way junction, leave Red Trail and continue straight to another junction at the reservation boundary, near a Mass Electric building and posted trail map. Turn left to begin the loop back to the main entrance on Margaret's Trail, which heads west along a stone wall.

After walking roughly 0.5 mile on Margaret's Trail, continue straight at the first junction with Greg's Trail, stepping up onto exposed bedrock. In another 200 feet or so, bear right at a fork and follow the trail to a tiny stream that drains the marsh on your left, with small cascades a short distance upstream. You also might want to explore a short side path that loops back to a partial view of the wetlands near a semicircle of stones around a fire pit.

Examine the edge of the stream for animal tracks, such as those made by raccoons and mink. A mink can grow as long as 35 inches, including the tail, although the weight of a mink that size would still be only about 2.5 pounds. Mink are crafty hunters and prey primarily on small rodents, but they will also eat birds, snakes, frogs, crayfish, and even muskrats.

Just beyond the stream, follow Margaret's Trail to the left at a fork and pass a dense pine grove. In about 300 feet, bear left again, cross a small stream at the outlet of a beaver wetland, and then continue across a short elevated boardwalk that offers fine views. A small glacial boulder rests on a nearby ledge. At 3.1 miles, complete the northern section of the loop at a four-way intersection with the white-blazed BCT. Turn left on the BCT, which rejoins Red Trail at an adjacent intersection. Backtrack to the paved road and the intersection with Yellow Trail, and then turn right and follow combined Red and Yellow trails to Prospect Road and the parking area.

DID YOU KNOW?

During the American Revolution, a large group of Andover townspeople climbed Holt Hill to watch the burning of Charlestown from the hill's summit.

NEARBY

The Addison Gallery of American Art (addison.andover.edu), part of Phillips Academy, was founded in 1931. Its holdings feature works by many prominent American artists, including John Singleton Copley, Winslow Homer, and John Singer Sargent. Numerous restaurants are in Andover along and off Main and Elm streets.

MORE INFORMATION

The reservation is open year-round, 8 A.M. to sunset; no restrooms. The admission fee is $5 for nonmembers of The Trustees of Reservations. Dogs are allowed but must be leashed.

THE LIFE AND TIMES OF A BOG

The bog at Ward Reservation formed 12,000 to 14,000 years ago as the glaciers from the most recent ice age retreated across New England. The bog rests in a glacial kettle hole, a depression made when a huge block of ice from a glacier melts. Unlike in other bodies of water, decay in a bog is extremely slow due to the lack of active flowing water. As plants die, they accumulate at the bottom of the bog, forming a thick organic matter known as peat. Over time, the amount of open water in the bog gradually decreases as plants that thrive in acidic boggy conditions, such as leatherleaf and sphagnum moss, take over. Sphagnum moss is very spongy and absorbent. American Indians used it to line babies' diapers, and doctors historically used it as a dressing for wounds.

Both black spruce and tamarack, trees that are more common in northern New England, grow in the Ward Reservation bog. The trees are small but quite old, because it is difficult to harvest trees in this environment. Some of the rare vegetation here includes rose pogonias, bog orchids, and two carnivorous plants: the sundew and the pitcher plant. (For more on the pitcher plant, see Trip 12 on page 53.) The sundew is much smaller than the pitcher plant, with round leaves and white or pink flowers. It traps insects in a sticky fluid and then closes its leaves around its prey. Insects provide both plants with some nutrients, such as nitrogen, that are lacking in the bog.

The low, shrubby vegetation bordering the bog is an excellent place to watch for dragonflies and damselflies, which together form the odonate order of carnivorous insects. One of the most visible species during midsummer is the blue dasher, a small and often abundant dragonfly. The males have light-blue bodies; females are brown, yellow, and black.

When exploring this and other bogs, be sure to stay on boardwalks and marked trails. Stepping onto the vegetative mats damages these fragile environments and is also dangerous, as it is possible to break through a mat and sink deep into the mud and peat.

BAKER'S MEADOW

Enjoy a trip around a shallow pond, bustling with life, and its associated uplands.

Features

Location Andover, MA

Rating Easy to Moderate

Distance 2.5-mile loop

Elevation Gain 30 feet

Estimated Time 1.5 to 2 hours

Maps USGS Andover; Andover Village Improvement Society: avisandover.org/ assets/maps/IndianRidgeWParishBakersMeadowSakowich.pdf

GPS coordinates 42° 38.145′ N, 71° 9.807′ W

Contact Bay Circuit Trail & Greenway: baycircuit.org

DIRECTIONS

Take Exit 39 from I-93 northbound; if coming from I-495, take I-93 south to Exit 39 and then turn east on MA 133 toward Andover. After 0.5 mile, turn right on Argilla Road. Oriole Drive is the second left. Less than 0.25 mile up Oriole Drive is a stand of pines on the right side at a paved driveway blocked by a chain. A sign points to AVIS Sakowich Reservation. A small turnout for parking sits along the road here, as well as the optimal entry point for the loop hike.

TRAIL DESCRIPTION

This hike links three contiguous Andover Village Improvement Society (AVIS) properties that center on Baker's Meadow Pond. The trails are obvious and easy to follow in most areas but can be rugged with pronounced rocks and roots, uneven ground, and wet patches. The properties are close to homes and well-kept neighborhoods on quiet culs-de-sac, with many side paths to nearby streets. Regardless of proximity to homes, the pond, teeming with life, is a surprisingly rewarding destination.

The Sakowich entrance leads through a disused property and down a hill toward the water. Just before the junction with the shoreline trail, there's a good vantage point to view the distant shore, scout for clusters of migrating ducks, or watch for the thin profile and deliberate movements of a heron stalking its prey in the marsh grasses.

Turn right on the trail around the shoreline and watch for trees chewed by a beaver near the first small bridge. A beaver dam, constructed of branches and sticks and covered with mud, sits to the left of the bridge, making an effective obstacle to water flow. Part of the

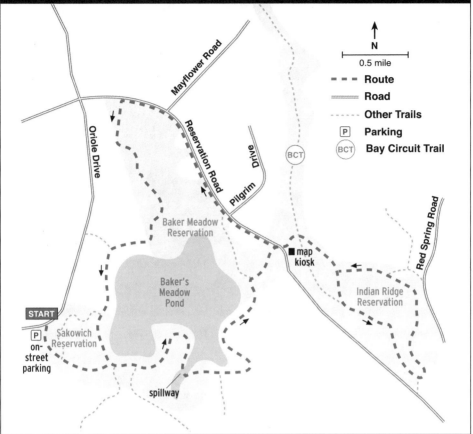

damage to trees appears to be several years old. Some trees have been killed and have fallen as a result, but others remain standing. Wire fencing has been wrapped protectively around tree trunks farther down the path. As you approach a small peninsula that juts into the lake, look to the left for the beaver lodge, a tall pile of branches that forms a mound. Beavers, which can stay underwater for up to 15 minutes, will store tender branches in the lodge for their winter food supply.

Among the beaver-chewed trees are a few pines, and experts agree that those are less favored by the rodents. Red maples and swamp maples are plentiful here along the water, making for a spectacular reflected contrast when in full fall color, around mid-October. The U.S. Forest Service says these trees are the most abundant native species in the eastern portion of North America, with a range stretching from Nova Scotia to Florida.

At the far end of the pond, near where the trail crosses a spillway, there's a bench and a partially submerged log that turtles and ducks use for sunning. In this area the trail skirts private property. Following the shoreline closely, it rounds another point of land and reaches a T intersection after a small bridge. To the left, the trail leads between the pond and Reservation Road, eventually intersecting with the road, for a shorter hike that stays close to the water. Turn right to go directly across the road and enter Indian Ridge

An active beaver lodge in Baker's Meadow Pond has resulted in many chewed trees on the perimeter of the water.

Reservation on the other side. The following loop around Indian Ridge adds about 0.75 mile to the total hike.

A helpful kiosk sits at the trail entrance. Pass the kiosk and look around: the terrain is very different here—a ridge with steep sides, likely glacial topography that was formed around giant chunks of ice. Go straight through the first trail intersection and turn right at the second, following the Bay Circuit Trail markers at the bottom of the hill. In this direction the trail loops the land between Reservation and Red Spring roads. Pay attention to the lack of underbrush as you slowly ascend the hill. Enjoy amazing views of tall, straight trees that have been untouched for a century, unlike the trees along many trails in eastern Massachusetts.

Follow the trail straight until it appears you're going to walk into someone's driveway, and then look left for a rocky path leading straight uphill. Climb the short, steep hill to another ridge that hugs Red Spring Road. Up here is a rock memorial to Alice Buck, one of Andover's early land conservation advocates. When you descend from the ridge, you're headed north toward school playing fields; continue straight at the next trail intersection and enter a wetter portion of the reservation, with more underbrush and fallen logs, all important habitat for native animals. Continue straight through two intersections where other trails come in from the left; you will briefly rejoin the white-blazed Bay Circuit Trail. Take the third left to return to the kiosk at the entrance.

Turn right on Reservation Road and walk about 0.4 mile past Pilgrim Drive and Mayflower Road on the right to reenter the Baker's Meadow trails at a culvert just before Oriole Drive, starting on Retelle Trail. Follow this trail, named for local conservation advocates Al and Evelyn Retelle, as it rounds the edge of the pond's very shallow, marshy waters, full of cattails. One intersecting trail on the right leads to Oriole Drive after 0.4 mile, but stay straight to return to the Sakowich Reservation, where the hike started.

DID YOU KNOW?

About 100 years ago, the stream that crossed a meadow here was dammed to create a pond. The property owner raised muskrats; muskrat fur was fashionable before 1920. Conservation-minded residents, for whom many of the trails are named, helped secure the land for future use by Andover citizens and visitors. Alice Buck was one of those early conservation advocates in the 1890s.

NEARBY

Several restaurants are in central Andover near the intersection of Red Spring Road and Brook Street, within walking distance of the Indian Ridge Reservation portion of this hike.

MORE INFORMATION

The Bay Circuit Trail, which intersects this hike at Indian Ridge, is a 231-mile adventure that links public-use properties through 57 communities around Boston.

18 BALD HILL RESERVATION

Sprawled across three towns in central Essex County, Bald Hill Reservation protects 1,700 acres of forested hills and low-lying swamps as conservation land.

Features

Location Boxford, MA

Rating Easy to Moderate

Distance 2.8 miles round trip

Elevation Gain 150 feet

Estimated Time 2 hours

Maps USGS Georgetown, USGS South Groveland; Greenbelt: ecga.org/files/galleries/Boxford_BaldHill_TrailMap.pdf; Massachusetts Department of Conservation and Recreation: mass.gov/doc/boxford-state-forest-trail-map/download

GPS coordinates 42° 38.405′ N, 70° 59.446′ W

Contact Essex County Land Trust: ecga.org/Property/bald-hill-conservation-area

DIRECTIONS

From I-95, take Exit 72 (formerly Exit 51). At the end of the ramp, follow signs toward Middleton (south) and then take the first right onto Middleton Road. Follow it 1.6 miles to a small roadside parking lot on the left at the Bay Circuit Trail crossing, where a sign welcomes you to Bald Hill.

TRAIL DESCRIPTION

The area encompassing Bald Hill and Crooked Pond, known as Bald Hill Reservation, lies within the quiet, largely undeveloped town of Boxford, near the Middleton and North Andover borders. The connected tracts of conservation land here include the John C. Phillips Wildlife Sanctuary (hunting prohibited), and Boxford State Forest.

Bald Hill Reservation is an excellent destination for wildlife enthusiasts and botanists, thanks to the wide habitat variety, including open hilltop meadows, rich forests, ponds, swamps, and beaver wetlands. Historians will enjoy exploring the site of the former Russell-Hooper farm. Each season offers a new set of attractions, including wildflowers, fall foliage, birdlife, and animal tracks. This hike features two connected loops that lead around Crooked Pond and a meadow and the farm site on Bald Hill. Waterproof footwear is highly recommended in early spring and during other high-water periods, as

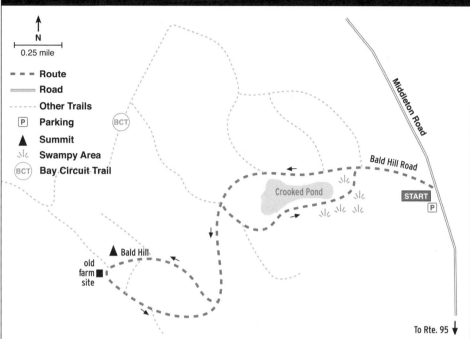

the trails at Crooked Pond are susceptible to flooding. Trail junction numbers are marked on posts or blazes on trees.

Begin by following the white-blazed Bay Circuit Trail (BCT) west along a woods road. Overhead, hemlock trees, some of which are infested with hemlock woolly adelgid, shade this wide, well-maintained trail as it heads west. About 0.25 mile into the walk, reach a junction at the east end of Crooked Pond, at the wildlife sanctuary boundary. This hike continues straight along the north side of the pond at marker 17, leaving the BCT, which goes up the slope on the right. (If water levels are high, the trail on the left—which is the return route for this hike—may offer a drier path along the south shore.) Follow the footpath along the pond edge, where you can scan the shallow water for a variety of wildlife, including the resident beavers, great blue herons, and visiting ducks.

Oaks, maples, and pines begin to join the hemlocks as the trail runs parallel to the pond. At marker 14, bear left at the junction with a connecting trail to the BCT on the right. Beavers have built a dam along the trail at the pond's west end; cross this area cautiously if the water is high. After you pass marker 13A, the walking becomes easier on a woods road, which leads up at a gentle grade toward Bald Hill. Blue markings on trees indicate the Boxford State Forest boundary. At marker 12, turn right to reach the crest of the hill at 1.3 miles. Look carefully for old apple trees, a legacy of the property's agricultural past, amid the small maples and oaks. An open field stretches along the ridge, providing a pleasant, sunny spot to picnic, despite the lack of spectacular views. It is especially inviting in autumn, when the trees bordering the field offer a vivid display of colors.

Because there are nearly 2,000 protected acres in the reservation, wildlife abounds. Ruffed grouse, goshawks, barred owls, woodcocks, deer, fishers, and coyotes all live here. One of the more conspicuous birds is the pileated woodpecker, a large, crow-sized woodpecker that is easily identified by its red head and loud, rasping call. Keep an eye out for wild turkeys, which have made a dramatic recovery after near-elimination during Colonial times.

One raptor to watch for is the northern goshawk, the largest member of the *Accipiter* genus of hawks. The goshawk is a rapid-flying predator that feeds on birds and small mammals, including gray squirrels. It can negotiate its way through thick forest understory or fly just above the treetops. If you are fortunate enough to see one of these magnificent and rather uncommon creatures, you won't forget the way its red eyes stare at you. Goshawks can turn anybody into an avid bird-watcher.

From the summit, bear left on a grass path that slopes downhill into the woods. Bear right at the junction with a trail that branches to the left and continue to a stone foundation at the Russell-Hooper farm site. After passing the foundation, continue to junction 10

Wild calla can be spotted around wetland edges at Bald Hill in spring.

and turn left onto a path along the field edge, with the remains of an old fireplace and chimney on the left. The trail leads away from the farm site and then bears left and continues through the woods back to the intersection at marker 12. From here, retrace your steps toward Crooked Pond.

At marker 13A at 1.9 miles, turn right to resume the loop around Crooked Pond (going left leads back to the trailhead via the north side of the pond). Bear left at marker 13B and follow the narrow treadway along the southwest end of the wetlands, remaining close to the water on the left. Wild calla, also known as bog arum or marsh calla, blooms along the water's edge from midspring to late spring. After passing rock outcroppings, follow the trail as it bears left to complete the loop at the junction with the Bay Circuit Trail at the eastern end of Crooked Pond. Turn right to return to the parking area.

DID YOU KNOW?

The Bald Hill area is one of the most diverse botanical sites in eastern Massachusetts, thanks to its combination of rich forests, limestone-nourished plants, and wetlands, such as vernal pools, brooks, bogs, and beaver ponds.

NEARBY

Witch Hollow Farm, at the intersection of Main Street and Ipswich Road, was once the home of a woman tried in the infamous Salem witch trials of 1693. Pizza restaurants are on Georgetown Road and Joseph Smith Way; several farm stands are in town.

MORE INFORMATION

The reservation is open dawn to dusk; no fee; no restrooms. Hunting is prohibited in the John C. Philips Wildlife Sanctuary but is allowed in Boxford State Forest in season. Maps are available at nearby staffed Massachusetts Department of Conservation and Recreation properties, including Bradley Palmer State Park and Harold Parker State Forest.

19 IPSWICH RIVER WILDLIFE SANCTUARY

This mostly forested path circles a pond and small island en route to the Rockery. Children will have fun exploring the maze of paths, bridges, and tunnels.

Features

Location Topsfield, MA

Rating Easy to Moderate

Distance 3.2-mile loop

Elevation Gain 100 feet

Estimated Time 2 hours

Maps USGS Salem; Mass Audubon: massaudubon.org/content/download/ 8050/145205/file/ipswich_trails.pdf

GPS coordinates 42° 37.875′ N, 70° 55.268′ W

Contact Mass Audubon: massaudubon.org/get-outdoors/wildlife-sanctuaries/ ipswich-river

DIRECTIONS

From I-95, take Exit 70 (formerly Exit 50) for US 1 and drive north for about 3 miles to the intersection with MA 97. Turn right (south) on MA 97, proceed 0.5 mile, and turn left onto Perkins Row. Go 1.0 mile to the entrance on the right. Check sanctuary hours and potential parking reservations before visiting (see "More Information" below).

TRAIL DESCRIPTION

The diverse habitats of the Ipswich River Wildlife Sanctuary include wetlands and unusual rock formations. Ten miles of trails wind through meadows, ponds, marsh, and forest and alongside Ipswich River. The area called the Rockery is a constructed maze of rocks and boulders formed into paths, bridges, and tunnels adjacent to a picture-perfect pond, surrounded by azaleas, rhododendrons, and mountain laurels.

The trip described here leads to several attractions, including Waterfowl Pond, a loop around Averill's Island, and the Rockery. If you are hiking with young children, you may want to shorten the route to its kid-friendliest features. One option is to walk directly to Waterfowl Pond and the Rockery, bypassing the Averill's Island loop (see map). Trail maps are available at the sanctuary headquarters, and trails are clearly signed.

The parking lot and nature center are on top of Bradstreet Hill, a glacial drumlin formed during the last ice age, when a glacier deposited debris and shaped it into a smooth,

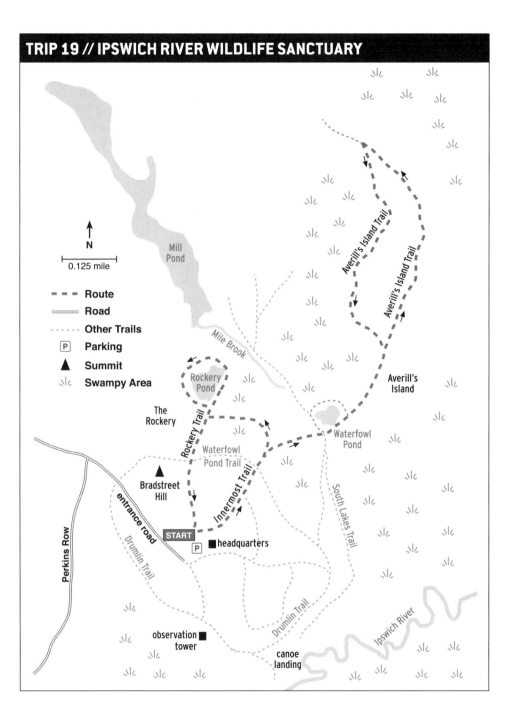

N
0.125 mile

- - - Route
——— Road
········ Other Trails
P Parking
▲ Summit
⅄ Swampy Area

Mill Pond

Mile Brook

Averill's Island Trail

Averill's Island Trail

Averill's Island

Rockery Pond

The Rockery

Rockery Trail

Waterfowl Pond Trail

Waterfowl Pond

Innermost Trail

Bradstreet Hill

South Lakes Trail

entrance road

Drumlin Trail

START

P ■ headquarters

Perkins Row

Drumlin Trail

observation ■ tower

canoe landing

Ipswich River

elongated mound. Also on the property are eskers, long ridges of sand and gravel. Eskers formed when meltwater streams in the glaciers deposited their debris in the ice, leaving raised streambeds after the ice melted.

From the entrance, follow the path toward the headquarters and turn left onto the driveway by the red buildings. At a signed trailhead, follow Innermost Trail along a wide, grassy path, passing through a field of goldenrod, Queen Anne's lace, and milkweed. (*Caution*: Be careful to avoid poison ivy here. Look for green leaves in groups of three that shine in the sun.) After roughly 50 feet, turn left at a junction at the edge of the field, and follow Innermost Trail downhill through a tunnel of dense foliage. Bear left at the junction with Ruffed Grouse Trail and continue on Innermost Trail beneath white pines and maples. Pass the intersection with Drumlin Trail and continue straight on Innermost Trail. The trail crosses a boardwalk through a swamp of cattails, purple loosestrife, yellow flag iris, and swamp maples and continues right at an intersection, passing more wetlands with standing dead timber.

At the intersection of several trails at a photogenic stone bridge at 0.4 mile, turn left to enjoy an overview of Waterfowl Pond from the bridge. Look for wading birds, such as great blue herons and night herons, and scan the water for frogs and painted turtles. Return to the junction and continue on Averill's Island Trail. A wooden observation platform on the left offers fine views across the water.

If you are visiting in May, inspect the edges of the path near the pond for recent signs of digging, indicating that a snapping turtle may have laid eggs in the dry ground adjacent to the pond. Once a female lays her eggs in a shallow depression, she covers them with dirt, but predators such as skunks and raccoons still manage to find many nests. "Snappers" play an important role in the health of ponds by eating dead fish, so teach children not to disrupt them or their nests. (Snapping and painted turtles are common in Massachusetts, but other turtle species are at risk due to habitat loss and fragmentation.)

Passing beneath white pines, hemlocks, and an occasional beech tree, Averill's Island Trail swings to the north and splits at a junction where a loop around Averill's Island begins. To make a counterclockwise circuit, bear right, passing towering white pines that give the forest an enchanted quality. In about a half-mile, you will see an open marsh on the right and, just beyond that, Ipswich River.

The trail now angles northwest through mixed woodland, where beeches and oaks display colorful fall foliage in late October. At a signed junction at the northern end of Averill's Island, turn left to continue the loop. (Going right onto White Pine Loop Trail leads to the northernmost portion of the sanctuary, where the trails are periodically flooded by beaver activity.) Head south to arrive back at Waterfowl Pond at 1.8 miles, completing the island loop.

To continue to the Rockery, bear right and retrace your steps past Waterfowl Pond to the intersection with Waterfowl Pond Trail. Turn right on Waterfowl Pond Trail and continue through the heart of a marsh to the intersection with Rockery Trail. Turn right again onto a boardwalk that leads to Rockery Pond at 2.4 miles. Circle the pond in a counterclockwise direction by bearing right. Colorful blooms of mountain laurels and rhododendrons make this an especially appealing walk in late spring. At the back end of the pond, cross a small

Oak-beech woodlands on Averill's Island Trail provide colorful fall foliage and resting areas for migratory songbirds.

bridge, walk through cedars and spruces, and arrive at the boulders of the Rockery. This spot offers a pleasant view of the pond's tranquil waters, and children will enjoy exploring its nooks and crannies. In one section, slabs of rock have been placed over the path, forming a dark tunnel. It's a magical place, made more so by the many evergreens.

Shintare Anamete, a Japanese landscape architect, designed the Rockery in 1902. Thomas E. Proctor, a former landowner, commissioned it as a setting for his collection of exotic shrubs, trees, and flowers. It took seven years to build. Proctor bought rocks from surrounding farms because there were no boulders or glacial erratics on his property. Some of the boulders were transported more than 10 miles by horse and cart. Mass Audubon bought the sanctuary from the Proctor family in 1951.

To return to the parking lot, from the rock tunnel retrace your steps over the boardwalk to the intersection of Waterfowl Pond Trail and Rockery Trail. Stay straight on Rockery Trail as it continues mostly uphill through woods and a field en route to the parking lot. It's about a half-mile walk from the Rockery to the parking area.

If you have additional time or plan on returning, the other sanctuary trails lead to attractions such as an observation tower overlooking Bunker Meadows and the banks of Ipswich River.

DID YOU KNOW?

The sanctuary protects a scenic 8-mile stretch of Ipswich River, which is excellent for canoeing. Like other rivers in eastern Massachusetts, the Ipswich is threatened by water withdrawals, with fourteen communities drawing water from its basin. Water conservation measures are necessary to protect the river and its aquatic life from the stresses of reduced flow.

NEARBY

The Topsfield Fair (topsfieldfair.org) takes place for approximately ten days in October at the Topsfield Fairgrounds (207 Boston Street). The town was originally chosen for the agricultural festival due to its location in central Essex County, which made access convenient for stagecoaches, and the event has been held almost continually since 1818. Several places to eat are on Main Street just west of the junctions of US 1 and MA 97.

MORE INFORMATION

Parking reservations are required between 9 A.M. and 4:30 P.M. as of 2021. Restrooms are available at the sanctuary entrance. Admission is free for Mass Audubon members; nonmembers pay a fee of $10 per vehicle.

20 BRADLEY PALMER STATE PARK

A network of well-maintained trails at a former estate lead to diverse attractions, including pastoral fields, forests, wetlands, and the Ipswich River.

Features 🚶 🐕 💧 📷 🎿 🏕 💲 🚴

Location Hamilton and Topsfield, MA

Rating Easy

Distance 3.3-mile loop

Elevation Gain 255 feet

Estimated Time 2 hours

Maps USGS Georgetown; Massachusetts Department of Conservation and Recreation: mass.gov/doc/bradley-palmer-trail-map/download

GPS coordinates 42° 39.202′ N, 70° 54.405′ W

Contact Massachusetts Department of Conservation and Recreation: mass.gov/locations/bradley-palmer-state-park, 978-887-5931

DIRECTIONS

From the junction of US 1 and Ipswich Road in Topsfield, follow Ipswich Road east for 1.2 miles. Turn right onto Asbury Street and continue 0.25 mile to the entrance road on the left. Bear right at a sign for the mansion and follow the road to the main parking area.

TRAIL DESCRIPTION

Situated amid a large expanse of conservation land in Essex County, Bradley Palmer State Park protects more than 720 acres in the Ipswich River watershed. The site was once the estate of Bradley Palmer, a prominent early-twentieth-century attorney who donated land to establish both the park and the adjacent Willowdale State Forest. Today, the park is a popular destination for a variety of recreational users, including hikers, horseback riders, mountain bikers, and cross-country skiers.

The extensive trail network includes old carriage roads and footpaths, some of which are maintained and improved by the Essex County Trails Association. More than 75 numbered junctions are marked on the Massachusetts Department of Conservation and Recreation (DCR) state park map, which is available at the park headquarters and on its website. Due to the numerous intersections, the map is strongly recommended for those unfamiliar with the area. This hike begins at the park's main entrance on Asbury Street and combines several trails, including a portion of the Bay Circuit Trail, to form a 3.3-mile loop. Walking on the well-maintained treadways is easy; the gentle climb of Moon Hill is the only significant elevation gain.

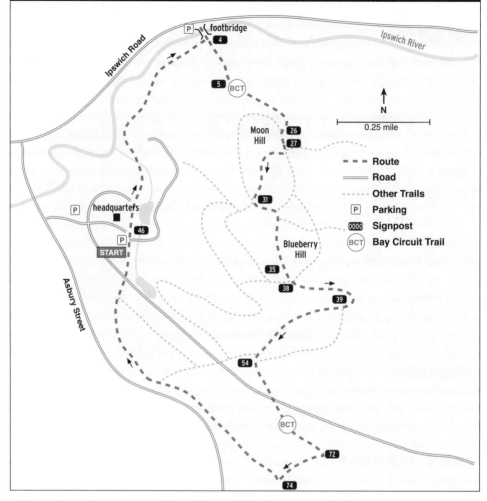

From the parking area, walk to the park headquarters and then continue around the right side of the building to a trailhead at marker 46. Enter the woods on an old interpretive trail, marked with periodic number posts, that overlaps with a portion of the park's Healthy Heart Trail (delineated with DCR Healthy Heart Trail signs). Follow this trail to the edge of a wetland associated with nearby Ipswich River, and cross a footbridge adjacent to a beaver dam. Bear right and traverse a low knoll; then descend to a junction with a trail that parallels Ipswich River. This hike continues to the right. (A short detour left leads to a bridge with fine views of the river and wetlands.)

Walk northeast on a pleasant, easy route through the mixed oak, pine, maple, and beech woodlands bordering the river. After passing a field, reach a four-way junction (markers 4 and 21) near a footbridge over Ipswich River at 0.7 mile. Here, the long-distance Bay Circuit Trail (BCT) enters the park from adjacent Willowdale State Forest at a crossing on Topsfield Road, where parking is available near the Topsfield-Ipswich town line. (This portion of the BCT is part of a connecting trail that joins the main BCT in Willowdale State Forest; the parking area is an alternate starting point for this circuit.)

Turn right onto the BCT and begin an easy ascent of the north side of Moon Hill, heading away from the river. This segment follows the BCT past numerous junctions. Watch carefully for the rectangular white BCT blazes, as there are also markers for the Essex County Trails Association and the Discover Hamilton Trail; the latter is a long-distance route that connects several conservation areas in the town of Hamilton. Traverse a large, open field and then reenter the upland woods and continue straight at marker 5, along an old carriage road. Old spruce trees shade the treadway.

At 1.1 miles, reach a broad, sunlit field at the top of Moon Hill, a 195-foot summit rising roughly 165 feet above Ipswich River. These forest-field habitats benefit a variety of wildlife, including eastern coyotes, red and gray foxes, white-tailed deer, and hawks and owls. Your best chance to see these and other species is in the morning or evening, when they are most active on feeding rounds and there are fewer park visitors. Following the BCT, bear left at marker 26 along the forest-field edge for a short distance; and then turn right at marker 27 and cross the heart of the meadow. Turn left at the next marker and follow the narrow grass path to the south side of the field.

At marker 31, bear left again and walk along the field edge; then reenter the woods and follow the BCT right at a fork along a gravel woods road. One of the familiar year-round resident birds here is the white-breasted nuthatch, whose loud, nasal, yammering call belies its small size. As with other nuthatches, these agile birds often maneuver sideways or upside down along tree trunks. Thanks to its habitat diversity, the park is part of a designated

Late fall foliage lines a pastoral meadow on the Bay Circuit Trail in Bradley Palmer State Park.

Massachusetts Important Bird Area that encompasses the largest contiguous forest in northeastern Massachusetts.

Continue to follow the BCT south and east over Blueberry Hill. Pass junctions 35 and 38, and then make an easy descent of the south slopes to the edge of a large, picturesque meadow at marker 39. Bear right at successive intersections and continue along another old woods road lined by tall oak trees. Roughly 0.25 mile from the meadow, reach a major junction at marker 54 in a small clearing where several roads and trails converge. The hike continues left here on the Bay Circuit Trail, which leads downhill and soon crosses the paved auto road at 2.2 miles. (To shorten the hike and return directly to the entrance from the junction at marker 54, turn right on either the woods road or the nearby paved park road at junction 52.) This section of the trail is especially attractive in late October and early November, near the end of the fall foliage season, when the numerous beech trees reach peak color. Beeches and oaks are the last of the main hardwood species to change color, and some trees even hold their dead leaves through winter.

You'll soon reach the edge of a large swamp at the park's southern end. (If the trail is flooded, backtrack to the paved road and return to the entrance.) At marker 72 turn right, leaving the BCT, and follow an unmarked trail through the heart of the wetland to a junction at a stone wall. Turn right at marker 74 and follow the trail northwest along the park boundary, roughly parallel to Asbury Street. After passing more stone walls and a pastoral view across the road, the trail bends to the right and follows the edge of another clearing that is partially shaded by a large, spreading oak tree. A quick descent leads to a junction at a small pond near the park entrance. Continue straight to complete the loop at the parking area.

DID YOU KNOW?

The former Bradley Palmer estate building, rehabilitated by Willowdale Estates, is now used for weddings and other events.

NEARBY

Willowdale State Forest (mass.gov/locations/willowdale-state-forest) abuts the park and offers many miles of trails. Visitors also can enjoy recreational activities at Hood Pond. The woods roads are excellent for skiing in winter. Restaurants are in Ipswich center along and off Route 1A.

MORE INFORMATION

The park is open year-round, dawn to dusk. A seasonal parking fee ($5 for Massachusetts residents, $20 for nonresidents) is charged at the main lot and at wading pool areas. Restrooms are available at the headquarters.

21 PARKER RIVER NATIONAL WILDLIFE REFUGE (PLUM ISLAND)

Plum Island is a premier destination for birding in the Northeast. A universally accessible trail leads to views of the island's natural barrier beach, dunes, marshes, and coastal forests.

Features 👫 ♿ 💧 🦋 ⬆ 💲

Location Newburyport, MA

Rating Easy

Distance 1.6 miles round trip

Elevation Gain 50 feet

Estimated Time 1 hour

Maps USGS Newburyport East; U.S. Fish and Wildlife Service: fws.gov/refuge/parker-river/map

GPS coordinates 42° 44.045′ N, 70° 47.509′ W

Contact Parker River National Wildlife Refuge: fws.gov/refuge/parker_river, 978-465-5753

DIRECTIONS

From I-95, take Exit 86 (formerly Exit 57) and follow MA 113 east for 2.5 miles into Newburyport. At the junction with MA 1A, follow MA 1A south for 1.3 miles, and then turn left onto Rolfe's Lane at a traffic light and sign for the refuge. Follow Rolfe's Lane for 0.5 mile to its end; then turn right onto Plum Island Turnpike and continue past the refuge visitor center on the right (opposite the Mass Audubon Joppa Flats visitor center). Cross the bridge over Parker River, turn right onto Sunset Road, and continue to the entrance gate and contact station.

TRAIL DESCRIPTION

Parker River National Wildlife Refuge, on Plum Island, encompassing a natural barrier beach, salt marshes, and coastal forests, is a place nature lovers should visit in all seasons. Plum Island is one of the foremost birding spots in the Northeast; more than 270 migratory and resident species have been seen there. Spring and fall, when many migrating birds fly low over the dunes, are the peak seasons for viewing. A winter walk amid white snow, golden-brown salt grass, and beach sand can be a cure for cabin fever. (*Note:* Be aware that greenhead flies can be very unpleasant during July and early August.)

This hike begins at the Hellcat Wildlife Observation Area (parking lot 4) on Refuge Road, 3.8 miles from the refuge entrance. The trail, a short loop with three signed

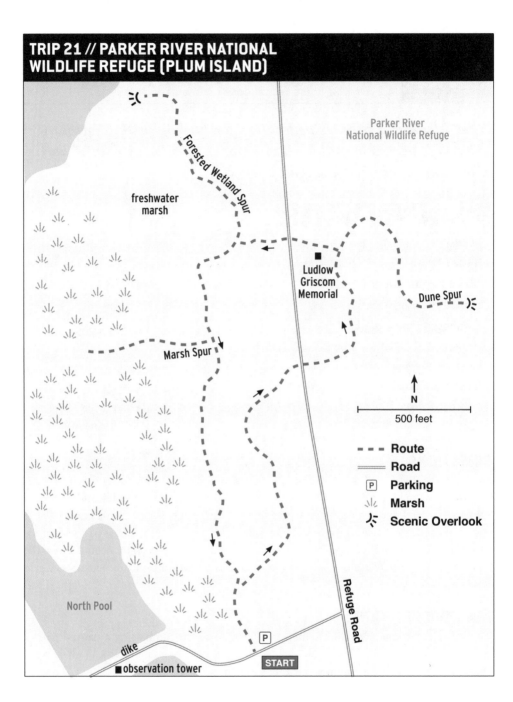

Parker River
National Wildlife Refuge

Forested Wetland Spur

freshwater
marsh

Ludlow
Griscom
Memorial

Dune Spur

Marsh Spur

N

500 feet

- - - **Route**
==== **Road**
P **Parking**
⊥ **Marsh**
⅄ **Scenic Overlook**

North Pool

dike

■ observation tower

START

Refuge Road

out-and-back side paths to viewing areas, follows a universally accessible boardwalk that was refurbished in 2020. Start at a posted map at the parking lot. At the first junction, a side path on the left, not part of the boardwalk trail but well worth the detour at either the start or end of the hike, leads to a dike and observation tower. The tower offers a fine overview of the refuge and habitats, including dunes, marshes, a beaver lodge, the ocean, and the mainland. Look for black ducks, green-winged teals, pintails, great blue herons, and green herons in the tidal marshes and pools during warmer months and migrations.

The circuit begins at the next intersection. To make a counterclockwise loop, take the right fork and follow the boardwalk for 0.2 mile through scrub oaks and freshwater wetlands to Refuge Road. Watch for raccoons foraging on the ground or resting in trees near wet areas. Cross the road and continue to a signed three-way intersection at a boulder dedicated to Ludlow Griscom, a Massachusetts ornithologist recognized as a pioneer in field identification of birds. Bear right on Dune Spur, a 0.1-mile out-and-back path that leads to an overlook with a panoramic vista of dunes and the Atlantic Ocean.

The spur and overlook offer excellent perspectives of the island, which was formed by glaciers. Additional sculpting occurred as the Merrimack River swept silt onto Plum Island. When the first Europeans arrived in the region, mature forests covered the island. Colonists quickly cleared the land, using white pine for ship masts and other lumber for wood fires; they set their sheep to graze on the rest of the vegetation. Today, Plum Island once again has trees, but only a few approach 50 feet tall. The best growing conditions are in hollows, where trees are sheltered from the wind and are closer to groundwater. The plants nearest the beach, including beach grass, seaside goldenrod, dusty miller, beach pea, and sea beach sandwort, are well-adapted to tolerate salt spray. In late summer, you may see southbound monarch butterflies migrating through the refuge.

Autumn is a good time to see rough-legged hawks and harriers hunting for small mammals and to see falcons wheeling in the sky as they migrate south. Lucky birders may be rewarded in winter with the sight of a snowy owl, a visitor from the Arctic. Although snowy owls breed in the tundra, they move south to New England in winter, when food sources are scarce in their home territories. Plum Island and nearby Salisbury Beach State Reservation are two of the best places to see snowy owls on the Massachusetts coast, particularly from December to the end of February. Some years they are fairly common at Plum Island, where they hunt in the open salt marshes, feeding on meadow voles and smaller birds.

Return to the intersection and turn right to resume the loop. Cross Refuge Road again and continue to the nearby intersection with Marsh Spur. Turn right and follow the second out-and-back path to an observation area at the edge of a freshwater marsh, an excellent place to scan for birds and other wildlife. The refuge entrance is visible in the distance to the north.

Retrace your steps to the loop and turn right again to follow the boardwalk on a winding course through maritime woodlands to the junction with the third and final spur path, which leads about 400 feet past growths of dense cattails and tall reed grass to another viewing area in the heart of a marsh. Purple loosestrife, an attractive but invasive species

A renovated boardwalk and observation areas provide outstanding bird-watching opportunities and views of marshes, dunes, and maritime forests.

that is colonizing wetlands throughout New England, blooms in August. Fortunate observers may glimpse Virginia rails and soras, both uncommon marsh birds that are often well camouflaged amid dense vegetation. The observation tower near the trailhead may be visible in the distance to the left.

From the intersection, follow the final segment of the circuit through woods bordering the marsh edge for about 0.2 mile to the trailhead and parking area.

For those who want to continue exploring, the refuge has many options. Pines Trail, with access from a marked trailhead on the auto road south of the Hellcat Wildlife Observation Area, offers an easy 0.3-mile walk through woods at the edge of a marsh. A connecting path links Pines Trail to parking area 5, where another boardwalk leads over dunes to an observation site with views of the beach and ocean.

Several other parking areas provide access to the beach, where a walk offers opportunities to watch for a variety of marine wildlife, examine the flotsam that has washed ashore, and listen to the surf—pounding and angry one day, gently lapping in rhythmic wavelets the next. Be on the lookout for piping plover, an endangered shorebird that is successfully reproducing on Plum Island. Piping plovers are small, sand-colored birds that nest on the beach and therefore are susceptible to being crushed by beach vehicles or disturbed by beachgoers. Other shorebirds, such as greater yellowlegs and willets, hunt for invertebrates along the shoreline and in tidal flats. Harbor seals are often seen bobbing in the surf beyond the breakers. Access to the beach is restricted during the spring and summer shorebird breeding season. Sandy Point State Reservation, which abuts the refuge at the island's southern tip, offers additional beach paths and ocean views.

DID YOU KNOW?

The refuge is one of New England's most prominent migrant traps—areas that are often visited by migrating birds accidentally or by vagrant bird species. Some of the more unusual species that have been spotted here include magnificent frigate birds, white pelicans, and western tanagers.

NEARBY

The historical Newburyport waterfront is a popular tourist attraction. Seasonal concerts are held in Waterfront Park. Restaurants are in town on and off Water and State streets. Maudslay State Park (mass.gov/locations/maudslay-state-park), on Curzon Mill Road, encompasses the grounds of the former Moseley Estate on the banks of the Merrimack River. Attractions include nineteenth-century gardens and plantings and a large natural stand of mountain laurel.

MORE INFORMATION

The refuge is open year-round. A $5 admission fee per car is charged, and annual passes are available. Restrooms are available at lot 4 and the main entrance; pets are prohibited. The headquarters and visitor center, at 6 Plum Island Turnpike across from Mass Audubon's Joppa Flats visitor center at the Plum Island Turnpike bridge, include information, exhibits, and a gift shop.

The refuge often fills to capacity during summer weekends and may temporarily close to vehicles when parking lots are full (pedestrians and bicyclists are admitted when the entrance gate is closed). The beach is usually closed from April 1 to July or August to protect nesting shorebirds, and public access is prohibited during an annual limited (two days as of 2021) deer hunt in early December.

OLD TOWN HILL

From scenic, three-state ocean views on Old Town Hill's summit to marshes in the Little River watershed, this walk leads to a variety of coastal attractions.

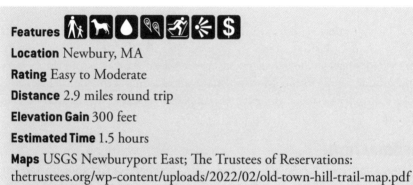

Features 👥 🐕 💧 🚣 🏃 ☀ 💲

Location Newbury, MA

Rating Easy to Moderate

Distance 2.9 miles round trip

Elevation Gain 300 feet

Estimated Time 1.5 hours

Maps USGS Newburyport East; The Trustees of Reservations: thetrustees.org/wp-content/uploads/2022/02/old-town-hill-trail-map.pdf

GPS coordinates 42° 46.164′ N, 70° 51.462′ W

Contact The Trustees of Reservations: thetrustees.org/place/old-town-hill, 978-526-8687

DIRECTIONS

From I-95 take Exit 86 (formerly Exit 54) and follow MA 133 east for 4.5 miles. Turn left and follow MA 1A north for 4.8 miles. After crossing a bridge over Parker River, turn left on Newman Road and continue to the roadside entrance and parking area on the left.

TRAIL DESCRIPTION

Old Town Hill, a glacial drumlin and prominent landmark of the northern Massachusetts coast, rises above winding Little River and the tidal marshes in Newbury. The hill is the centerpiece of a 531-acre property (The Trustees of Reservations) with outstanding habitat diversity. This hike combines several trails, including a portion of the long-distance Bay Circuit Trail (BCT), as a 2.3-mile circuit over Old Town Hill and through surrounding forests, meadows, and wetlands. A short out-and-back segment leads to the banks of Little River. Maps are posted at the entrance and main junctions.

From the gate and Trustees sign at the parking area, cross Newman Road and bear right on the white-blazed BCT (the section of the BCT from the entrance to Old Town Hill's summit, also known as Ridge Trail, is part of the Red Trail loop). Pass the first of many stone walls, indicators of past agricultural clearing by early settlers, and a former pine plantation interspersed with hardwoods. After briefly paralleling Newman Road, turn left and follow the BCT/Ridge Trail along an old cart road. In autumn, the foliage of mixed hardwoods, including oaks, maples, birches, and aspens, offers a potpourri of color. Heavily

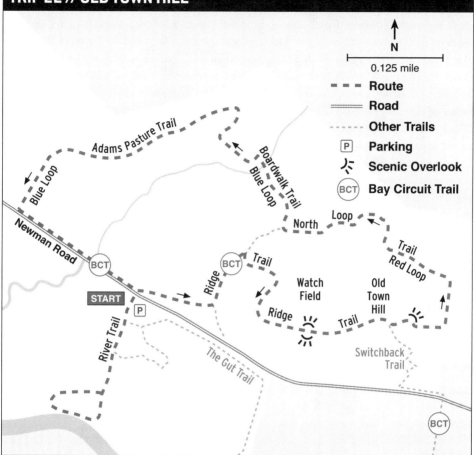

browned leaves and rapid drop, as occurred in 2020 and several other recent years, indicate drought effects. The loud, chattering call of territorial red squirrels is a familiar sound, especially in pine woods. Oak acorns provide sustenance for blue jays, eastern chipmunks, and gray squirrels.

At the next intersection, turn right and follow the BCT/Ridge Trail on a quick ascent to the edge of Watch Field, a former hilltop pasture now maintained as a meadow, at 0.3 mile. The BCT/Ridge Trail continues right for about 500 feet to the field's southwest corner and then turns left (east) along the southern side, which is lined with a few cedars. A small opening on the right affords a partial view of the Little River valley and a home abutting the reservation. From another outlook at a maple tree ringed with boulders, enjoy sweeping northeasterly vistas across the field to Newburyport, Plum Island, and the Atlantic Ocean.

Continue along the field edge to a grassy clearing and two trail junctions at the 168-foot summit at 0.6 mile. On clear days, visible distant landmarks include the Isle of Shoals off New Hampshire and Mount Agamenticus in southern Maine. Fall foliage peaks in late October, later than in most other New England regions due to the mild coastal climate and low elevation.

To continue the circuit, from a posted map follow red-blazed Red Loop into upland hardwood forest. (The BCT branches right at the adjacent junction to follow a switchback route down to Newman Road east of the main entrance.) Pass a stone wall and make a moderately steep descent to North Field, a meadow at the base of Old Town Hill's northeast slopes. Bear left along the field edge and then left again to reenter the woods on Red Loop. Follow the winding path past a large, twin-trunked white pine, several boardwalk bridges, and a small footbridge over a seasonal stream. These forests provide crucial habitats for songbirds traveling on the coastal Atlantic flyway during spring and fall migrations. Watch Field is just out of view atop the slope on the left as you pass through a portion of an old spruce plantation.

At 1.3 miles, reach a three-way junction with Blue Loop at a posted map. (A left turn here on Red Loop leads back to the BCT/Ridge Trail and the trailhead.) This hike continues right on blue-blazed Blue Loop, which leads downhill through pine-hardwood forest to a narrow boardwalk across a portion of the Newman Road Marshes, wetlands in the Little River watershed. Salt marshes are crucial ecosystems that support a rich food web and mitigate flooding. Great egrets (distinguished from similarly all-white snowy egrets by their larger size and black beaks), great blue herons, and other wading birds feed on frogs, snails, crabs, mussels, and other prey.

Bear left to follow Blue Loop along the forested wetland edge and past more stone walls. Ascend past a few cedars to a reservation boundary sign and turn left to continue on Blue Loop. Enter Adams Pasture, a large field at the reservation's northern boundary, and walk along the south edge of the field, with views of marshes through trees on the left. The field

From Watch Field atop Old Town Hill, scenic, three-state coastal views extend north to Mount Agamenticus in Maine.

provides crucial habitat for bobolinks, grassland birds that arrive to breed during spring and summer. White-tailed deer, wild turkeys, barred owls, and red-tailed hawks are among many other species that benefit from open areas and forest-edge habitats.

At the field's southwest end, bear left and follow an old road across the marsh to a trailhead and posted map on Newman Road. Muddy or wet spots may lie along the path, which is just a few feet above sea level. Turn left and walk east along Newman Road (usually light traffic) for 0.3 mile, with fine views of wetlands on both sides. Watch for a variety of birds, including Virginia rails and glossy ibises in summer and horned larks in winter. At 2.3 miles, complete the circuit portion of the hike at the main entrance.

To make an easy out-and-back walk (0.6-mile round trip) to Little River, from the gate and posted map follow yellow-blazed River Trail south to a junction where a short loop begins. Follow either fork to open views from the muddy banks of Little River and a former pasture. Little River empties into Parker River near the reservation boundary. Both waterways are part of the Great Marsh, an expansive complex of salt marshes and tidal rivers along the northeastern Massachusetts coast.

DID YOU KNOW?

Newbury's first settlement was at the base of Old Town Hill. Colonial settlers cleared the summit and built an observation tower for sentries during the seventeenth century. A tall elm tree on the hilltop served as a navigational landmark for mariners.

NEARBY

Salisbury Beach State Reservation (mass.gov/locations/salisbury-beach-state-reservation), off MA 1A in Salisbury, encompasses a barrier beach and marshes where the Merrimack River empties into the Atlantic Ocean. The reservation is an excellent destination for viewing winter wildlife. Amenities include a large seasonal campground, boardwalks, boat ramps, and a playground, as well as accessible beach, camping, and picnicking facilities. The reservation is open year-round; a seasonal parking fee ($14 for Massachusetts residents, $40 for nonresidents) is charged from May 15 to October 31.

MORE INFORMATION

The property is open year-round, sunrise to sunset; no fee. Hunting is permitted in season. Dogs are allowed but must be leashed from April 1 to August 15.

23 CRANE BEACH

Five miles of trails wind through more than 1,200 acres of white-sand beach and dunes along both sides of Castle Neck.

Features 🐕 💧 🔍 🎿 ❄️ 🦅 🛖 🚌 💲

Location Ipswich, MA

Rating Moderate

Distance 3-mile loop

Elevation Gain 270 feet

Estimated Time 2.5 hours

Maps USGS Ipswich; The Trustees of Reservations: thetrustees.org/wp-content/uploads/2020/07/crane_estate_trailmap_2019.pdf

GPS coordinates 42° 41.024′ N, 70° 46.042′ W

Contact The Trustees of Reservations: thetrustees.org/place/crane-beach-on-the-crane-estate

DIRECTIONS

From MA 128, take Exit 45A (formerly Exit 20A) and follow MA 1A north for 8.0 miles to Ipswich. Turn right onto MA 133 east, continue 1.8 miles, and then turn left onto Northgate Road. Drive 0.7 mile, turn right onto Argilla Road, and continue 2.5 miles to the entrance at the end of the road.

By public transportation, take the Newburyport/Rockport line of the MBTA Commuter Rail to Ipswich Station, and then take the Ipswich Essex Explorer bus to Crane Beach. For schedule and rates, visit ipswichessexexplorer.com.

TRAIL DESCRIPTION

At scenic Crane Beach, part of a network of properties owned by The Trustees of Reservations, finger-shaped Castle Neck juts into the ocean at the mouth of Castle Neck River and Essex Bay. Diverse flora, including an extensive pitch-pine forest, carnivorous plants, and cranberries, can be found here. The area is also known for its birdlife and fall foliage. Check fees before your visit (see "More Information" below).

This hike combines the reservation's Green and Red trails to form a 3-mile loop that explores the western portion of the neck. Although the trip isn't overly long and can be completed in less than two hours at a good pace, don't underestimate it. Most of the route traverses soft sand, exposed areas, and rolling terrain as the trails wind along and over a series of dunes. Bring plenty of water and sunscreen. For a shorter outing, hike Green Trail alone or follow a portion of Red Trail to the beach and walk back along the shore to the

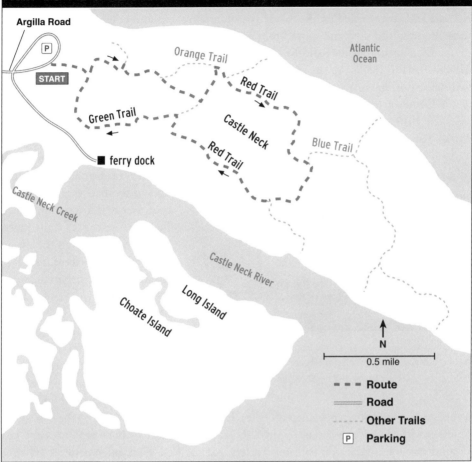

Argilla Road

P

Orange Trail

Atlantic
Ocean

START

Red Trail

Green Trail

Castle Neck

Red Trail

Blue Trail

ferry dock

Castle Neck Creek

Castle Neck River

Long Island

Choate Island

N

0.5 mile

- - - Route
Road
Other Trails
P Parking

entrance. The trails are well marked, with posted maps and numbers. Please stay on the marked trails and do not walk along the crests of the dunes or step on the vegetation.

Begin at a trailhead on the east side of the large parking lot, across from the beach offices and walkways. Follow a connecting path into the woods and across a short boardwalk to the start of the Green Trail loop in an open area. Turn left on this green-blazed trail to make a clockwise circuit. The ocean soon comes in sight to the north, with Crane Beach's wooden walkways visible on the left. The trail curves to the right, and beautiful views unfold as it crosses the dunes. The fragile dunes, which prevent the land from being engulfed by the sea, are held together by long, connected plant roots.

At marker 2, turn right to continue on Green Trail, which descends into a shaded grove of pitch pine and scrub oak. This forest type is common on Cape Cod and the southeastern Massachusetts coast, but less so along the North Shore. These trees are well adapted to the sandy soils that few other species can tolerate.

The trees and shrubs offer food and cover for a variety of wildlife that calls Castle Neck home. Eastern coyotes are fairly common; watch for their tracks and droppings along the trail, especially near junctions within their territories. Another midsize predator that is present, but quite elusive, is the bobcat, which makes its dens well off the beaten path. Bobcats and coyotes feed on prey such as cottontail rabbits and mice. Look for tracks of these mammals in sand and snow. From midsummer to late fall, watch for meadowhawk dragonflies flitting around shrubs, especially near wet areas. The hardy yellow-legged meadowhawk is the last of the state's 170 dragonfly species to remain active as the warm weather winds down. You might see it in late November or even early December in mild years. The beach itself is an important nesting site for endangered piping plovers and least terns. In 2019, 49 piping plover pairs raised 96 chicks, and in 2020, 69 pairs raised 89 chicks. Follow Green Trail straight past the junction with the western end of Orange Trail

Massachusetts beaches serve as important breeding grounds for piping plovers. Be aware that certain beach areas may be closed to protect nests and chicks. *Photo by Tim Saxton, Creative Commons on Flickr*

on the left and continue through a grove of overhanging pitch pines to another open area. At 0.7 mile, arrive at a junction where the Green and Red trails meet. This hike continues to the left on Red Trail. (For a shorter outing, turn right and return to the parking area via Green Trail for a 1.7-mile round trip.)

Red Trail crosses a series of dunes as it leads you back toward the ocean. Beach grasses and shrubs, such as beach rose, help stabilize the dunes, which exist in a variety of ever-changing shapes and sizes. The red-blazed path curves to the east at the junction with the eastern end of Orange Trail, and the ocean again comes into view. Just beyond the junction, a side path on the left, part of Red Trail, offers a quick 0.1-mile (approximately 5-minute) walk to the beach. (Another option for a short outing is to take this path and then turn left and walk along the beach back to the parking area.) Red Trail continues to the right and follows moderately steep terrain over a series of dunes along the north side of the neck. At the crest of the climb, enjoy fine sweeping views across rolling dunes. Watch for red admiral and monarch butterflies in the patches of shrubs.

Follow Red Trail as it curves away from the ocean and winds to a Y junction at 1.5 miles. At this intersection, roughly an hour's walk from the trailhead, 0.3-mile Blue Trail leaves left to connect with Yellow Trail and Black Trail in the remote eastern portion of Castle Neck. (These out-and-back trails offer optional extensions to the trip; be sure to have plenty of water.) This hike continues along Red Trail, which follows rolling terrain across the heart of the neck. Bear right again at the next junction (marker 21), where another out-and-back path branches to the south. Just beyond this junction, a short but steep climb up a dune rewards you with a beautiful, panoramic vista overlooking the mouth of Castle Neck River and its associated marshlands to the south.

Descend the dune and continue northeast over more rolling terrain and soft sand. After another short but steep climb, Red Trail weaves along Wigwam Hill, where American

A favorite of locals and visitors alike, Crane Beach is home to protected dunes and sandy beaches.

Indians once built signal fires at overlooks. Pass a view of the ocean to the right (north); more vistas unfold as the trail descends the hill and rejoins Green Trail at marker 25.

Turn left onto green-blazed Green Trail and continue past marker 6 into a pine grove that offers a stretch of easy walking and a much-needed break from the sun. Note the lack of plant diversity, the result of the sandy soils and acidic pine needles in the grassy woods here. The trail emerges back onto another open dune and curves to the right (north) to cross the center of the neck. At the three-way junction at the end of the Green Trail loop, turn left to return to the parking area.

DID YOU KNOW?

The Castle Neck area was actively farmed from the time of European settlement through the early twentieth century. Salt hay cut from the marshes was used to feed cattle.

NEARBY

Castle Hill, just west of the beach at the end of Argilla Road, is home to the historical Crane Estate and its beautifully landscaped grounds. The nearby Crane Wildlife Refuge consists of 697 acres of islands, salt marsh, and intertidal environments. More than 3 miles of trails explore this area, where more than 200 species of birds have been observed. For more information about the estate and refuge, visit thetrustees.org. Restaurants are in central Ipswich along and off MA 133 and MA 1A.

MORE INFORMATION

The reservation is open year-round, 8 A.M. to sunset. Admission fees, as much as $50 per car on summer weekends, are charged year-round. Reduced rates and a yearly parking sticker are available for members of The Trustees of Reservations. Fees are lower for bicyclists, pedestrians, and visitors arriving after 4 P.M.

During peak season (Memorial Day through Labor Day), Crane Beach is a popular swimming beach, especially on weekends, with lifeguards and rangers on duty. In-season amenities include bathhouses, showers, picnic tables, refreshments, merchandise, water fountains, and transportation for visitors who are mobility impaired or challenged. Portable toilets are available in the off-season. Horseback riding is allowed from October through March with a permit and fee. Dogs are allowed from October 1 through March 31 (free for Trustees members, $5 fee for nonmembers) and are not allowed between April 1 and September 30 to protect nesting shorebirds. Limited seasonal bow hunting is permitted.

24 RAVENSWOOD PARK

This ecologically diverse slice of wilderness includes a magnolia swamp, rocky ledges and boulders, and a large forest.

Features

Location Gloucester, MA

Rating Easy to Moderate

Distance 2.7-mile loop

Elevation Gain 360 feet

Estimated Time 2 hours

Maps USGS Gloucester; The Trustees of Reservations: thetrustees.org/wp-content/uploads/2022/02/ravenswood-park-trail-map.pdf

GPS coordinates 42° 35.493' N, 70° 41.911' W

Contact The Trustees of Reservations: thetrustees.org/place/ravenswood-park, 978-526-8687

DIRECTIONS

From MA 128, take Exit 53 (formerly Exit 14) and follow MA 133 east for 3.0 miles to MA 127. Turn right and proceed south for 1.9 miles to the reservation entrance on the right.

TRAIL DESCRIPTION

Ravenswood Park is a pocket of forested wilderness within the suburbs of the North Shore. Large hemlock trees, miles of winding trails, and a rare magnolia swamp are all reasons to visit the 500-acre property, owned by The Trustees of Reservations. History lovers will enjoy the story of Mason A. Walton, the Hermit of Gloucester, who lived on the property for 33 years. Samuel E. Sawyer, a wealthy merchant who summered here, preserved this land. In 1889, Sawyer's will created Ravenswood Park as a property "laid out handsomely with drive-ways and pleasant rural walks." Following Sawyer's death, the property was managed by a dedicated group for 104 years. It was transferred to The Trustees of Reservations in 1993.

This 2.7-mile walk first goes through Great Magnolia Swamp and then leads to the hermit cabin site before looping back to the parking area through old trees and rocky terrain. A detailed trail map is posted on a sign at the parking area. The walking is mostly easy, over mildly rolling terrain. Trails are clearly signed, although number markers at junctions have been removed.

From the parking area, follow Old Salem Road, a wide, historical carriage road, into the woods. At 0.2 mile, turn left at a four-way junction (opposite Ledge Hill Trail, which enters

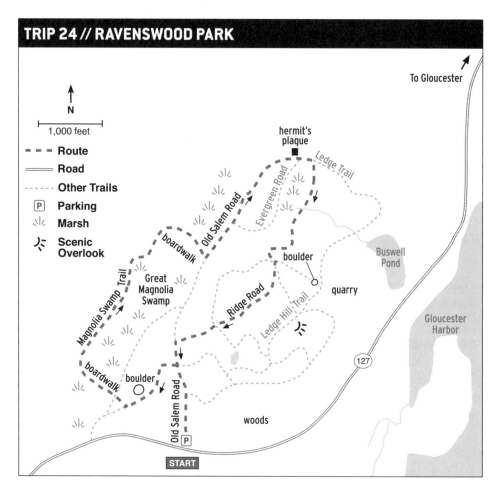

To Gloucester

N

1,000 feet

--- Route
=== Road
···· Other Trails
P Parking
Marsh
Scenic Overlook

hermit's plaque

Ledge Trail

Evergreen Road

Old Salem Road

boardwalk

Great Magnolia Swamp

Magnolia Swamp Trail

boulder

Buswell Pond

Ridge Road

Ledge Hill Trail

quarry

Gloucester Harbor

127

boardwalk

boulder

Old Salem Road

woods

P

START

from the right) and follow narrow, yellow-blazed Magnolia Swamp Trail beneath large hemlocks as it winds up and down small hills in a southwesterly direction. Just 300 feet down the trail, a narrow path enters on the left; continue straight to an exposed ledge where a car-sized glacial boulder is perched on the bedrock. Such boulders are known as glacial erratics due to the haphazard way they were deposited by glaciers roughly 15,000 years ago.

Follow Magnolia Swamp Trail along a rocky treadway to the right of the boulder, heading toward the swamp and passing through an understory of mountain laurel and blueberry. Continue straight at an intersection and follow a narrow boardwalk that traverses the ferns and thick foliage in the wet area of the swamp. Red maples and sweet peppers grow along the boardwalk, and the low-lying swamp has a decidedly different feel than the upland terrain. The regionally uncommon magnolia trees for which the swamp and the nearby village of Magnolia are named grow here. This species is the sweet bay magnolia (*Magnolia virginiana*), a primarily southern species that is native to lowlands and prefers rich, moist soil.

In the mid-nineteenth century, Henry David Thoreau visited the swamp to see the magnolias. During the 1800s and early 1900s, many magnolias were harvested from the swamp, and the population was on the verge of extinction before protective measures and replanting ensured the survival of a limited number of specimens. (They are on the state's endangered species list.) In this northern climate, magnolias do not grow very tall and can be difficult to distinguish from other trees. Perhaps the best time to spot one is in June, when their creamy white flowers are blooming, giving off a delicate scent. (Please do not bend the branches to see the flowers up close, as this can damage growth.)

The narrow boardwalk continues 0.25 mile before reaching dry ground. At 0.7 mile, Magnolia Swamp Trail bears right and traverses the edge of the swamp in a northerly direction, passing more large hemlocks, boulders, and rocky outcroppings. At the intersection with blue-blazed Fernwood Lake Trail on the left, turn right to stay on Magnolia Swamp Trail, which follows a boardwalk across the upper portion of the swamp. Continue uphill, past more hemlocks with winterberry growing below, to the intersection with Old Salem Road at 1.2 miles.

Turn left onto Old Salem Road and continue past the lower junction with Evergreen Road, which enters from the right. Look for some yellow birches to your left, followed by another wet area where red maple and a few white pines grow. Stone walls lace the woods, indicating this was once pasture or farmland. Chances are, the soil was too stony for growing crops, so farmers used it as sheep or cattle pasture.

After walking 0.5 mile from the Magnolia Swamp Trail junction (1.7 miles overall), arrive at a boulder with a plaque dedicated to the Hermit of Gloucester, Mason A. Walton. This scholarly man initially came to Gloucester to cure himself of tuberculosis after his wife and child died early in his marriage. As his health improved, and with the permission

Oak and red maple trees grow along the boardwalk in Ravenswood Park.

of the landowner, he built a cabin in 1884 on land that subsequently became part of Ravenswood Park and spent his days writing and studying wildlife. People came to the cabin to listen to him discuss the flora and fauna of the area, and he contributed to the magazine that became *Field & Stream*. He died in 1917 at age 79, and the cabin was destroyed by a fire in 1948.

One of the animals that was absent in Walton's day but is increasingly common now is the fisher, a large member of the weasel family. Its muzzle is pointed, its ears are broad and rounded, and its legs and feet are stout. It has a glossy, brownish-black coat, with small white patches on the neck. Fishers are one of the few animals that prey on porcupines. They do so by circling the porcupine, biting its exposed face, and tiring it out before moving in for the kill. The hemlocks along the trail are a chief food source for porcupines, and the exposed ledges offer good denning areas.

From the boulder and plaque, begin the return leg of the loop by turning right off Old Salem Road onto the upper end of Evergreen Road, a wide carriage road that leads southwest. About 0.1 mile down this road, traverse a tiny stream where a stand of mountain laurel grows beneath the canopy of tall hemlocks. At the next intersection, turn left off Evergreen Road and continue about 75 feet to the intersection of Ridge Road and Quarry Road. This hike continues right on Ridge Road. (For a longer, more rugged return route, follow Quarry Road east to a small former quarry site, and return to the parking area via orange-blazed Ledge Hill Trail—a narrow, snaking path through very rocky terrain.)

Well-maintained Ridge Road leads southwest for about 0.4 mile, passing beneath more impressive pines and hemlocks, to the intersection with Old Salem Road. Turn left and follow Old Salem Road south to the end of the loop at the junction with Magnolia Swamp Trail. Continue straight on Old Salem Road and retrace your steps to the entrance.

DID YOU KNOW?

Ravenswood Park contains many relics of Cape Ann history, including American Indian burial mounds and artifacts, rock walls and cellar holes built by early settlers, and old carriage roads that are now park trails.

NEARBY

The Gloucester Fisherman's Memorial on South Stacey Boulevard was established in 1925 in recognition of both the town's 300th anniversary and its many sailors who have been lost at sea. Restaurants are on Main and Rogers streets near the waterfront.

MORE INFORMATION

The park is open year-round, sunrise to sunset; no fee; no restrooms. Dogs are allowed but must be leashed. Mountain biking is permitted in designated areas except during the March and April mud season.

25 HALIBUT POINT STATE PARK AND RESERVATION

Enjoy magnificent views of the ocean, a historical granite quarry, and a walk along the rocky coastline at the northern tip of Cape Ann.

Features

Location Rockport, MA

Rating Easy

Distance 1.5-mile loop

Elevation Gain Minimal

Estimated Time 1 hour

Maps USGS Gloucester OEN; Massachusetts Department of Conservation and Recreation: mass.gov/doc/halibut-point-map/download

GPS coordinates 42° 41.199′ N, 70° 37.902′ W

Contact Massachusetts Department of Conservation and Recreation: mass.gov/locations/halibut-point-state-park, 978-546-2997; The Trustees of Reservations: thetrustees.org/place/halibut-point-reservation, 978-526-8687

DIRECTIONS

Take MA 128 (Yankee Division Highway) to Gloucester. After crossing the bridge over Annisquam River, turn north at the Grant Circle rotary onto MA 127 (Washington Avenue), following signs for Annisquam and Pigeon Cove. Continue on MA 127 for 6.1 miles then turn left to reach the state park entrance on Gott Avenue. From Rockport Center, take MA 127 north for 0.5 mile to Gott Avenue on the right.

By public transportation, Cape Ann Transit Authority (CATA) offers bus service, but riders must request Halibut Point because the park is not a scheduled stop. For more information, call CATA at 978-283-7916 or visit canntran.com.

TRAIL DESCRIPTION

On the rugged Cape Ann coast, which is more reminiscent of Maine than Massachusetts, Halibut Point offers walkers, beach explorers, birders, and history buffs a wonderful network of trails. The state park and the adjacent shoreline owned by The Trustees of Reservations collectively form a unique area of open space on this rocky headland. From 1840 until the mid-twentieth century, Halibut Point was the site of numerous quarry operations sourcing granite as old as 450 million years.

From an information sign on Gott Avenue opposite the parking area, follow a wide, flat path north toward the former Babson Farm Quarry and the Atlantic Ocean. Dense

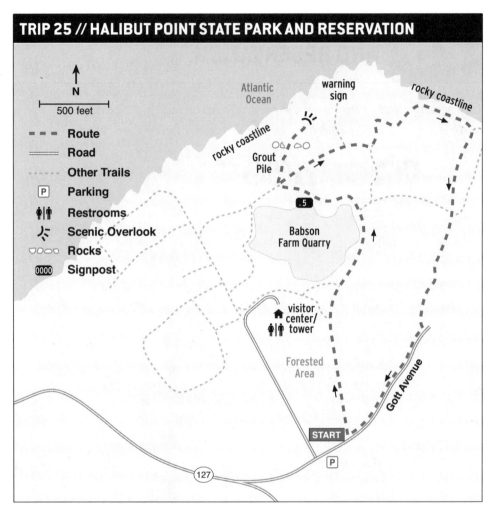

foliage, including red cedar, wild apple, dogwood, oak, mountain ash, wild cherry, and draping grapevines lines the path. Watch for eastern cottontail rabbits, especially early and late in the day. After 0.25 mile, reach a T intersection at a view overlooking the granite quarry, now filled with water.

Turn right and follow the path, which is marked with several interpretive signs, along the quarry's edge. One of the pieces of granite on the left has visible grooves created by past cutting and drilling. Continue on the path halfway around the quarry, just past marker 5 (the number is painted on a rock on the right), to a fork in the trail. Turn right and follow a sign to an overlook. The jumble of rocks you are standing on is called the Grout Pile, where discarded pieces of granite were dumped over the years and now form the perfect vantage point to admire the coastline and ocean. On clear days, you can see the New Hampshire coast, including the Isle of Shoals, and the low profile of Mount Agamenticus in Maine, 80 miles distant. If you have binoculars, scan the shoreline for seals or watch the lobster anglers checking their traps. If you see a seal on the rocks below, do not approach it. Young harbor seal pups often rest on the rocks while their mothers feed offshore. The pups nap and then return to the sea and join their mothers.

During winter, Halibut Point is an excellent place to watch for wintering seabirds and waterfowl, including northern gannets, loons, scoters, red-breasted mergansers, red-necked and horned grebes, common eiders, and purple sandpipers. The common loon winters off Halibut Point, but it does not make its haunting cry in winter, and its distinctive black-and-white-patterned plumage is replaced by a dull brown color on its back, with its throat and chest white. Loons migrate in small flocks and continue to dive beneath the water's surface even in winter, hunting for fish. Another distinctive seabird to watch for is the harlequin duck, which has brilliant colors and feeds at the rocky shoreline. Razorbills, which resemble penguins in shape and color, are occasionally seen around Cape Ann. Be sure to bring binoculars or a spotting scope, as the birds may be far out at sea or hidden in the coves.

Once you have enjoyed the overlook, retrace your steps 200 feet to the intersection near the quarry. Turn left and follow a signed path east toward the rocky shores and ocean. The path slopes downward through small scrub oaks and shadbushes to a more open area of large rocks. After about 500 feet, a short out-and-back path on the left leads to the shore. (Use caution when exploring the shoreline. The pounding surf can sweep over the rocks and make walking hazardous, especially after storms, and at low tide black algae make rocks slippery.) Look for wildflowers, such as trout lily, violet, aster, and goldenrod, growing at edges and gaps in the rock during spring and summer.

Halibut Point's shores constitute a landscape unique to the southern New England coast. Cape Ann is the largest outcropping of rocky headland between Cape Cod and Maine's

Tide pools in Halibut Point's rocky shores provide opportunities for explorers of all ages.

Cape Elizabeth. These ledges are resistant to wave erosion, unlike the sandspits and dunes that make up the rest of the Massachusetts coastline. The slablike granite rocks and toppled ledges at Halibut Point are a testament to the ice sheet that moved through the land 10,000 years ago. The bedrock tended to break along parallel cracks, which is why the granite slabs look layered. Just a few hundred feet farther inland, huge, round boulders that litter the landscape are another legacy of glaciers. The Cape Ann area has an abundance of these boulders, called glacial erratics, which were deposited haphazardly by the retreating glaciers.

The rocky ledges offer some of the finest tide-pool habitat in Massachusetts, and during low tide, you can observe the marine organisms—starfish, barnacles, algae—that survive this harsh environment by clinging to the rocks.

After exploring near the ocean, backtrack along the path for about 200 feet and turn left to continue east along the point. Carefully cross the open rocks and walk parallel to the ocean for about a quarter-mile toward a lone house farther down the coast. (This portion of Halibut Point Reservation is owned by The Trustees). At 1.0 mile, reach a sign at the reservation boundary with Sea Rocks, an oceanfront tract of land and right-of-way path owned by the town of Rockport. Turn right onto a narrow path that leads south, away from the ocean, through a grove of low trees. After about 0.25 mile of easy walking, turn right onto Gott Avenue and complete the loop by walking another 0.25 mile back to the parking area. Please respect the private residences along the road.

DID YOU KNOW?

The Halibut Point area was originally called "Haul About" by sailors because they had to carefully tack around the treacherous, rocky shoreline.

NEARBY

Picturesque Rockport Harbor's best-known attraction is Motif No. 1, an iconic red fishing shack that has long been a popular subject for painters and photographers. Cape Ann is home to five lighthouses, including the Eastern Point Lighthouse at the tip of Eastern Point in Gloucester and the Annisquam Lighthouse, off MA 127 near the Gloucester–Rockport town line. Restaurants are along and off MA 127A in Rockport center.

MORE INFORMATION

Open year-round, 8 A.M. to sunset. A parking fee ($5 for Massachusetts residents, $20 for nonresidents) is payable at a self-serve station. Admission is free for members of The Trustees of Reservations, pedestrians, bicyclists (bike rack at the entrance), and vehicles with disabled veteran and handicap license plates. Portable restrooms are available. Bicycling on trails and swimming are not permitted. Pets are allowed but must be leashed. Free natural history and education programs are offered.

Not much about Boston's busy western suburbs still resembles the region's natural, original state. Rock was
blasted to make interstate highways flatter and smoother,
land was excavated for reservoirs, rivers were dammed for
industry, and wet areas were filled in to make more human habitat. Still, there is beauty in the way nature
healed around those scars: highway medians filled with
flowers; bluebirds flitting around the large lawns of new
developments; the sky reflected in the water of human-made
canals, reservoirs, and deep quarries.

Our ancestors, including famous figures such as Ralph
Waldo Emerson and Henry David Thoreau, knew to seek out the quiet places and the land
that was deemed unfit for farms or homes. They walked in the evenings and on Sundays,
watching the sky turn from indigo to black and listening to the wind that foretold the
change of season. Thoreau was well known for mucking about in swamps and marshes in
search of wildlife, and his observations are used today to calculate climate change.

We are fortunate that the residents in this densely packed region, on their own and in
cooperation with conservation nonprofits, have looked past progress and profits to the
future, preserving areas important to wildlife and to peace of mind.

The Metro West region is home to open spaces and preserved land reflecting the wide
range of Massachusetts's history, including the location of American Indians' encamp-
ments near the Charles River in Natick's Broadmoor Wildlife Sanctuary, the early European settlements along Lexington's Battle Road, and the long chain of reservoirs that filled
Boston's need for drinking water: Wachusett, Whitehall, Hopkinton, Ashland, Sudbury,
and Lake Cochituate. Now the string of aqueducts used to channel that water is also considered a wildlife corridor and recreational space. Farmland that once fed local residents is
quickly being converted to housing tracts, but a few large parcels are set aside for wildlife
habitat and open space, such as Easton's Wheaton Farm, Northborough's Mount Pisgah,
and Carlisle's Great Brook Farm. In these places, we can witness nature reclaiming fields
and watch the steady progression of reforestation. In others, such as Audubon's Moose Hill
in Sharon, the property still includes working farmland where visitors can explore a
moment suspended in time: when the food people consumed came from down the street.

Move back yet another step by visiting the national wildlife refuges in Lincoln, Concord,
and Maynard. These sites are the least disturbed properties in this region, kept closest to
their natural states for wildlife habitat. Here, humans are the visitors and wildlife are the

residents. Careful observation may reveal herons and other migrating birds. You may hear wood thrushes, spy turtles sunning on rocks, or find coyote tracks in the snow.

More than a kind afterthought for animal habitat, conservation land is key to our peace of mind as well. Massachusetts started setting aside land for human recreation in the late 1800s, beginning with Mt. Greylock State Park and near Boston with Middlesex Fells and Blue Hills reservations. Even more than 100 years ago, it was clear that people need nature as much as nature needs people to conserve it.

26 WACHUSETT RESERVOIR AND RESERVATION

More than 4,000 acres of water and woods, maintained by the Massachusetts Department of Conservation and Recreation, offer outstanding hiking, snowshoeing, and wildlife watching.

Features

Location West Boylston, MA

Rating Easy

Distance 4.2 miles round trip

Elevation Gain 225 feet

Estimated Time 2.25 hours

Maps USGS Worcester North; Massachusetts Department of Conservation and Recreation: mass.gov/doc/wachusett-reservoir-forest-roads-and-gates/download

GPS coordinates 43° 49.71′ N, 71° 29.06′ W

Contact Massachusetts Department of Conservation and Recreation: mass.gov/locations/wachusett-reservoir, 508-792-7806

DIRECTIONS

From I-190, take Exit 9 (formerly Exit 5) and follow MA 140 south for 2.4 miles past Wachusett Reservoir's Thomas Basin and Old Stone Church. At the intersection with MA 12 and MA 110, turn right and follow MA 140/MA 12 across a bridge. Turn at the first left to enter the parking area at gate 25.

TRAIL DESCRIPTION

Wachusett Reservoir was created in 1905 as part of the water supply for the greater Boston area. Along with Quabbin Reservoir, to which it is connected, it also serves as an important wildlife reservation. The Massachusetts Department of Conservation and Recreation manages the lands surrounding the reservoir, protecting the water quality and enhancing the ecological integrity of this crucial natural resource. Please check rules before visiting, as the reservoir is a heavily regulated water supply area.

The 4,135-acre reservoir's forest buffer includes a network of unmarked, informal trails, most of which lead to the reservoir's shores. This 4.2-mile out-and-back walk, which follows a portion of the southwest shore, leads to fine views across the water, to one of the reservoir's source brooks, and to a pond. Trails are unblazed, but most junctions are numbered. The combination of woods and wetlands provides excellent habitat for a variety of wildlife.

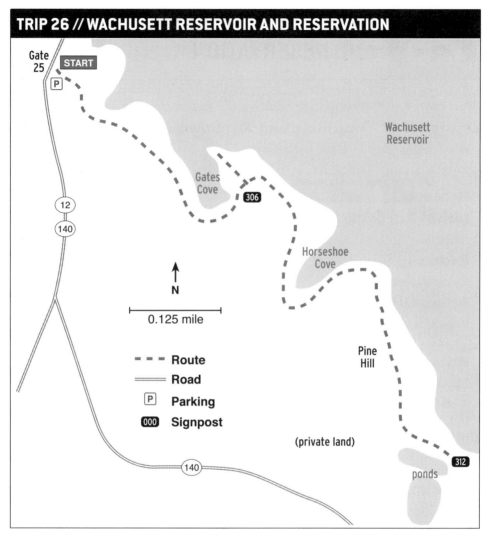

Gate 25
START
P
Wachusett Reservoir
Gates Cove
306
Horseshoe Cove
↑ N
0.125 mile
Pine Hill
- - - Route
═══ Road
P Parking
000 Signpost
(private land)
12
140
140
312
ponds

From the parking area, walk around gate 25 and follow the woods road across a wide power-line clearing. The mixed habitat of field, open water, and forest is a good place to look for wildlife, including white-tailed deer, wild turkeys, and a variety of songbirds, including common yellowthroats, wood thrushes, and prairie warblers. Colorful New England asters bloom in late summer and early autumn. The road curves left, crosses a small brook, and then follows a straight and level course through a pine plantation. Several short paths on the left lead to the reservoir shore.

At 0.5 mile, cross a bridge over Scarlett's Brook and ascend a small hill above the ravine. At the crest of the climb, bear left at a junction and descend to an intersection at marker 306. Turn left here to make a short out-and-back detour to Gates Cove on an unmarked path. From the shoreline at the end of the path, enjoy fine views across the water to historical Old Stone Church and Wachusett Mountain.

Wildlife sightings are frequent in Wachusett Reservoir. Here, common loons swim the southwest shore.

Due to its size, Wachusett Reservoir attracts many birds, including bald eagles and nesting pairs of common loons. The common loon can be identified by its sleek black head with a long, pointed bill and the black-and-white markings on its back. If you are fortunate, you might hear one or more of its calls. At night it tends to emit a mournful wail; in the daytime you are more apt to hear its tremolo, which sounds like a demented laugh. Both can send shivers up your spine.

Watching loons is fascinating, whether they are taking off, flying, or diving. These large birds weigh about 9 pounds and have difficulty getting into the air. That's why you never see a loon on a small body of water. It needs up to a quarter-mile to flap its wings and run along the lake's surface to become airborne. Once in the air, the bird is at home, traveling at speeds in excess of 60 mph. Equally impressive is the loon's ability to dive in search of fish. It uses its wings to propel itself underwater and usually stays beneath the surface for about 40 seconds, although loons have been known to stay submerged for up to five minutes.

Wachusett Reservoir's deep, clear waters support thriving populations of lake trout, brown trout, salmon, and some very large smallmouth bass. (Fishing is permitted seasonally in designated areas; see "More Information" below.) The adjacent forests are home to a variety of woodland mammals, including coyotes, deer, bobcats, squirrels, and chipmunks. In winter, watch for flocks of snow buntings around open areas.

To continue the hike, backtrack to marker 306 and follow the wide dirt road through the woods. At approximately 0.25 mile from marker 306 (1.4 miles overall), the trail curves to the left, crosses a small brook lined with skunk cabbage, and follows the shore at Horseshoe Cove. Check the low vegetation for migratory songbirds and colorful dragonflies.

Approximately 170 species of odonates—the collective order of dragonflies and damselflies—are active in Massachusetts throughout the warm months. Blueberry shrubs produce fruit in summer and offer colorful foliage in fall. When the trail splits, follow the left fork along the shoreline to more open views across the water. The path narrows as it continues along the reservoir edge and then curves to the right and rejoins the woods road near a small sand beach.

Continue on the woods road, with the water to your left and the steep slopes and outcroppings of Pine Hill to your right. After passing an emerald-colored pond in the base of a ravine on the right, reach marker 312 at a fire hydrant and the pumping station building at 2.1 miles. A narrow path drops down to the edge of the pond, and a short trail on the left leads to the reservoir's edge. This marks the end of this hike, although more trails stretch beyond for visitors who have time to explore. (Follow the woods road to left turns at markers 314 and 315 to reach more shore views in approximately 0.5 mile; this adds about 30 minutes total walking time to the hike.) Backtrack to the parking area, keeping the water to your right as you retrace your steps. At marker 306, you can save time by turning left to bypass the side trip to the shore.

DID YOU KNOW?

At the time of its creation, Wachusett Reservoir was the world's largest artificial reservoir. Anticipating the need for more water sources, state planners included an aqueduct intake from the west, which eventually became Quabbin Reservoir.

NEARBY

Old Stone Church, on the reservoir shore near the intersection of MA 140 and MA 110, is a favorite destination for history buffs and photographers. Only the church's stone exterior remains; the structure was abandoned and its interior stripped bare when the reservoir was created.

To reach the bluffs at the reservoir's south end, which offer a good perspective of the reservoir's size, park on MA 140 (just west of the intersection with MA 70) and walk along the shoreline to the right, or enter from gates 13 through 15 off MA 70.

Wachusett Mountain State Reservation and Ski Area, featuring 17 miles of hiking trails and long views from the region's highest summit, is off MA 140 in Princeton. Restaurants are in Clinton, reachable via MA 62, 70, or 110.

MORE INFORMATION

Public access is allowed from one hour before sunrise to one hour after sunset; no fee. Dogs are prohibited. The administration building is on 180 Beaman Street (MA 140) in West Boylston. Hiking is allowed at gates 6 through 16 along MA 70, gates 17 through 24 along MA 140, and gates 25 through 42 along MA 12/MA 110. Shore fishing is permitted from the first Saturday in April (if the ice is melted) to November 30 at gates 6 through 35 and at the Thomas, Oakdale, and Stillwater basins in West Boylston. Maps are available at mass.gov/info-details/dcr-watershed-public-access-maps, and a fishing guide is available at mass.gov/dcr/wachusettfish.

MASSACHUSETTS'S WATERSHED WILDERNESS

The history of the water supply in Massachusetts is as old as the state itself. In the years following European settlement, the city of Boston used a variety of local sources for drinking water, including Jamaica Pond. As the region's population rapidly grew, these sources proved incapable of meeting the increased demand, and state planners began searching outside the metropolitan region for future sources.

A series of reservoirs west of the city reached their capacity by the end of the nineteenth century, so planners recommended creating an extensive water supply network in central Massachusetts. In 1897, construction began on Wachusett Reservoir, which was formed by the impoundment of the South Branch of the Nashua River, near Worcester. The work was completed by 1905, and when the new reservoir was filled to its capacity in 1908, it became both the world's largest artificial reservoir and the largest freshwater body in Massachusetts. Water was delivered from Wachusett Reservoir to Weston Reservoir, near Boston, via a long aqueduct. To build Wachusett Reservoir, several neighborhoods in the towns of West Boylston and Clinton had to be abandoned and flooded. Today, one building from these neighborhoods, the Old Stone Church in West Boylston, remains standing near the water's edge; it is one of the town's best-known landmarks.

In spite of Wachusett Reservoir's size, it was only a matter of time before more regional water sources were necessary. During the early 1920s, the state began planning for the much larger Quabbin Reservoir in the Swift River valley. This was an especially controversial project, as it required four towns—Enfield, Dana, Prescott, and Greenwich—to be abandoned and flooded. Roughly 3,500 people were displaced, the buildings were razed, and in 1938 the towns officially ceased to exist. Although the state compensated residents, the amount they received was low. The 40-square-mile reservoir was filled during the mid-1940s.

With the completion of Quabbin Reservoir, Boston's water needs seemed satisfied. But due to the prolonged drought of the 1960s, water supply again became an issue, and a proposal was put forward to divert portions of the Connecticut River to Quabbin Reservoir. This time there was considerable sustained opposition from a variety of interests in western Massachusetts, and the project was never approved. A fortunate byproduct of the debates was the adoption of water conservation measures in eastern Massachusetts that have significantly reduced the region's water demand in recent decades.

27 MOUNT PISGAH CONSERVATION AREA

Hike along old stone walls and woodland streams to the summit of Mount Pisgah and enjoy seasonal views of the towns of Hudson and Marlborough and the Worcester Hills.

Features

Location Northborough, MA

Rating Easy

Distance 1.75-mile loop

Elevation Gain 115 feet

Estimated Time 1 to 1.5 hours

Maps USGS Marlborough; Sudbury Valley Trustees: town.northborough.ma.us/sites/g/files/vyhlif3571/f/uploads/mt._pisgah_trails_area_trail_map.pdf

GPS coordinates 42° 21.587′ N, 71° 40.267′ W

Contact Sudbury Valley Trustees: svtweb.org/properties/page/mount-pisgah-conservation-area-berlin-and-northborough, 978-443-5588

DIRECTIONS

From I-290, take the Church Street/Boylston/Northborough exit (Exit 27). At the end of the exit, follow signs toward Boylston. Turn right onto Ball Street at the sign for Tougas Family Farm. Follow Ball Street for 1.7 miles to its end. Turn left onto Green Street, continue 0.5 mile to where the road forks, and bear right onto Smith Road. Drive 0.3 mile to the parking area on the right.

TRAIL DESCRIPTION

Mount Pisgah is in the hilly northwest section of Northborough, adjacent to the Berlin town line. It is the highest point in Northborough and offers seasonal scenic views across the hills of southern Worcester County. A mix of narrow footpaths and old dirt roads traverse a forest of red oak, white pine, maple, and beech. Other features, such as forest streams and stone walls marking the old farms that once operated on these grounds, also await visitors.

The 83-acre Mount Pisgah Conservation Area abuts other conservation land, including a 92-acre tract owned by the Massachusetts Division of Fisheries and Wildlife, that forms a fairly large patch of contiguous second- or third-growth forest with habitat for a variety of wildlife. The reservation's trails also connect to other recreational trails in the town of Berlin. This hike, which combines several well-marked trails, is a fairly easy circuit (albeit with rugged, rocky footing in many areas) that includes a short climb to the ridge of Mount Pisgah.

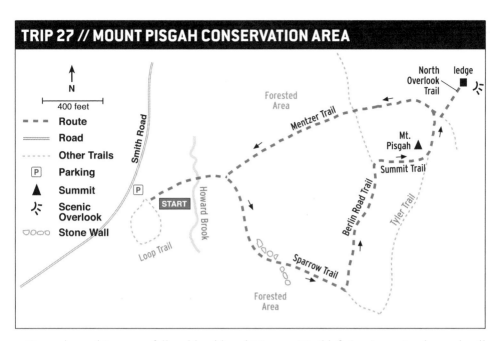

From the parking area, follow blue-blazed Mentzer Trail left (east), passing beneath tall white pines (the trail on the right is a short loop). Soon on your left will be a small grove of young trees that have sprung up from what was once a field cleared for agriculture. Opportunistic (also known as "early successional" or "pioneer") tree species, including gray birch, poplar, pine cherry, and white pine, are the first to establish themselves in such areas, later followed by oak and maple. Look for eastern cottontail rabbits in the tangle of undergrowth and in the thick grasses.

Within 0.25 mile, the trail crosses Howard Brook and then splits. Go right on white-blazed Sparrow Trail. Red maples, oaks, and pines line this path, which is rocky in places. On the forest floor are blueberry bushes, sheep laurels, and herbaceous plants, such as partridge berry, mosses, and princess pine. (Avoid the red-blazed trail to private property on the right.) After a zigzagging rerouted 0.25 mile, the path comes to a stone wall and curves to the left, following the wall.

Walk along the stone wall for a couple of minutes and then continue to the right through an opening in the wall. The route now heads primarily eastward again and soon intersects with an old logging road called Berlin Road Trail. Turn left onto the logging road and follow it for 0.5 mile until you come to Summit Trail on the right. Turn right onto Summit Trail, walk about an eighth-mile to a T intersection, and then turn left onto signed Tyler Trail. A rock a few feet to the left of the trail is embedded with a U.S. Geological Survey marker indicating the summit of Mount Pisgah (there may be a cairn of rocks nearby). After about five more minutes of walking, arrive at the next T intersection, where Mentzer Trail, your return route, enters on the left. Here, turn right and go 20 feet to where the trail forks. Bear left, proceeding about 200 feet to the exposed rock ridge, where there's a vista overlooking Hudson and Marlborough to the east when foliage does not obscure it.

The walk down from the hilltop takes only 20 to 25 minutes. From the overlook, backtrack to the intersection of Tyler and Mentzer trails and continue straight on Mentzer Trail, following yellow markers. Keep straight where the trail crosses Berlin Road Trail. The rocky path leads through a stand of hardwoods.

Deer and raccoon tracks are not uncommon here. The elusive fisher, a large member of the weasel family, has been observed in the vicinity. (Fishers are great hunters of squirrels, porcupines, rabbits, mice, and birds.) Barred owls, great horned owls, hawks, and foxes also have been sighted. Of the two types of foxes that live in Massachusetts, red foxes are fairly common, while gray foxes, which have catlike claws enabling them to climb trees, are shyer and less often seen. Foxes occasionally establish dens close to human dwellings, including in barns and backyards. The best opportunities for seeing wildlife and hearing calls are dawn and dusk.

Mentzer Trail enters the shade of a pine grove and then, 0.3 mile from the Berlin Road Trail crossing, returns to the stream junction you encountered at the start of the hike. Turn right here and cross the stream to return to the parking lot.

DID YOU KNOW?

The conservation area's trails are named for families with historical connections to the land. The Mentzer, Sparrow, Bennett, and Tetreault families all operated farms in the region, and legacies of their activity, such as stone walls and old farm equipment, remain along the trails. The Mentzer farmhouse is still standing near the center of Northborough on Green Street.

Easterly views from central Massachusetts's Mount Pisgah can extend as far as Boston.

NEARBY

Much of the land surrounding Mount Pisgah is still actively farmed. From June to November, the nearby Tougas Family Farm offers fruit picking, including apples, strawberries, peaches, raspberries, and blueberries. The farm has animals for children to visit and a kitchen that serves country dishes. For more information, call the farm at 508-393-6406 or visit tougasfamilyfarm.com. Restaurants are along US 20 and MA 9.

MORE INFORMATION

Mount Pisgah Conservation Area is open year-round, dawn to dusk; no fee; no restrooms. Dogs are allowed, but owners must clean up after them.

28   OXBOW NATIONAL WILDLIFE REFUGE

Part of the Eastern Massachusetts National Wildlife Refuge Complex, Oxbow National Wildlife Refuge protects wetlands and forests along the Nashua River.

Features

Location Harvard, MA

Rating Easy

Distance 1.9-mile loop

Elevation Gain Minimal

Estimated Time 1.25 hours

Maps USGS Ayer; U.S. Fish and Wildlife Service: fws.gov/refuge/oxbow

GPS coordinates 42° 29.744′ N, 71° 37.565′ W

Contact Oxbow National Wildlife Refuge: fws.gov/refuge/oxbow, 978-443-4661

DIRECTIONS

From MA 2 in Harvard, take Exit 109 and follow MA 110/111 south for 1.6 miles. At Harvard Center, turn right and continue on MA 110 for 2.0 miles to the village of Still River. At the post office, turn right onto Still River Depot Road, following signs for the refuge. After passing the refuge's open fields, cross the railroad tracks and then bear right to the main parking lot, where maps, brochures, and restrooms are available.

TRAIL DESCRIPTION

If you're an enthusiast of wetlands and wildlife, you'll enjoy Oxbow National Wildlife Refuge, a nearly 1,700-acre property of wetlands, forests, and fields along the banks of the Nashua River in the picturesque town of Harvard. From 1917 until 1974, much of the refuge was part of the Fort Devens military reservation, and the military still has land on the other side of the river. You may hear target practice and drills during your visit.

Please note that dogs are not allowed at national wildlife refuge properties.

This hike follows the refuge's 1.9-mile trail, which comprises three short paths, each exploring a different habitat. Along the way are continuous views of a variety of habitats, including the river and its associated swamps, ponds, and beaver wetlands; floodplain and upland forests; and fields, which sustain a diverse wildlife community. Portions of this route, especially near the junction of the river and the causeway paths, may be wet during early spring. Be prepared for bugs during late spring and summer.

From the information kiosk at the parking lot, walk around the metal gate to your right onto Tank Road Trail and then quickly bear left at a signed junction onto Riverside Trail.

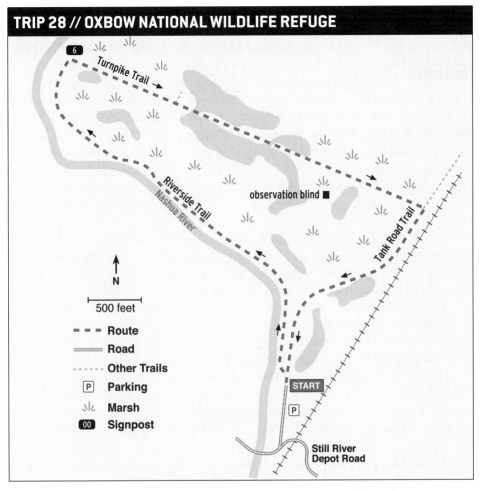

This narrow treadway follows the east bank of the Nashua River, offering fine views across the water. Walk quietly, and you may well see a great blue heron or a flock of ducks. Along the bank is a cluster of silver maples, one of the trees characteristic of floodplain forests. Riverside Trail parallels Tank Road Trail, which is a short distance through the woods to your right, for 0.2 mile (a short crossover path connects the two trails) and then bears left to follow a bend in the river.

Riverside Trail soon passes a large clearing on the right, maintained as a field for the benefit of wildlife. Before the military acquired the refuge property, it was productive farmland; the valley offered much more fertile soil than the surrounding rocky hills. Among the many upland species that benefit from mixed habitats are eastern coyotes, red and gray foxes, white-tailed deer, bluebirds, monarch butterflies, and numerous birds of prey. Field wildflowers, such as Queen Anne's lace and goldenrod, bloom during summer and nourish a variety of insects.

From the field, the trail continues north along the river. Another tree that grows in the floodplain is shagbark hickory, whose overlaying sections of bark do indeed give it a shaggy appearance. During late spring and early summer, you'll likely see many ebony jewelwing damselflies—easily identified by their brilliant, dark-green bodies and black wings—flitting around the vegetation that borders the river. Damselflies are distinguished from dragonflies by their smaller size and their practice of perching with their wings folded vertically. (Dragonflies spread their wings out horizontally.) Another insect to watch for is the small, orange-and-black pearl crescent butterfly. Frogs and toads scamper across the grassy path below.

At 0.8 mile from the trailhead, the path turns sharply to the right at marker 6 and leads away from the river to the adjacent floodplain. You are now on Turnpike Trail, originally built by farmers to transport hay out of the wet meadows. This section of the route is prone to flooding in early spring, and if it is impassable, you can backtrack to the start and walk the rest of the hike in reverse. The muddy areas here offer plenty of opportunities to look for animal tracks; some of the most common are those of white-tailed deer and raccoons. The trail traverses a series of wooden bridges and short boardwalks before continuing east in a straight line along a causeway.

Turnpike Trail passes near two large beaver lodges (unless the beavers have moved on), offering excellent close-up views of their architecture. Hard as it may be to believe now, beavers once were nearly eliminated from much of Massachusetts and the rest of New England due to unregulated hunting and trapping. Wars and settlement of North America were influenced by access to beavers and their pelts. Look carefully for trees that have been cut by beavers—these animals affect their landscape more than any other, apart from humans. Wading birds and waterfowl benefit from beaver-created wetlands, however; keep an eye out for great blue herons, green herons, and wood ducks.

A few minutes farther along, a short side path on the right leads to an enclosed wooden observation blind at the edge of a wetland where you can watch for ducks, birds, river otters, turtles, raccoons, and muskrats. Turnpike Trail continues along the north shore of this wetland pool and ends at a three-way junction with Tank Road Trail, 1.5 miles from the trailhead and 0.7 mile from the river.

Here, you have the option of continuing the loop by turning right or extending the outing by making a one-way detour on Tank Road Trail. For the latter option, the route continues north for approximately 0.8 mile to a beaver pond and the Route 2 overpass. On the north side of the overpass, it connects with recently established Goddard Trail and a trail to Mirror Lake, a kettle pond that abuts the refuge (follow signs at junctions).

For those following the circuit, Tank Road Trail—the name of which is a holdover from the old military reservation—leads past a grove of large white pines, briefly parallels the Boston and Maine Railroad tracks, and then follows the edge of another wetland. Black-eyed Susans and other wildflowers such as daisies grow along the trail's edge in summer. The river and Riverside Trail soon come into view on the right, and for a last look at the water, take the short crossover path on the right. After 0.4 mile of easy walking from the Turnpike Trail junction, you'll be back at the main parking area.

DID YOU KNOW?

Biologists at the refuge monitor a variety of birds, reptiles, amphibians, and mammals. Their findings are used to plan future management practices for this and other refuges, such as creating freshwater impoundments for waterfowl and fields for American woodcocks and bluebirds.

NEARBY

Fruitlands Museum, a short distance from the refuge at 102 Prospect Hill Road, is a National Historic Landmark with exhibits related to New England's landscape. This was also the site of a utopian experiment by Bronson Alcott and Charles Lane in 1843. The museum is open from mid-April to mid-November; visit fruitlands.org for more information. Restaurants are on Ayer Road (MA 110/111) north of the junction with MA 2.

MORE INFORMATION

The refuge is open year-round, dawn to dusk. No visitor center is on-site; maps and brochures, including a bird checklist, are available at the parking lot. A boat launch is near the parking lot. Camping, fires, dogs, and swimming are prohibited; fishing is allowed in the river but not in ponds or wetlands; skiing is allowed. The refuge is part of the Eastern Massachusetts National Wildlife Refuge Complex. The headquarters and visitor center are at the Great Meadows National Wildlife Refuge Sudbury Unit, 73 Weir Hill Road, Sudbury. Annual passes to this and other refuges and national parks can be purchased through the Sudbury office. A map of Mirror Lake is available at harvardconservationtrust.org/maps/mirror_lake.pdf.

Beaver wetlands and floodplain forests make up a large portion of Oxbow National Wildlife Refuge.

Great Brook Farm State Park offers a wide variety of flora and fauna for nature study as well as groomed trails for cross-country skiing.

Features

Location Carlisle, MA

Rating Easy

Distance 2.25-mile loop; 3-mile loop with extension

Elevation Gain Minimal

Estimated Time 1.5 hours; 2 hours with extension

Maps USGS Billerica; Massachusetts Department of Conservation and Recreation: mass.gov/doc/great-brook-farm-state-park-summer-trail-map/download

GPS coordinates 42° 33.365′ N, 71° 20.889′ W

Contact Massachusetts Department of Conservation and Recreation: mass.gov/locations/great-brook-farm-state-park, 978-369-6312

DIRECTIONS

From I-495, take Exit 32 to MA 225 and follow it to Carlisle Center. At the rotary, bear right on Lowell Street (following the sign for Chelmsford) for 2.0 miles to the park entrance on the right.

TRAIL DESCRIPTION

Purchased by the Commonwealth of Massachusetts in 1974, Great Brook Farm is rich in history and has more than 10 miles of trails. Pine Point Loop, the popular trail named for its passage beneath towering white pines, is a pleasant 2-mile ramble around Meadow Pond. A designated Healthy Heart Trail, Pine Point Loop has blue markers and painted blazes. At numbered junctions, it connects with numerous less traveled park trails, including Tophet Swamp Loop at the southern end of the property.

From the parking area, walk around a small pond toward the red farm buildings. Turn right onto Lantern Loop Trail near a kiosk (maps may be available), a bike rack, and a sign for the ice-cream stand. Continue a short distance to North Road. Cross the road in front of the farm and begin Pine Point Loop at the sign "Trails Open to Hiking," with a blue blaze. Follow the path about 600 feet and then bear right onto a dirt farm road. Continue past part of Meadow Pond, a shallow body of water with fingers stretching in various directions. The treadway is wide and flat, making it an excellent place for cross-country skiing. Picnic tables are scattered about the fields and woods; one sits on a point of land jutting toward the water.

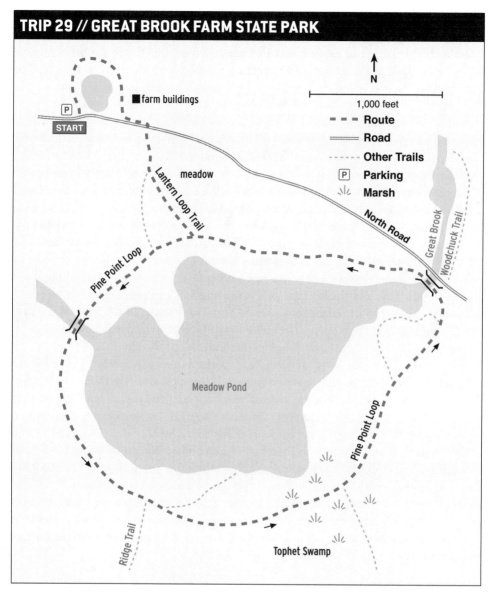

Watch carefully for great blue herons, which can blend in perfectly with dead trees at the edge of Meadow Pond. Another fascinating bird sometimes seen here is the wood duck. Nest boxes have been erected on posts in the ponds to help these colorful birds reestablish in New England. They had declined due to both hunting and the widespread cutting of the large trees in which they nest. The males are especially beautiful, with iridescent greens, purples, and blues, and a white chin patch. Females are a grayish-brown color with a white eye ring. Their habitat includes wooded rivers, ponds, and swamps. They are fast flyers and quite agile as they navigate between trees.

Follow Pine Point Loop past wetlands and then bear left at a cornfield on the right at marker 21. In past centuries, American Indians planted corn and other crops in the fertile meadows here. Listen for the screeches of the red-tailed hawks that often perch on tree limbs adjacent to the open cornfield. Various side paths on the left will bring you closer to the water if you wish to extend your exploration. After about 1 mile, the trail passes through more low-lying wetlands and junctions with Keyes Loop and Beaver Loop trails on the left. (The latter leads to the pond's eastern shores and then rejoins the main loop near North Road.) Glacial erratics, including a large boulder at the pond shore, add diversity to the scene.

Return to Pine Point Loop and follow it to a wooden bridge crossing near North Road, where the waters of Great Brook tumble over a dam and out of the pond. Next to the bridge is a small parking area with access to the trail. (A parking pass is required in season.) Here, you have the option of detouring off the pond loop to explore the trails on the opposite side of the road at marker 13. If you follow Woodchuck Trail across the road and along Great Brook, it soon reaches the site of an old mill on a small pond. At the back end of the pond, the water cascades over a waterfall lined with stones erected by the settlers. Imagine the work that must have gone into its construction. The pattern of the lichen-covered rocks and the whitewater below makes for an interesting scene.

In 1691, John Barrett built one of the first fulling mills in America here; fulling is the process of shrinking and thickening cloth. A sawmill and a gristmill were erected in the early 1700s. The power of Great Brook was also put to work in the 1800s, when mills made wheels, nail kegs, and birch hoops. The mill site is still visible at the northeastern end of the property, just beyond where Great Brook passes under North Road.

As you retrace your steps toward North Road, notice a small sign for the garrison, where the pioneers erected a stone house for protection. If the approximately 15-foot-wide cellar hole was the entire size of the house, it must have been cramped inside, but tight quarters would have been the least of the settlers' worries during a raid by American Indians, which was not uncommon during the earliest years of settlement here.

To complete the hike, return to Pine Point Loop and follow it past a small field and through the woods on the north side of the pond. (You can also walk along North Road for 0.5 mile, back toward the parking area.) You'll soon return to the junction with the dirt road at the start of the loop. Bear right and retrace your steps to the parking area. The farm and pastures provide pleasant scenery along the way. Children enjoy seeing the cows in the fields and the ducks in the pond near the barn. Top off your trip with a visit to the ice-cream stand at the back of the farm.

DID YOU KNOW?

Several American Indian sacred sites are on the grounds, and agriculture has been practiced here for centuries. Holstein cattle have been kept on-site for the past 60 years, through the present day.

NEARBY

Carlisle is a small, rural town with little development. Ferns Country Store, a classic New England general store that has operated at its present location on the town-center rotary since 1844, offers sandwiches, soups, salads, and dinners.

Great Brook Farm State Park's 1,000 acres feature more than 20 miles of trails. *Photo by Joanna Poe, Creative Commons on Flickr.*

MORE INFORMATION

Great Brook Farm State Park is open year-round, dawn to dusk; a $3 parking fee is charged from April 1 to December 1.

The Great Brook Ski Touring Center is open from December 1 to March 20 (snow conditions permitting) on Mondays, Wednesdays, and Fridays from 10 A.M. to 5 P.M.; Tuesdays and Thursdays from 10 A.M. to 9 P.M. (with night skiing on Lantern Loop); and weekends and holidays from 9 A.M. to 5 P.M. It offers ski rentals and a lodge and snack bar. Call 978-369-7486 or visit greatbrookski.com.

30 GREAT MEADOWS NATIONAL WILDLIFE REFUGE

The trails at Great Meadows, one of the region's richest wildlife refuges, offer continuous views of the Concord River, its floodplain, and two ponds.

Features

Location Concord, MA

Rating Easy

Distance 1.7-mile loop

Elevation Gain Minimal

Estimated Time 1 hour

Maps USGS Maynard; U.S. Fish and Wildlife Service: fws.gov/refuge/great_meadows

GPS coordinates 42° 28.507′ N, 71° 19.770′ W

Contact Great Meadows National Wildlife Refuge: fws.gov/refuge/great_meadows, 978-443-4661

DIRECTIONS

From the center of Concord, follow MA 62 east for 1.4 miles and then turn left onto Monsen Road. Continue 0.3 mile to a sign for the refuge. Turn left and follow the refuge entrance road to the parking area.

By public transportation, take the Fitchburg line of the MBTA Commuter Rail to Concord, walk northeast on Sudbury Road, turn right on MA 62 through the town center, and continue on MA 62 to Monsen Road. Turn left onto Monsen Road and follow it to the trailhead. The refuge is approximately 2.3 miles from the Concord station.

TRAIL DESCRIPTION

The 3,800-acre Great Meadows National Wildlife Refuge comprises two divisions, known as the Concord Unit and the Sudbury Unit, that include portions of the Concord and Sudbury rivers. It's part of the Eastern Massachusetts National Wildlife Refuge Complex, which also includes nearby Assabet River National Wildlife Refuge and Oxbow National Wildlife Refuge. These refuges protect more than 7,000 acres of habitat for wildlife in the heart of New England's most populous region. The regional office is at the Sudbury Unit. (See "More Information" below.) The route described here follows Dike Trail at the Concord Unit, an easy circuit through prime wildlife habitats. Please note that dogs are not allowed at national wildlife refuge properties.

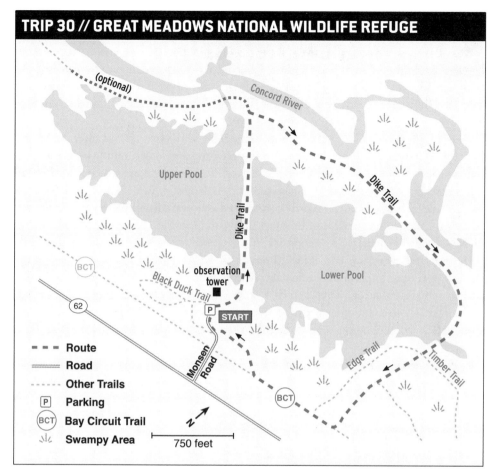

At the start or finish of your hike, be sure to climb the observation tower adjacent to the parking lot to admire sweeping vistas across the refuge. Dike Trail begins at a gate next to an information sign across the parking lot from the tower and follows a straight causeway between Upper Pool and Lower Pool. The impoundments are drained into the river during summer, opening up extensive mudflats that are heavily used by southbound migratory waterfowl and songbirds.

This is one of the region's richest wildlife areas. More than 220 bird species have been recorded here, including the tiny but loud marsh wrens that breed at only a handful of other sites in Massachusetts. Watch for them in clumps of cattails during warm months. Thanks to an active nest box program, the refuge hosts a healthy population of wood ducks, which have recovered from decline caused by hunting and the loss of mature nesting trees. Other breeding waterfowl include blue-winged teals, mallards, grebes, black ducks, American coots, and Canada geese; American wigeons and gadwalls pass through during migrations. During spring and late summer, you may see migrating shorebirds, such as dunlins, greater and lesser yellowlegs, and sandpipers, in muddy areas. The often-elusive marsh birds include soras, Virginia rails, great blue herons, green herons, and black-crowned night herons. Characteristic songbirds of wetland edges include northern water thrushes, swamp sparrows, yellow warblers, and great-crested flycatchers.

After 0.4 mile, Dike Trail arrives at a three-way junction on the narrow strip of land between the impoundment pools and the Concord River. The main loop continues to the right here, but if you have time, consider adding a mile to the outing by turning left and following the one-way path west, along the shores of Upper Pool, for 0.5 mile to the refuge boundary and then backtracking to the junction.

From the junction, Dike Trail continues to the right, with views across Lower Pool to the right and the river and floodplain forest to the left. Stop and look carefully for giant snapping turtles swimming below the pool's surface. The marshy edge adjacent to the trail offers excellent close-up views of muskrats and their lodges, which are much smaller than those made by beavers and are mostly constructed from cattails. Other mammals present in the wetlands include beavers, river otters, mink, and raccoons. The refuge is home to one of New England's largest populations of threatened Blanding's turtles, distinguished by their bright yellow throats and chins. Although the turtles spend most of their lives in the shallow, vegetated impoundment, females venture onto land to make nests in open areas, such as agricultural fields and backyards. Watch for other reptiles and amphibians, including painted, spotted, and snapping turtles; leopard frogs; and northern water snakes. In late April, you may see thousands of exotic carp attempting to enter the impoundment from the river.

At 0.6 mile from the three-way junction, Dike Trail curves to the right, around the northern tip of Lower Pool. It then reaches junctions with two side paths, both of which

Crucial freshwater wetlands make up about 85 percent of Great Meadows' 3,600-plus acres along the Concord and Sudbury rivers.

offer short, optional diversions from the main route. On the right is 0.35-mile Edge Trail, which explores the woods along the edge of Lower Pool. To the left is Timber Trail, which makes a 0.4-mile loop through oak, pine, and maple woodlands. The oak-pine woods add to the refuge's habitat diversity and are home to red foxes, white-tailed deer, and songbirds (northern orioles, red-breasted grosbeaks, scarlet tanagers, phoebes, and eastern wood pee-wees). Year-round residents include great horned owls, eastern screech owls, red-bellied and pileated woodpeckers, and wild turkeys.

At 1.3 miles, Dike Trail joins the white-blazed Bay Circuit Trail at a junction near the refuge boundary. Turn right and follow both trails southwest along the old Boston and Maine Railroad line for 0.4 mile to the refuge entrance road. The Bay Circuit Trail continues south from the refuge to Minute Man National Historical Park and Walden Pond.

DID YOU KNOW?

The Concord and Sudbury rivers have a long history of human use, as evidenced by relics of American Indian activity dating to 5,500 BCE. In pre-Colonial times, the meadows were used as agricultural fields and burned to create habitat for game animals.

NEARBY

The Concord Unit is a short drive from Minute Man National Historical Park (Trip 31) and Walden Pond (Trip 32). The Old North Bridge and the Minute Man statue, which mark the site of the first battle in the American Revolution, are just west of the refuge off Monument Street. Restaurants are in Concord Center.

MORE INFORMATION

A parking fee ($4 daily, $12 annual) is now charged at the Concord Unit. Passes may be purchased at a self-serve pay station, at the Great Meadows and Assabet River refuge offices, or at refuge headquarters, 73 Weir Hill Road, Sudbury, MA 01776, for $12 or by appointment. Checks made out to the U.S. Fish and Wildlife Service can be sent in the mail to the refuge headquarters address. Other federal passes, including Duck Stamps, are accepted. The trails are open dawn to dusk.

The refuge headquarters and visitor center are at the Sudbury Unit on 73 Weir Hill Road. Two short trails at the Sudbury Unit can be combined into an easy 1-mile circuit exploring wetlands along the Sudbury River and a low glacial hill along its banks.

Boat launches are available on the river roads near both units. A launch for cartop boats is available at the Sudbury Unit; it requires a 5-minute walk from the entrance over easy terrain.

31 MINUTE MAN NATIONAL HISTORICAL PARK: BATTLE ROAD TRAIL

This woodland-and-meadow trek with a historical focus doesn't stray far from settled areas but is quaint and pleasant nonetheless, particularly in spring and fall.

Features

Location Concord, Lincoln, and Lexington, MA

Rating Moderate

Distance 5-mile loop

Elevation Gain Minimal

Estimated Time 3 hours

Maps USGS Maynard; National Park Service: nps.gov/mima/planyourvisit/maps.htm

GPS coordinates 42° 27.606' N, 71° 19.424' W

Contact Minute Man National Historical Park: nps.gov/mima, 978-369-6993

DIRECTIONS

From I-95, take Exit 46 for MA 2A west to Concord. Follow MA 2A approximately 0.3 mile. Enter the park and follow signs to the Minute Man Visitor Center, less than 1 mile from I-95/MA 128. From the visitor center, follow MA 2A west 1.9 miles, bear right onto Lexington Road, and continue 0.9 mile to Meriam's Corner in Concord. Turn right onto Old Bedford Road and enter the parking area on the right.

By public transportation, take the Fitchburg line of the MBTA Commuter Rail to the Concord stop. Walk northeast along Sudbury Road to the center of town (Sudbury Road converges with Main Street) and turn right onto MA 2A. Stay left when the Cambridge Turnpike diverges to the right after the Alcott House. Pass the Wayside Visitor Center on your right and soon come to Meriam's Corner, where this hike begins. The trailhead is 2.5 miles from the Concord station.

TRAIL DESCRIPTION

Congress created Minute Man National Historical Park in 1959 to preserve and interpret the events, ideas, significant historic sites, structures, properties, and landscapes associated with the start of the American Revolution.

The theme of the trail on this hike, Battle Road Trail, is the Battle of April 19, 1775, which launched the American Revolution, but the trail interprets the broader story of the people whose lives were altered by the events that took place here, including their relationship with the landscape. Much of the trail follows remnants of Battle Road, although some

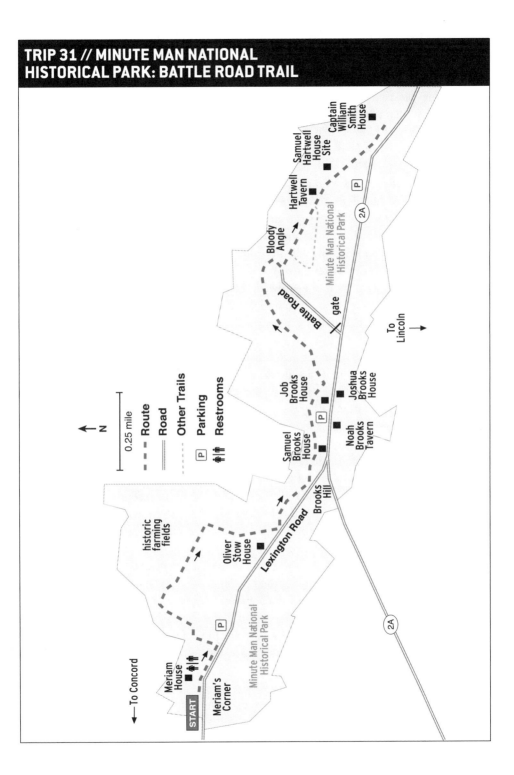

Captain William Smith House

Samuel Hartwell House Site

Hartwell Tavern

Bloody Angle

Battle Road

gate

To Lincoln

Minute Man National Historical Park

2A

N

0.25 mile

- - - Route
— Road
····· Other Trails
P Parking
Restrooms

Job Brooks House

Joshua Brooks House

P

Noah Brooks Tavern

Samuel Brooks House

Brooks Hill

Lexington Road

historic farming fields

Oliver Stow House

P

2A

To Concord

Meriam House

Meriam's Corner

START

Minute Man National Historical Park

sections leave the historic road to follow the route of the minutemen, traversing a mosaic of farming fields, wetlands, and forests. Fall foliage can be particularly spectacular here, but it can also bring crowds on weekends. Winter is quieter, and the park's trails are great for snowshoeing. The route as described here is a 5-mile round trip from the Meriam House to the Captain William Smith House and back.

From the Meriam House, follow the trail as it winds to the east. The route soon passes a series of historical farm fields that have been continuously used for agriculture since the seventeenth century. By the turn of the eighteenth century, approximately 90 percent of the land within what is now Minute Man National Historical Park had been converted to agricultural use. Although extensive meadows existed in the area before European settlement, acres of forest were cleared to create pasture and cultivated cropland.

The trail turns right and winds south toward MA 2A, passing the first of two Bloody Angle historical sites and crossing a boardwalk over protected wetlands as it nears the Job and Joshua Brooks houses. After passing the houses and briefly paralleling MA 2A, the trail turns northeast onto another boardwalk. Here, you'll follow the route of the minutemen northeast through woods of sugar and silver maple, white oak, and American beech. The dominant shrubs in the understory are mostly non-native species, including buckthorn and honeysuckle.

Although history is the main attraction here, naturalists will find plenty to observe as well. The park's habitats support a wide variety of terrestrial and freshwater aquatic wildlife. Common mammals include species typically associated with both rural and developed areas, such as eastern cottontail, gray squirrel, deer mouse, beaver, red fox, coyote, and white-tailed deer. Less common species, such as bobcat and fisher, also inhabit the area. All told, roughly 70 species of birds, 12 species of fish, and more than 30 species of reptiles and amphibians have been documented in the park. Bird-watching is especially good in spring, when many migratory species are present.

The trail bears right along a stone wall and soon arrives at the second Bloody Angle site, where it joins Battle Road. You'll pass Hartwell Tavern, a restored eighteenth-century home and tavern that was standing on Battle Road at the start of the war and is therefore known as a witness house. A short distance farther along is the Captain William Smith House, another witness house, which was built in the late seventeenth century and was the home of Captain Smith, commander of the Lincoln Company.

The Smith House marks the end of the outbound segment of the round trip, although the trail continues to the eastern boundary of the park in Lincoln. As you retrace your steps to the parking area near the Meriam House, you can explore the other trails that branch off Battle Road, such as Vernal Pool Trail near the second Bloody Angle.

DID YOU KNOW?

The British militia was in Concord in April 1775 because it had been sent to seize military stores and ammunition kept by colonists. The British general Thomas Gage was under pressure from his superiors in England to maintain control of Massachusetts.

Captain William Smith House is one of several notable homes in Minute Man National Historical Park.

NEARBY

The Old North Bridge and the Minute Man monument, which mark the site of the war's first battle, are off Monument Street. Another historic feature of note adjacent to the bridge is the Old Manse, at 269 Monument Street. Built in 1770 for the minister William Emerson, it then served as a meeting place for mid-nineteenth-century transcendentalists, such as Henry David Thoreau, Bronson Alcott, and Margaret Fuller. It is now a National Historic Landmark and is managed by The Trustees of Reservations. The 231-mile Bay Circuit Trail passes the bridge and house. Restaurants are in Concord Center.

MORE INFORMATION

Visitor centers in the park include the North Bridge (174 Liberty Street in Concord), Minute Man (250 North Great Road, Lincoln), Hartwell Tavern, Whittemore House, and Wayside. Some are open only seasonally. The grounds are open sunrise to sunset; the parking lot gate closes at sunset. Pets are allowed in the park and in all visitor centers but must be on a leash no longer than 6 feet at all times.

 **WALDEN POND**

Although Walden Pond is not remote and you won't be alone, on a quiet day you will feel miles away from civilization. Indeed, you are at the heart of the beginnings of the American conservation movement.

Features

Location Concord, MA

Rating Easy

Distance 3-mile loop

Elevation Gain 270 feet (Emerson's Cliff)

Estimated Time 1.5 hours

Maps USGS Maynard; Massachusetts Department of Conservation and Recreation: mass.gov/eea/docs/dcr/parks/trails/walden.pdf

GPS coordinates 42° 26.451′ N, 71° 20.123′ W

Contact Massachusetts Department of Conservation and Recreation: mass.gov/locations/walden-pond-state-reservation, 978-369-3254

DIRECTIONS

From I-95, take exit 29B for MA 2 west toward Acton. Follow MA 2 west about 9 miles and then turn left onto MA 126. The Walden Pond State Reservation parking lot is on the left in a quarter-mile.

By public transportation, take the Fitchburg Commuter Rail line to the Concord station, which is near the corner of Thoreau Street and Sudbury Road. Walk away from town on Thoreau Street and cross MA 2 (wait for signal at crosswalk). Walden Pond State Reservation will soon be on your right. The pond entrance is about 1.5 miles from the Concord station.

TRAIL DESCRIPTION

Starting in 1845, Henry David Thoreau lived in a small cabin at Walden Pond for two years, two months, and two days. He wrote *Walden* after his experiment to live "deliberately" and simply in the woods. Today, the park is run by the Massachusetts Department of Conservation and Recreation. It includes the pond, trails, a swimming area, a boat launch, and the original house site of Henry David Thoreau. A replica of Thoreau's cabin stands in the main parking area. The Thoreau Society runs a gift shop that is part of Walden Pond Visitor Center.

Pond Path takes you around the pond and up to a vantage point from which you can view the area. For decades, the trails and slopes around the pond have been eroded by overuse. In recent years, major efforts have been made to quell the erosion and to restore

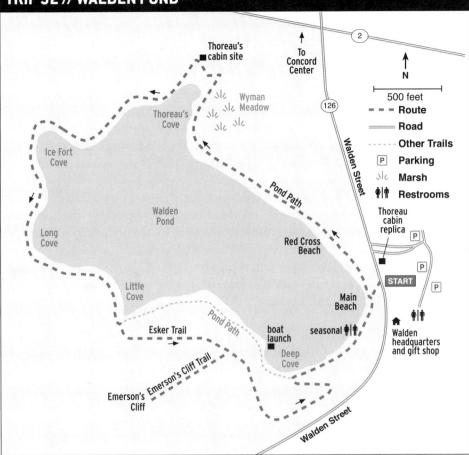

the vegetation. A visit reveals some success but also shows that restrictions are still warranted. Stay on the designated trails and roads or on the beach.

From the parking lot, use the crosswalk to reach the ramp down to the pond's beach area. Turn right and walk along Red Cross Beach or on the path just above it. As the beach ends, make sure you are following the path, not the shore. You are now skirting the north shore of the pond on Pond Path.

Walden is one of many kettle ponds in eastern Massachusetts. These were formed more than 10,000 years ago, when ice blocks melted in sand or gravel deposits, leaving behind depressions that filled with water and became the ponds we see today. Kettle ponds usually have no streams flowing in or out of them, and this is true of Walden Pond. Walden Pond also holds the distinction of being the deepest naturally occurring lake or pond in the state.

The route turns right (north) along a cove called Thoreau's Cove; the site of Thoreau's cabin is nearby, just off the main Pond Path. When Thoreau lived here, Walden was surrounded by one of the few remaining woods in the area, the other lands having been cleared for farming. By the time the Emerson, Heywood, and Forbes families donated the property to the Commonwealth of Massachusetts in 1922, much of this forest had been cut. Now the woods have grown back and include berry bushes, sumac, pine, hickory, and oak. Thoreau planted 400 white pines beyond his cabin, but these were leveled by a hurricane in 1938. The stone chimney that marked the site of the original house was unearthed in 1945 by an archaeologist after a three-month search.

Along the trail, keep an eye out for the reservation's wildlife, including squirrels, chipmunks, rabbits, skunks, raccoons, woodchucks, red foxes, and white-tailed deer. Many of these animals were present in Thoreau's day, although some, such as deer, were nearly eliminated by hunting and habitat loss due to forest clearing. Scan the trees for chickadees, red-tailed hawks, and migratory songbirds (spring to early fall), and check the pond for kingfishers, geese, and flocks of migratory waterfowl. The pond is stocked by the state and otherwise would have few fish. The best time to see wildlife at this well-trafficked spot is early morning or early evening.

From the house site, Pond Path turns south and ascends uphill slightly. To the right are the train tracks of the Commuter Rail. The tracks originally were laid by the Boston and Fitchburg Railroad in 1844, just one year before Thoreau moved to the woods. Pond Path then winds south and west along the western shore of the pond, passing Ice Fort Cove and Long Cove. After Long Cove, Pond Path turns east. At Little Cove, the trail dips southward, and a side path to the right leads to Esker Trail. Here, you have the option of continuing left on Pond Path and following it to Deep Cove or going right to explore Esker Trail and an overlook.

To climb to the overlook, take the side path and turn left onto Esker Trail, which runs parallel to and just uphill of Pond Path. Soon Emerson's Cliff Trail leads to the right and uphill to the overlook. In summer, the view can be obscured by vegetation. Return to Esker Trail and turn right onto it, following it as it parallels Route 126 to the boat-launch ramp. Turn left and walk down the ramp to the beach at Deep Cove. From here, reconnect with Pond Path, which leads to the main beach and the ramp, back up to the road and parking lot.

DID YOU KNOW?

Thoreau's cabin was later acquired by farmers who moved it to the other side of Concord to use for storage. It was dismantled in 1868.

NEARBY

Thoreau Farm, the site of Thoreau's birth in 1817, is at 341 Virginia Road in Concord. It was built around 1730 and was part of an active farm into the twentieth century. It is now managed by the Thoreau Farm Trust; visit thoreaufarm.org for information on tours. Restaurants are in Concord on Thoreau Street, Walden Street, and other roads near the town center.

If this easy hike around Walden Pond doesn't slake your thirst, consider the Emerson–Thoreau Amble, a trail that starts at the Thoreau house site and ends at the Emerson House.

MORE INFORMATION

At Walden you can find the commonwealth's first net-zero visitor center, which uses a solar canopy in parking lots and includes electric vehicle charging. A book and gift shop in the visitor center is managed by the Thoreau Society. The center shows a film about Thoreau and provides a slate of interpretive exhibits. Interpretive rangers are on-site as well. Be sure to visit the replica of Thoreau's cabin near the main parking area.

Hours vary according to season, and visitors are encouraged to call for current hours. A parking fee is charged ($8 for Massachusetts residents, $30 for nonresidents). The lot fills up on summer days, and a 1,000-visitor cap has been set, so it is advisable to plan ahead; call first or check the live Twitter feed @waldenpondstate to determine if a visit is feasible. All organized groups must make reservations in advance. Restrooms are attached to the visitor center in the main parking area, and seasonal restrooms are by the main beach. Dogs are prohibited year-round (service dogs exempt). Fires, camping, bikes, and alcoholic beverages are not allowed in the park. No trash receptacles or picnic tables are on the grounds.

The Department of Conservation and Recreation built an accessible trail to Thoreau's original house site. From the main parking area, turn right after the crosswalk. The trail runs parallel to the road for a short distance and then leads into Woods Path at the first gate. Interpretive and directional signs lead you on an interesting walk through the woods to the house site.

At times, Walden Pond evokes the tranquility that inspired Henry David Thoreau. *Photo by Matthew Grymek/AMC Photo Contest.*

HENRY DAVID THOREAU:
NATURALIST, EXPLORER, AND WRITER

Walden Pond is well known as the site of the esteemed writer Henry David Thoreau's mid-nineteenth-century retreat. From his self-built cabin, he wrote, observed nature, and explored the area, often heading south-southwest along the Sudbury River toward Fairhaven Bay and the hilly region of Mount Misery.

In his essay "Walking," Thoreau wrote, "I can easily walk ten, fifteen, twenty, any number of miles, commencing at my own door, without going by any house, without crossing any road except where the fox and the mink do: first along by the river, and then the brook, and then the meadow and the woodside."

Thoreau walked every day and wondered how anyone could stay indoors: "I confess that I am astonished at the power of endurance, to say nothing of the moral insensibility of my neighbors who confine themselves to shops and offices the whole day for weeks and months, aye, and years almost together." Thoreau probably would be even more astonished by our society's development and commercialization of open space, but at least the acres around Walden Pond, Mount Misery, and many other places in eastern Massachusetts have been saved.

Thoreau was born in Concord, Massachusetts, in 1817. He attended Harvard University during the 1830s and lived in the cabin at Walden Pond, on land owned by Ralph Waldo Emerson, from 1845 to 1847. During this time, he recorded detailed observations about the natural year that ultimately served as the source for essays he wrote later. His book *Walden*, published in 1854, was not widely acclaimed at first but is now regarded as one of the classics of American nature writing.

Thoreau's interest in natural history and travel increased during the 1850s. He visited Cape Cod several times, and his vivid descriptions of a treeless, barren landscape with long, open views are an invaluable record of what the Cape looked like following centuries of intensive timber harvesting. His other trips in New England included expeditions to the Katahdin–Moosehead Lake region of Maine and to the White Mountains. He visited New Hampshire's Mount Monadnock several times and wrote one of the first detailed natural descriptions of the mountain.

His carefully recorded observations of nature, including the dates of first blossoms and peak fall foliage, are still used by scientists to track climate change.

After contracting bronchitis in 1859, Thoreau spent his final years writing in his journals and writing and editing essays, such as those in *The Maine Woods*. He died in 1862 at age 44.

33 LINCOLN CONSERVATION LAND

The conservation land surrounding Mount Misery provides excellent views of the Sudbury River, Fairhaven Bay, and forests, ponds, and marshes.

Features

Location Lincoln, MA

Rating Moderate

Distance 3-mile loop

Elevation Gain 50 feet

Estimated Time 1.5 hours

Maps USGS Maynard; Lincoln Land Conservation Trust and Rural Land Foundation: lincolnconservation.org (see Map 5 at this website)

GPS coordinates 42° 25.054′ N, 71° 21.236′ W

Contact Lincoln Conservation Commission: conservation@lincolntown.org, 781-259-2612; Lincoln Land Conservation Trust and Rural Land Foundation: lincolnconservation.org

DIRECTIONS

From I-95, take Exit 26 for US 20 east. Turn left onto Stow Street and then left again onto MA 117 west (West Main Street). Follow MA 117 for 5.9 miles to the Lincoln Conservation Land–Mount Misery parking entrance on the right (0.7 mile after MA 117 crosses MA 126). If the parking area is full, head west toward Concord for two more parking areas on the right.

By public transportation, take the Fitchburg line of the MBTA Commuter Rail to Lincoln. Walk 0.5 mile southwest on Lincoln Road and turn right onto MA 117. Walk another 0.5 mile to the intersection of MA 117 and MA 126. Continue on MA 117 west 0.7 mile to the parking area on the right.

TRAIL DESCRIPTION

The quiet rural town of Lincoln is home to numerous conservation areas that protect approximately one-third of its total acreage, with about 80 miles of trails and roadside paths for hikers to explore. At the Mount Misery conservation area, well-marked trails offer views of the diverse habitats of 284-foot Mount Misery, one of the prominent hills of the Sudbury Valley. This route, which includes a portion of the Bay Circuit Trail, circles the base of Mount Misery and loops westward toward the Sudbury River.

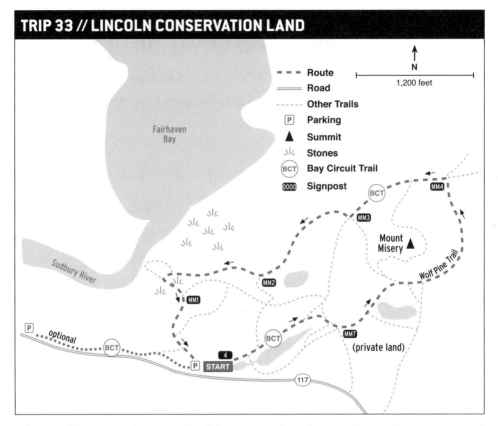

The trail begins on the east side of the main parking lot on MA 117. From gate post 4 and the bike rack, follow the white-blazed Bay Circuit Trail along the north shore of a small pond; turn right at the first junction and cross the small stream that feeds the pond. Turn left at junction MM7 and left again at the next intersection, continuing past the western shore of another pond (the water will be on your right) to a four-way junction at the base of Mount Misery.

Turn right onto an old cart road. (The trail continuing straight ahead quickly climbs to the summit of the hill, where trees block almost all the views, and then descends to rejoin the route described here on the north side of the hill.) The cart road draws an easy, nearly level circle around the base of Mount Misery, passing rock ledges and a beaver wetland. White-tailed deer are sometimes seen at dusk in the field on the right. Oak, white pine, and the occasional white birch and beech compose the woods. (Many hemlock trees have been killed by the hemlock woolly adelgid.) After walking about 1.5 miles from the parking lot, rejoin the Bay Circuit Trail at junction MM4, at the edge of a large field. Turn left and continue straight past the next junction, where the aforementioned trail over Mount Misery's summit enters on the left.

Keep an eye out for barred owls, which nest in the tree cavities of mature forests and forested wetlands such as those at Mount Misery. Barred owls often roost by day and make their hunting rounds at night. Their call, which sounds like *who-cooks-for-you?*, is one of the

Wild turkeys evade a young hiker on Lincoln conservation land. *Photo by Maury Eldridge/AMC Photo Contest.*

most distinctive bird songs. Cooper's hawks also nest in the area. They feed on birds and small mammals, including doves and squirrels. The adult Cooper's hawk is identifiable by its dark blue-gray back, long banded tail, relatively short wings, and rufous bars on its breast.

Continue west on the Bay Circuit Trail to junction MM3 and then turn right onto another old cart path. Bear right at junction MM2 and continue to follow the path, which winds west to the edge of a broad marsh and floodplain along the Sudbury River, with good views across the wetlands. The trail soon leads to the river itself, where you can watch for waterfowl flying over the waters. After enjoying the scenery, follow the trail away from the river to junction MM1, bear right, and continue for a short distance to complete the loop and return to the parking area.

DID YOU KNOW?

Mount Misery was named in the 1780s when, according to local lore, two yoked oxen wandered there and wrapped themselves around a tree. Unable to escape, they perished.

NEARBY

Mass Audubon's Drumlin Farm is a great place to introduce children to farm animals. It is on MA 117 in Lincoln, 4.5 miles west of the MA 117 overpass at I-95. The 180-acre property also includes trails that wind through fields, pastures, ponds, and woods; a gift shop; and a nature center where programs are held. Restaurants are near Lincoln MBTA Station.

MORE INFORMATION

The conservation land is open year-round, dawn to dusk; no fee. Dogs are allowed, but they must remain leashed on marked trails and in the agricultural fields. A boat launch is at Farrar Pond on MA 117, 0.2 mile west of the conservation area. You can walk along the Bay Circuit Trail to the pond. See a posted information sign for the most current rules.

34 NOBSCOT HILL AND TIPPLING ROCK

The rocky ridges of Nobscot Hill, the highest point on the Bay Circuit Trail, and Tippling Rock offer outstanding views and wildlife habitat.

Features 🚶 🐕 👁️👁️

Location Sudbury and Framingham, MA

Rating Moderate

Distance 4-mile loop

Elevation Gain 515 feet

Estimated Time 2.25 hours

Maps USGS Framingham; Sudbury Valley Trustees: svtweb.org/sites/default/files/Nobscot.pdf

GPS coordinates 42° 21.638′ N, 71° 26.498′ W

Contact Sudbury Conservation Office: sudbury.ma.us/conservation, 978-440-5471; Bay Circuit Trail: baycircuit.org.

DIRECTIONS

From I-495 in Marlborough, take Exit 26 to US 20 east. Follow US 20, which becomes Boston Post Road, for 7.8 miles. After the yellow flashing light at Grinnell Road on the right, immediately turn right on the gravel driveway and enter the unpaved parking area on the south side of the highway. (Watch for a small sign denoting town of Sudbury conservation land and Tippling Rock Trail.) If you reach the quaint Barnstead Shoppes shopping center, you've gone too far.

TRAIL DESCRIPTION

Nobscot Hill, which at 602 feet is the highest point along the entire 231-mile Bay Circuit Trail, is part of a series of rocky hills and ridges in Sudbury and Framingham, the heart of the Metro West region. From outlooks near its summit and from the nearby open ledges of Tippling Rock, hikers can enjoy long views to Mount Monadnock, Wachusett Mountain, and Boston.

Several contiguous conservation areas, including Weisblatt Conservation Land and Nobscot Conservation Land (managed by the town of Sudbury), Nobscot Scout Reservation (owned by the Knox Trail Council), and the Nobscot Hill tract (a Massachusetts Department of Conservation and Recreation property, marked as Callahan State Park on some maps), collectively protect more than 700 acres. This moderately rugged hike (many tree roots and rocks) begins at Weisblatt Conservation Land and follows the Bay Circuit Trail (BCT) over Tippling Rock to the summit of Nobscot Hill. Numerous junctions

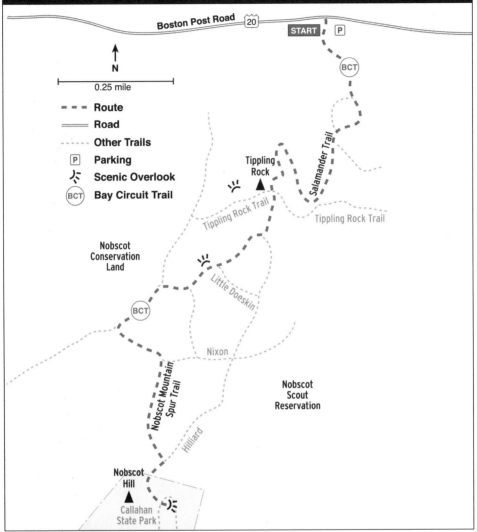

Boston Post Road 20

START P

BCT

N

0.25 mile

- - - Route
═══ Road
······ Other Trails
P Parking
⚡ Scenic Overlook
BCT Bay Circuit Trail

Salamander Trail

Tippling Rock ▲

Tippling Rock Trail

Tippling Rock Trail

Nobscot Conservation Land

BCT

Little Doeskin

Nixon

Nobscot Mountain Spur Trail

Nobscot Scout Reservation

Hilliard

Nobscot Hill ▲

Callahan State Park

connect with other trails, and carrying a map is strongly recommended. (See "More Information" below for landowners' rules and contact information.) The BCT is blazed with white squares featuring the BCT logo, and its signage is plentiful, providing helpful navigation along the entire route.

Begin at the Weisblatt Conservation Land trailhead by following the BCT and Salamander Trail south on an easy ascent through the property's northwest corner. Salamander Trail gets its name from the conservation area's vernal pools, one of which you can view a short distance from the trailhead. These wetlands offer critical breeding habitat for wood frogs, spring peepers, and spotted salamanders. Large, undeveloped, and roadless areas are especially important for vernal pool wildlife because they offer protected travel corridors that enable animals to safely disperse in an otherwise heavily developed region.

After Salamander Trail leaves to the left, looping back to the parking area, continue on the BCT southwest toward the boundary of adjacent Nobscot Scout Reservation, at roughly 0.5 mile. Bear right and follow the BCT as it briefly bends northwest and ascends the base of a ridge, curves sharply left, and continues south along the ledge.

This rocky habitat, which is relatively uncommon in eastern Massachusetts, offers ideal denning habitat for wildlife such as fishers, porcupines, coyotes, and bobcats. As with many other species, fishers (members of the weasel family) were extirpated from Massachusetts during Colonial times but have returned to the region in recent decades. While the animals themselves are rarely seen, their tracks are visible in the winter forest and around stone walls, where they hunt porcupines and other small mammals.

At 0.8 mile, after 20 to 25 minutes of walking, you will reach the rugged crown of Tippling Rock at the south end of the ridge. At 426 feet, it is the highest point in the town of Sudbury. (Nobscot Hill, which is 602 feet, is just across the town line in Framingham.) According to local lore, a farmer split this giant boulder to keep it from tipping onto his cattle. From this overlook, admire easterly panoramic vistas across the Metro West region to the Blue Hills and the skyscrapers of downtown Boston. To the west is a partial view of the sloping profile of 2,006-foot Wachusett Mountain, the highest point in Massachusetts east of the Berkshires.

After enjoying the scenery, continue on the BCT down the west end of the rocky ridge, following the white BCT markers carefully at junctions. After the junction with Tippling Rock Trail, turn right and traverse an adjacent ridge. A stone chimney just off the trail marks the site of an old cabin. Pass a boulder and then turn right and descend into the northeast corner of Nobscot Conservation Land, a 118-acre tract managed by the town of

Nobscot and Tippling Rock offer long-range views to those willing to make the hike.

Sudbury. Follow the blazes left at a junction. (The trail straight ahead continues 0.3 mile to a parking area off Brimstone Lane.)

After another 0.1 mile, reenter Nobscot Scout Reservation at the base of Nobscot Hill. After crossing a stream, turn sharply right at the next junction and begin a moderately steep ascent of the northeast slopes. Amid the dense woodlands, stone walls offer evidence of this landscape's past, when even the rocky hills were cleared for agriculture. A forest fire in 1930 burned a large portion of the reservation, but the forests have rebounded strongly over the past 92 years. Early morning and evening are the best times to watch for wildlife, including migratory songbirds and owls, which often nest in the tall pines.

Shortly after crossing the Framingham town line, continue past two more trail junctions and enter Department of Conservation and Recreation land on the upper slopes. At 1.9 miles from the trailhead, reach the 602-foot summit of Nobscot Hill, which is capped by communications towers and a fire tower. Although there are no views from the summit proper (unless you're invited up to the fire tower by rangers during the tower's seasonal operations), you can follow the trail to the left roughly 125 yards to reach a ledge with a partial easterly view of the Boston skyline. On clear days, another overlook on the south side of the summit offers long-distance views of Wachusett Mountain to the west, Mount Monadnock to the northwest, and distant Mount Kearsarge in central New Hampshire to the north.

From the summit, retrace your steps along the BCT to Tippling Rock and the trailhead. If you decide to explore the other trails, be sure to have a map and to follow markers carefully at the numerous junctions.

DID YOU KNOW?

Nobscot Scout Reservation is divided into two management areas. The Open Space Zone, which includes the Bay Circuit Trail, is a wildlands area. The Program Zone hosts scout activities and is managed for wildlife habitat and firewood.

NEARBY

Longfellow's Wayside Inn, a nonprofit historical landmark, offers many attractions, including a photogenic gristmill that was built by Henry Ford in 1929, a restaurant and inn with overnight lodging, and a 125-acre park. It is on Wayside Inn Road off US 20. Restaurants are on US 20 (Boston Post Road) in Sudbury.

MORE INFORMATION

Skiing is not permitted on Weisblatt Conservation Land. Skiing and biking are allowed at Nobscot Scout Reservation, but swimming, wading, and horseback riding are prohibited; pets must be leashed; and visitors must keep away from buildings, facilities, and campsites.

CALLAHAN STATE PARK

This route explores a traditional New England mix of carriage roads and trails under a canopy of pines and hardwoods.

Features

Location Framingham, MA

Rating Moderate

Distance 2.75-mile loop

Elevation Gain 230 feet

Estimated Time 2 hours

Maps USGS Framingham; Massachusetts Department of Conservation and Recreation: mass.gov/doc/callahan-state-park-trail-map/download

GPS coordinates 42° 20.583′ N, 71° 26.916′ W

Contact Massachusetts Department of Conservation and Recreation: mass.gov/locations/callahan-state-park, 508-653-9641

DIRECTIONS

From the Massachusetts Turnpike (I-90), take Exit 111 to MA 9 west toward Southborough/Worcester. The exit takes you on a long figure-8 loop; when you reach MA 9 west, get in the left lane to turn left at the exit for MA 30 toward Southborough. Turn right at the intersection of Pleasant Street Connector and MA 30. About 1 mile farther, turn left on Pine Hill Drive. After 1.5 miles, turn right on Parmenter Road, which becomes Edmands Road. The parking area known as Pipeline Trail parking is 0.5 mile ahead on the right.

The closest public transportation is the MBTA Commuter Rail line that stops in downtown Framingham, 6.0 miles away. You may want to take the train and then ride a bike to the trailhead. Trains may accommodate bicycles when space is available; see mbta.com/bikes/bringing-your-bike-the-train.

TRAIL DESCRIPTION

Beginning at the left side of the parking area, broad and unshaded Pipeline Trail stretches up over a hill where short yellow markers protruding from the ground mark an underground gas line. If visiting in spring, look for a vernal pool on the left not far up the trail. On pleasant days in March and April, you may hear loud confirmation of wood frogs and peepers in the vicinity of the pool.

Pass signs for Sudbury Valley Trustees trails and continue up Pipeline Trail toward the high hill in the distance.

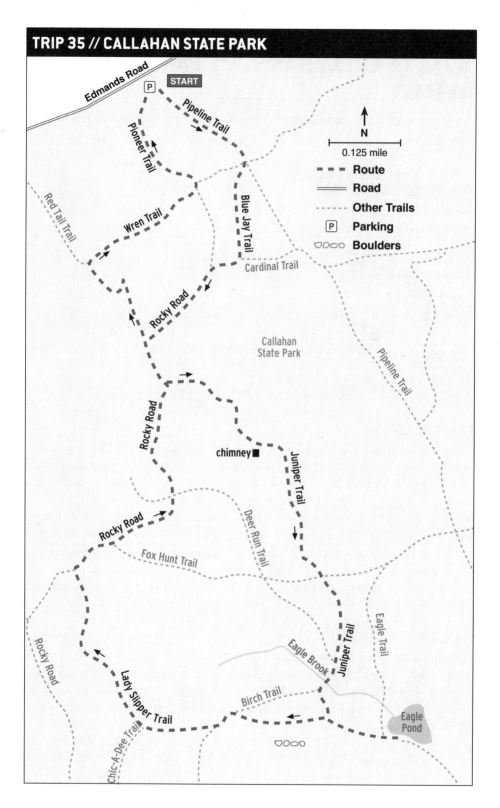

Edmands Road

P START

Pipeline Trail

Pioneer Trail

Red Tail Trail

Wren Trail

Blue Jay Trail

Cardinal Trail

Rocky Road

Callahan
State Park

Pipeline Trail

N

0.125 mile

- - - Route
==== Road
····· Other Trails
P Parking
◦◦◦ Boulders

Rocky Road

chimney ■

Juniper Trail

Rocky Road

Deer Run Trail

Fox Hunt Trail

Rocky Road

Lady Slipper Trail

Chic-A-Dee Trail

Eagle Brook

Juniper Trail

Eagle Trail

Birch Trail

◦◦◦

Eagle
Pond

At about 0.25 mile, reach the forked intersection of Blue Jay and Wren trails on the right. Follow Blue Jay Trail left. This trail is a rugged, uphill former cart path that follows the contour of a broad basin on the left side, allowing a view into the bowl. On the right is the first of many long stone walls crisscrossing the park. Blue markers on this wall delineate the boundary of the state forest portion of the property.

As you approach the upper portion of the path, watch on the left side for a large oak with a vertical scar marking its surface and a rock embedded in the base of its trunk.

At the intersection with Cardinal Trail, go right to stay on Blue Jay Trail. At the top of the hill, in a clearing, a wooden sign at a T intersection points out Rocky Road. Go left through a gap in a stone wall to follow Rocky Road across the level area and as it begins to descend the hilltop. Roots protrude across the treadway here, making footing challenging on wet days. Go through a gap in another stone wall and walk down the broad trail surrounded by tall pines.

Two intersections lie in rapid succession here. At the first, where Red Tail Trail meets Rocky Road on the right, continue straight on Rocky Road, going downhill. A low wooden bridge crosses a stream at the bottom of the hill. The second intersection, marked by a sign on a tree as F21, is here, along with a helpful trail map. Take Juniper Trail on the left at this intersection of multiple trails.

Juniper Trail continues uphill through more pines, but there's a small reward for going this far: when the trail levels out you will find an old stone chimney to the right. After pondering about the remnants of this structure, continue through a gap in a stone wall and start downhill again. The trail curves to the right, and you'll notice, regardless of the season, that the pines give way briefly to a vine-covered area of thick underbrush. After one more curve, this time to the left, you arrive at a triangular junction.

This intersection of Juniper and Fox Hunt trails is marked with a sign (F12). Continue on Juniper Trail through three more intersections: Deer Run Trail on the right, Connector Trail on the left, and Lady Slipper Trail on the right. (Taking Fox Hunt Trail at the intersection shortens this hike significantly; you can head back to the parking lot by going right on Rocky Road at the second intersection.)

Just before Lady Slipper Trail, cross Eagle Brook, which has a small bridge and can be quite muddy. Stop before

Fragments of buildings, such as this chimney, found on Juniper Trail, indicate historical uses of the land that is now a state park.

crossing the bridge to look for a "hugging tree" here, where a pine and adjacent hardwood have intertwined roots showing above the surface. Just after the bridge, near the intersection with Birch Trail, look for trees that have deep, V-shaped bark. These are black gum trees, which produce small clusters of round, blue-colored fruit and display bright red leaves in fall.

The intersection with Lady Slipper Trail isn't a perfect four-way. The trail intersects with Juniper Trail on the right, but you continue a short distance before turning left on Lady Slipper Trail. Here, it passes through some underbrush before opening to a meadow. Stroll down to the water's edge near a bench and enjoy the sunshine and view of Eagle Pond for a few minutes. You may hear frogs croaking or see a belted kingfisher searching for lunch.

Return to the wooded trails via Lady Slipper Trail, and cross Juniper Trail to stay on Lady Slipper Trail. Notice the difference in the white pines along this section—many have double or triple trunks. On a windy day the branches may creak and whine as they rub together or whistle as the wind passes through many small branches and needles.

After an intersection with Birch Trail, pass an interesting collection of ledge boulders and smaller glacial erratics. Near the next intersection, where Chick-A-Dee Trail is on the left, watch for wetlands on the right. Years of fallen leaves, branches, and trees provide the perfect habitat for water-dwelling frogs that may be heard in the area from April to September. Birds gravitate to the area for its ample supply of insects.

Continue on Lady Slipper Trail through a gap in a stone wall and past oak trees with multiple trunks. Some of these, called gemels, develop a little well between the dual trunks where other plants may thrive. On the ground near oaks you may also find little tan balls that are very lightweight. These are called galls and are created by the trees when wasps inject larvae into the tree trunk or branches.

Farther ahead, Lady Slipper Trail goes over a small rise and around a pine tree in the middle of the treadway. As you climb uphill again, look to your left for a large boulder broken in a diamond shape along a seam, as if cut with a chisel. Just after this point, Lady Slipper Trail turns left and parallels a stone wall on the left as it approaches a junction with Rocky Road. Go to the right at the junction to follow Rocky Road and pass through a gap in another stone wall. In a short distance, Fox Hunt Trail intersects on the right at marker F10. Continue straight on Rocky Road. Look to the left on the next hill to see a deep well. That side of the trail is a steep slope down; you are at about the 2-mile mark of the hike.

As Rocky Road curves left about 250 feet ahead, it is intersected by Deer Run Trail. Continue straight on Rocky Road. Signs indicate that this is now Sudbury Valley Trustees property. Papery, light-yellow leaves on the ground are evidence of a beech tree nearby. Keep watch on the right for a very large oak tree along a stone wall, a tree that was likely left standing because it was at the edge of a pasture when this area was completely deforested for farming.

Juniper Trail enters from the right just after you pass tall pines that seem like sentinels guarding the route. This is the wide intersection you passed through earlier, with the trail map, a low wooden bridge, and the F21 sign. Cross the bridge and stay left at the next intersection to take Red Tail Trail where Rocky Road turns right.

Red Tail Trail turns sharply left and zigzags downhill just after the stone wall. (Trail planners and builders often create zigzag patterns to reduce erosion and to make climbing or descending hills easier.) At the bottom of the hill, where Red Tail Trail continues straight to Edmands Road, turn right onto Wren Trail, follow it a short distance, and then take the first left onto Pioneer Trail (you may see the remnants of a wire fence here in the underbrush) to return directly to the parking lot.

DID YOU KNOW?
An 1875 map of Framingham shows a 500-acre farm owned by the Bowditch family near the Framingham–Sudbury town line, an area that still hosts several farms.

NEARBY
The Garden in the Woods, a 45-acre botanical garden nearby on Hemenway Road, offers landscaped trails, tours (including by golf cart), and plant information. Visit nativeplanttrust .org/visit/garden-woods for more details.

MORE INFORMATION
The 800-acre park is adjacent to many parcels of conservation land controlled by different groups, allowing visitors to create longer-range trail hikes, such as from Tippling Rock on MA 20 in Sudbury (see Trip 34) to Sudbury Reservoir Trail (see Trip 36). The Bay Circuit Trail, which climbs Gibb Mountain, provides one of these opportunities. See baycircuit .org/pdf/section8.pdf for details. According to the Massachusetts Department of Conservation and Recreation, no ranger is specifically assigned to Callahan State Park. An active dog owners group claims that 85 percent of the park's 100,000 annual visitors bring dogs. Visit callahandogs.com/callahan-state-park for more information.

A gentle walk leads along a quiet historical reservoir guarded by cedar trees.

Features

Location Southborough and Framingham, MA

Rating Easy

Distance 4 miles round trip

Elevation Gain 75 feet

Estimated Time 2 hours

Maps USGS Framingham; Bay Circuit Alliance: baycircuit.org/wp-content/uploads/2020/02/BCT_Map8_2020.pdf; Sudbury Valley Trustees: svtweb.org/properties/page/boroughs-loop-trail

GPS coordinates 42° 18.666′ N, 71° 29.500′ W

Contact Massachusetts Department of Conservation and Recreation: mass.gov/locations/sudbury-reservoir, 508-792-7806

DIRECTIONS

From the Massachusetts Turnpike (I-90), take Exit 111 to MA 9 west toward Southborough/Worcester. The exit takes you on a long figure-8 loop; when you reach MA 9 west, get in the left lane to turn left for MA 30 toward Southborough. Turn right at the intersection of Pleasant Street Connector and MA 30. About 1 mile farther, turn left on Pine Hill Drive, and then quickly turn left onto Clemmons Street (Southborough). The trail begins at a yellow gate on the left where Clemmons and Nichols streets intersect. A small turnout provides space for parking.

TRAIL DESCRIPTION

Sudbury Reservoir is an oasis of tranquility along the 231-mile Bay Circuit Trail's route through the crowded suburbs west of Boston. Enjoy water views while surrounded by lush native greenery on this easy out-and-back walk.

The simple, straightforward cart path with no interruptions is perfect for quiet contemplation, trail running, or cross-country skiing. This portion offers connections to more trails in Callahan State Park across Parmenter Street and to Boroughs Loop Trail, a newer option that will eventually encircle the "borough" towns (Marlborough, Northborough, Southborough, and Westborough) with a 33-mile route. Ambitious hikers may be enticed to explore more of the Bay Circuit Trail (BCT), which can be accomplished in sections because it has many access points.

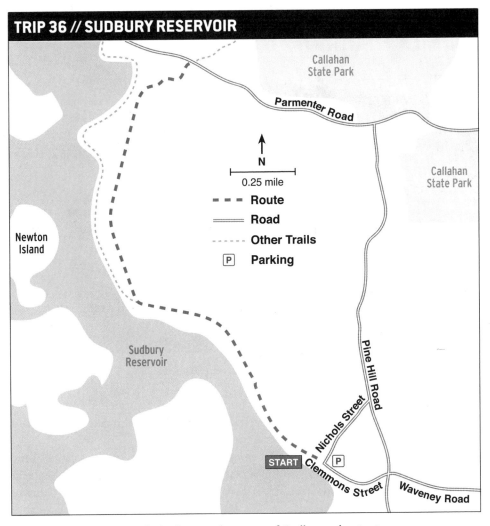

The reservoir—none of which is in the town of Sudbury, despite its name—was constructed beginning in 1898 as part of a system to supply drinking water to the growing city of Boston. This 2-square-mile body of water is fed both by aqueducts siphoning off Wachusett Reservoir water to the west and by local tributary streams. It has an average depth of 17 feet but is up to 65 feet deep in places. Sudbury Reservoir was discontinued as a source of Boston's water in the mid-1970s but is considered an emergency reserve, so activities in and around it remain restricted. Shoreline fishing is allowed, but boating is not; swimming and skating are also prohibited. Anglers may fish for largemouth and smallmouth bass and chain pickerel.

From the yellow gate, turn right and go slightly downhill. (The trail to the left leads to Fayeville Dam, marked "Southborough Historic Dam District" on some maps. The dam itself has no access (fenced off with No Trespassing signs), but Boroughs Loop Trail passes by the near end; the BCT (northbound) comes up Clemmons Street and enters Sudbury Reservoir Trail at the yellow gate.) Signs near the gate indicate that horses, dogs, campfires,

The 1,800-foot dam at Fayville was built in 1894 and includes a 300-foot spillway.

camping, and bicycling are prohibited. Deer hunting is allowed during fall and winter, so be watchful during these months, particularly at dusk and dawn. Also take precautions to avoid tiny deer ticks that may spread Lyme disease.

The early portion of the walk just after the gate is neither pretty nor indicative of the route, which improves significantly within several hundred feet. Here, the path is bordered by masses of vines, particularly invasives, such as poison ivy and bittersweet, the latter of which bears red and yellow berries in late fall. Bittersweet vines are sometimes featured in holiday decorations, but do not disturb or cut these, as stray berries easily spread the choking weed to new locations.

At the 0.3-mile mark, the route passes underneath power lines and goes through a stand of pines. The treadway is grassy, one vehicle wide, with wheel ruts worn to bare earth. The walking is easy, with almost no elevation change or rocks or roots underfoot, allowing visitors to let their minds wander or let their eyes stray to the left to gaze at the reservoir visible between the trees.

Because this manufactured body of water has always been protected from encroachment, the trees surrounding it likely avoided logging for generations, allowing a variety of hardwoods to grow unhindered. Some are stunning specimens of oak and maple, but the most memorable are the straight rows of arborvitae that line the path.

On the northbound route from the Clemmons/Nichols area toward Parmenter Street, you'll pass through a disorganized stand of cedars mixed with pines and then will see long stretches of sentinel-like cedars alongside the path. Many of these rows are in the first mile. These cedars are particularly remarkable for their size because the species is known for growing a foot or less per year. In the distant past, cedars were valued by American Indians and early European settlers for their resistance to rot and decay, making the wood preferable for fence posts, shingles, and even the earliest water pipes. Many of New England's oldest homesteads have cultivated plots of cedars for these purposes.

A stone wall parallels the path on the right side for much of the route and then inexplicably appears on the left for a short time. A hand-drawn 1875 map shows a handful of property owners along "Pleasant Street," which backed up to a narrow and undammed Stony Brook, but provides no details about farmland.

The width of the trail and age of the surrounding forest generally allow for long sight lines that could be helpful in observing wildlife. Animal paths can be seen in several areas where there is more underbrush along the shoreline. Here, you may catch sight of native white-tailed deer, raccoons, fishers, or coyotes. Closer to the water, encountering a frog or snake is likely; birds heard during a recent stroll included blue jays high in the trees and a belted kingfisher scouring the waterfront for a fish or frog. Winter cross-country skiing or snowshoe hiking might reveal more animal tracks in snow than are visible in other seasons.

New England's ubiquitous *Acer rubrum*, commonly known as red or swamp maple, proliferates here along the water, making for a spectacular reflected contrast when in full fall color around mid-October. The U.S. Forest Service says the red maple is the most abundant native tree in the eastern portion of North America, with a range stretching from Nova Scotia to Florida.

In the first mile along Sudbury River Trail, there is only one intersecting trail, which is challenging to find due to underbrush. It is on the right side near a large fallen tree around the 0.75-mile mark and leads to the Graystone Way neighborhood. At about 1.25 miles, the longer shoreline trail (marked with BCT signage) diverges from Sudbury Reservoir Trail, but both intersect Parmenter Street. The BCT route is preferable if one wants to connect with Wayside Woods/Callahan State Park trails on the other side of Parmenter Street.

Turn around at Parmenter Street to complete the out-and-back route (approximately 4 miles).

DID YOU KNOW?

Natick's Lake Cochituate was Boston's original reservoir, but in the mid-1800s industries, such as tanneries, polluted the water, prompting officials to make a dike across the lake to better contain the waste that flowed in from sources close to the town center. Whitehall, Hopkinton, and Ashland reservoirs were all created to supplement the water supply of Boston and did so until they became state parks in 1947.

NEARBY

Numerous restaurants are on MA 9 in Framingham and MA 20 in Sudbury. Farms in the area of Parmenter Road, Nixon Road, and Broadmeadow Street on the Framingham–Sudbury town line may also sell food and locally grown vegetables.

MORE INFORMATION

The Massachusetts Department of Conservation and Recreation manages Sudbury Reservoir Trail and the surrounding property. Fishing is allowed along the trail except in the area near Fayeville Dam. State officials recommend limiting consumption of fish from this location due to elevated levels of mercury. See mass.gov/doc/sudbury-reservoir-fishing -map-and-rules/download for fishing regulations.

BROADMOOR WILDLIFE SANCTUARY

Broadmoor is a sanctuary rich in both natural and human history. Walk through forests and along fields that were farmed for hundreds of years on land that native peoples occupied for thousands of years.

Features 🚶 ♿ 💧 🦆 ⛷ 🚻 💲

Location Natick and Sherborn, MA

Rating Moderate

Distance 3-mile loop

Elevation Gain 50 feet

Estimated Time 1.5 to 2 hours

Maps USGS Framingham; Mass Audubon: massaudubon.org/content/download/43822/1088237/file/MA_Broadmoor_color.pdf

GPS coordinates 42° 15.368' N, 71° 20.421' W

Contact Broadmoor Wildlife Sanctuary: broadmoor@massaudubon.org, 508-655-2296

DIRECTIONS

From I-95, take Exit 37 to MA 16 west. Continue on MA 16 west 7.0 miles into South Natick. The parking lot and signs welcoming you to Broadmoor will be on your left. The sanctuary is on Route 16 (280 Eliot Street), 1.8 miles west of the center of South Natick.

TRAIL DESCRIPTION

Broadmoor Wildlife Sanctuary is a popular hiking destination due to its diverse terrain and wildlife. The sanctuary is home to more than 175 varieties of birds, including 60 breeding species. At the nature center building, or online before your visit, you can get a map detailing all 9 miles of trails. The trails have color-coded markers, with blue heading away from the parking lot and yellow heading back.

The most scenic area is at the eastern end of the property. To reach it, follow Mill Pond–Marsh Trail past Mill Pond and the mill sites, and cross South Street to the Charles River Trail loop, traveling down along the river. Even when the parking lot is full, the trails going to the western end of the property rarely have more than a few hikers. One such trail is Indian Brook Trail, which leads to the even more secluded Glacial Hill Trail. Views of Little Farm Pond from Glacial Hill Trail make it a beautiful destination in any season.

Begin your walk by checking in at the nature center. Turn right a few feet down the main trail onto Indian Brook Trail, near the boardwalk (signpost 2). The beginning of Indian Brook Trail passes through a beautiful open field where eastern kingbirds, northern

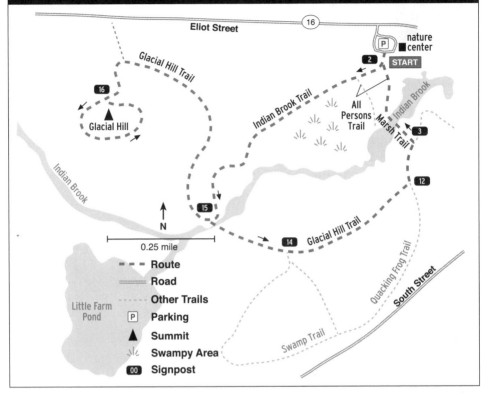

mockingbirds, cedar waxwings, and indigo buntings can be seen, in addition to the resident woodchucks. A short spur path on the left is an extension of All Persons Trail, which leads to an observation platform overlooking the field. Soon Indian Brook Trail enters a wooded area with oaks on the right and the Indian Brook marsh on the left. A short boardwalk on the right offers close-up views of a vernal pool. During a visit in spring, you may hear the loud "quacking" of wood frogs courting in the pool.

The Indian Brook marsh and the sanctuary's other wetlands are habitat for wood ducks, painted turtles, kingfishers, great blue herons, raccoons, muskrats, and river otters. In 1989, beavers moved into the Indian Brook marsh. This was big news for Charles River watershed lovers, as these were apparently the first beavers to inhabit the area in nearly a century. A beaver family built a dam at the junction of Indian Brook Trail and Glacial Hill Trail and then built a lodge a short distance upstream. Today, there are many more lodges, one of which is especially visible in winter from the accessible boardwalk.

At signpost 15 is a junction with Glacial Hill Trail. This hike continues to the right (northwest) along the northern portion of Glacial Hill Trail. (You will return to this junction after looping over Glacial Hill.) The trail winds its way through oaks for about a half-mile before reaching a small hill, or drumlin—a doughnut-shaped glacial deposit rising up from the marshy forest below. Common but often elusive inhabitants of these woodlands include deer, foxes, great horned owls, and wild turkeys.

After traversing a wetland at the base of the hill (an area that may be flooded in spring), Glacial Hill Trail runs below the top of the hill, forming a 0.6-mile loop with views of Little Farm Pond. Retrace your steps to Indian Brook Trail at signpost 15.

From here, turn left to go back to the parking lot, or turn right to continue the loop by crossing a bridge over Indian Brook—a great spot for birding and photography—and hiking the southern portion of Glacial Hill Trail. Follow Glacial Hill Trail left at signpost 14 (Blueberry Swamp Trail makes a 0.8-mile loop to the right here) and continue to the junction at signpost 12, at the edge of a clearing. Turn left here and then bear left again on Marsh Trail at the junction at signpost 3.

As the trail winds back to the nature center, it crosses a boardwalk with fine views of the wetlands. Shortly before reaching the center, be sure to make the short detour onto the All Persons Trail boardwalk. This is an excellent wildlife-viewing area, where muskrats, northern water snakes, and large groups of basking painted turtles may be seen at close range.

Another little-known section of the sanctuary is Little Farm Pond, a 23-acre kettle pond in Sherborn. To reach this pond from the main parking lot, drive 1.1 miles west on MA 16, turn left onto Lake Street, and continue 0.8 mile to Farm Road. Turn left onto Farm Road and look for a small parking area on the left side of the road, about 100 yards from the intersection of Lake Street and Farm Road. From here you can hike down Little Farm Pond Trail to the pond and explore a marked trail loop along its west side. This quiet, special place is rich with wildlife, including the Virginia rail, and unusual vegetation, such as carnivorous sundews and pitcher plants. Look for migrating ducks in late fall and early winter.

The painted turtle (*Chrysemys picta*) is commonly found in sunny, shallow bodies of water throughout Massachusetts and can spend as many as six hours a day basking in the sun.

DID YOU KNOW?

The nature center is a state-of-the-art building with 128 solar panels providing electricity. In fact, the panels produce more energy than is used, making the nature center carbon negative. Composting toilets save an estimated 100,000 gallons of water annually, and rainwater is collected from roof runoff to water the native plants garden.

NEARBY

Restaurants are in central Natick along and off Main Street. The historical (circa 1881) Bacon Free Library is in a pleasant setting along the Charles River in South Natick, at 58 Eliot Street (MA 16). The library is also the home of the Natick Historical Society. The Center for the Arts in Natick, in the former Central Fire Station on Summer Street, hosts a variety of musical and theatrical performances.

MORE INFORMATION

The wildlife sanctuary is open Tuesday through Sunday, dawn to dusk; it is closed on Mondays except for holidays. Admission is free for Mass Audubon members; fees for nonmembers are $6 for adults, $4 for children ages 2 through 12, and $4 for seniors); pets are prohibited. The nature center is open Tuesday through Friday, 9 A.M. to 5 P.M.; Saturday and Sunday, 10 A.M. to 5 P.M.; and Monday holidays, 10 A.M. to 5 P.M. Winter hours may vary.

38 ROCKY NARROWS RESERVATION AND SHERBORN TOWN FOREST

The rugged hillsides of the remote Rocky Narrows, reachable by foot or by canoe or kayak, are a highlight of the Charles River valley.

Features

Location Sherborn, MA

Rating Moderate

Distance 2.7-mile loop

Elevation Gain 165 feet

Estimated Time 1.5 hours

Maps USGS Medfield; The Trustees of Reservations: thetrustees.org/wp-content/uploads/2021/09/RockyNarrows_TrailMap_2020.pdf

GPS coordinates 42° 13.557' N, 71° 21.241' W

Contact The Trustees of Reservations: thetrustees.org/place/rocky-narrows, 508-785-0339

DIRECTIONS

From I-95, take Exit 31B and follow MA 109 west 8.0 miles to the junction with MA 27 in Medfield. Turn right on MA 27 north and drive 3.1 miles to the junction with MA 115 in Sherborn. Continue on MA 27 0.3 mile past the reservation's south entrance on the right and then turn right onto Snow Street. After 0.4 mile, bear right onto Forest Street and continue another 0.4 mile to the parking area (room for six cars) on the right.

TRAIL DESCRIPTION

The contiguous Rocky Narrows Reservation (owned by The Trustees of Reservations) and Sherborn Town Forest offer hikers a relatively wild section of more than 400 acres of woodlands to explore. One highlight is King Philip's Overlook, an open ledge atop a steep valley (see essay on page 177) that affords a fantastic view of the Charles River. Hemlock trees cover much of the hillside in the reservation, and a walk here feels more reminiscent of northern New England than suburban Boston. Although this route is fairly straightforward, the property has many trails, and carrying a map is strongly recommended for first-time visitors. Maps are also posted at the trailhead and at some junctions.

The hike, which begins at the Rocky Narrows Reservation Forest Street entrance, combines the local Red Trail and Blue Trail and the long-distance Bay Circuit Trail (BCT). The walking is mostly easy, with a couple of quick climbs. A few areas may be muddy or wet, depending on the season, although the largest of these can be bypassed easily.

TRIP 38 // ROCKY NARROWS RESERVATION AND SHERBORN TOWN FOREST

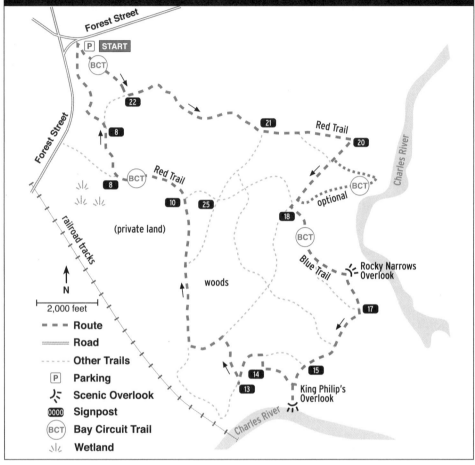

Follow the path across the field adjacent to the parking area and then bear right onto a gravel road. After passing more fields, the trail, marked with white BCT blazes and red blazes, enters the woods at marker 22 and descends to a small wetland. These types of areas, where different habitats meet, are especially rich in wildlife. Skunk cabbage blooms in abundance in early spring, and frogs will likely jump off the path into the water as you approach.

Follow the route east, through woods of oak, pine, and scattered hemlock, continuing through junction 21. At junction 20, turn sharply right opposite a wetland, where in spring and summer you'll probably hear the distinctive *conk-la-ree* call of red-winged blackbirds. When you come to a junction after another 500 feet, turn left to follow the BCT to a canoe landing on the bank of the Charles River or, if conditions are wet, simply continue straight on Red Trail to junction 18, where it rejoins the BCT.

There is a healthy population of white-tailed deer here. During spring, you might see their heart-shaped tracks in the damp earth. The narrow part of the print is made by the

Fall foliage, seen here from King Philip's Overlook, makes for a stunning hike in Rocky Narrows Reservation.

front of the deer's hoof and indicates the direction the animal was traveling. Another large mammal in residence is the coyote, which can be found throughout Massachusetts. Coyotes are very adaptable, eating whatever food source is available, including house cats. They are secretive animals and do most of their hunting at night. A coyote howl in the wee hours is a sound you won't soon forget.

At marker 18, turn left off Red Trail and follow blue-blazed Blue Trail and the BCT (white markers with BCT logo) upslope along a stone wall. Continue high above the west bank of the Charles River, passing through shady groves of large eastern hemlocks. Rocky Narrows Overlook and other viewpoints provide vistas across the Charles River valley. The woods on the far side of the river are part of Medfield State Forest. Hemlocks thrive in these rocky ridges and ravines, growing to a height of 70 feet in cool, moist spots. To distinguish hemlocks from other evergreens, examine the needles closely. Hemlock needles are flat with blunt tips, typically a quarter-inch to a half-inch long—shorter than spruce and fir needles. Usually several needles sit upside down on the branchlet, and they have dark-green tops and silvery undersides. Because the needles are acidic, there is often little undergrowth beneath trees where needles have fallen year after year. Hemlocks have brown cones, about 0.75 inch long, which hang from the tips of the branches. They mature in fall and stay on the tree until spring. Another way to distinguish hemlocks from fir trees is to look at the crown of the tree. The hemlock will be rounded, while the fir comes to a sharp, dense point. Unfortunately, hemlock is declining significantly in southern New England due to infestation of the hemlock woolly adelgid (see page 38).

At junction 17, bear right and follow the combined Blue Trail and the BCT away from the river, entering Sherborn Town Forest. At marker 15, bear left and follow the white-blazed BCT on a quick descent to King Philip's Overlook. Enjoy the fine vista south across the valley, taking in the fields and more of Medfield State Forest. A railroad bridge is visible to the right. This is a good place to look for hawks soaring above the water. Great blue herons also make their way up and down the river. Their population has increased due to cleaner waters and because the proliferating beaver population has led to more ponds with standing timber, the herons' preferred nesting spot.

Begin the return leg by following the left fork of the BCT to junction 14, where you'll rejoin Blue Trail. Turn left here and then bear right at a posted map at junction 13 and continue to junction 10, where Blue Trail ends at its second junction with Red Trail. Turn left and follow the combined Red Trail and BCT downhill to a large wetland along Seawall Brook; then turn right and follow the combined trails north along the wetland edge to marker 10. After passing the wetland, bear right (marker 9), then left (marker 8) at successive junctions to return to the parking area. (*Note*: If the trail at marker 10 is flooded during spring, you can avoid a wet crossing by going right at junction 10, left at junction 25, continuing to Red Trail at junction 21, and then going left to the reservation's entrance.)

DID YOU KNOW?

As you follow the trail atop the Rocky Narrows, you're traversing a landscape that is 650 million years old. Colonists referred to the Narrows as "the Gates of the Charles."

NEARBY

The town centers of Medfield and Sherborn have many historical buildings. Several of these old homes were part of the Underground Railroad in the nineteenth century and have trapdoors, secret rooms, and hidden passages. Restaurants are in central Medfield along Main Street (MA 109) and North Street.

MORE INFORMATION

Rocky Narrows Reservation is open year-round, dawn to dusk; no fee; no restrooms. Dogs are allowed but must be leashed.

KING PHILIP'S WAR: AN EARLY AMERICAN CONFLICT

Rocky Narrows is one of several nature preserves in eastern Massachusetts that also have historical connections to King Philip's War. The conflict began in 1675, when Metacomet, an American Indian leader whose English-given name was Philip, led an uprising of Wampanoags, Nipmucks, and Narragansetts in an effort to regain tribal lands from European settlers. The war, which cost the lives of an estimated 600 colonists and 30,000 American Indians, eliminated or severely weakened many native tribes. Although more than half of New England's then-90 established towns were damaged by the battles, colonists rapidly rebuilt.

King Philip's Overlook at Rocky Narrows Reservation is one of many hilltops, viewpoints, and rock formations in Massachusetts named for the American Indian leader. Medfield, which lies in front of you as you look across the river, was hard hit by the uprising. Many homes were burned and several settlers were killed, but the American Indians could not overpower the colonists' garrison.

Another site of interest is at nearby Noon Hill Reservation. Many historians believe that King Philip launched his raid on the town of Medfield from Noon Hill. Others argue the raiders gathered on the west side of the Charles River. No matter where the attack came from, this was an important area for the American Indians, who preferred to live near the confluence of major streams and rivers. Here, Stop River enters the Charles River below Noon Hill.

After the American Indians withdrew from Medfield, one fighter who had learned English left a note near a burned bridge over the Charles River that read: "Know by this paper, that the Indians that thou hast provoked to wrath and anger, will war this twenty-one years if you will: there are many Indians yet, we come three hundred this time. You must consider the Indians lost nothing but their life; you must lose your fair houses and cattle." Despite these bold words, the American Indians were outnumbered by the British.

The attack on Medfield occurred in February 1676. By August of that year, so many American Indians had been killed, including Philip, that the war ended. Ironically, Philip was the son of Massasoit, the Wampanoag leader who had showed kindness to the Pilgrims during their first disastrous year in Plymouth.

An extensive network of trails leads to a millpond and a waterfall and up to modest Noanet Peak, where there are views across forested hills to the Boston skyline.

Features

Location Dover, MA

Rating Moderate

Distance 3.5-mile loop

Elevation Gain 230 feet

Estimated Time 1.75 hours

Maps USGS Framingham, USGS Medfield; The Trustees of Reservations: thetrustees.org/wp-content/uploads/2020/07/Noanet-Trail-Map.pdf

GPS coordinates 42° 14.878′ N, 71° 16.161′ W

Contact The Trustees of Reservations: thetrustees.org/place/noanet-woodlands, 508-785-0339

DIRECTIONS

From I-95/Route 128: Take Exit 31B (109 West). Follow MA 109 for less than 1 mile and turn right on Dover Road. Follow Dover Road for 2.3 miles to the parking lot on the right. (Dover Road becomes Powisset Street in Dover.)

From Medfield Center: Take Route 109 East, and then turn left onto Hartford Street. Follow Hartford Street for 1.5 miles, and then turn left onto Walpole Street. Follow Walpole Street for 0.8 mile, and then turn right onto Powisset Street. After 0.6 mile, turn left into the Noanet parking lot.

Parking at Noanet is limited to 30 cars, and the lot can fill up in the busy spring or fall season when the weather is pleasant. The lot is closed once it reaches capacity. Consider arriving early in the morning or late in the afternoon during this time. (If the lot is full, other Trustees properties, including Rocky Woods Reservation and Powisset Farm, are nearby for an equally enjoyable visit!) Please do not park along the street—this is strictly enforced. Cars may be ticketed, towed at the owner's expense, or both.

TRAIL DESCRIPTION

The diversity of terrain makes Noanet Woodlands special: swamplands, brooks, millponds, a waterfall, upland forests, and a 387-foot hill are all here. These features provide excellent opportunities for nature study, as well as hiking, jogging, and cross-country skiing on the reservation's extensive trail network. The property abuts Powisset Farm, also owned by The

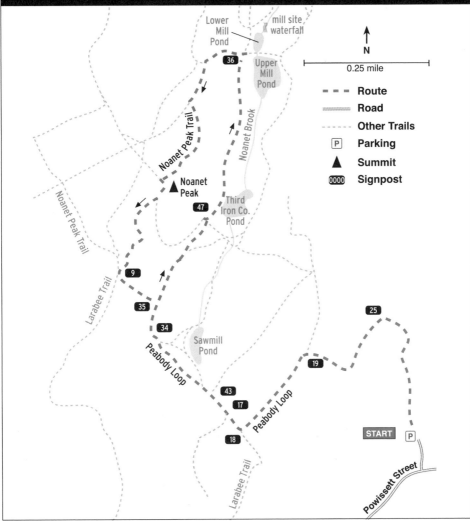

Trustees of Reservations, and the privately owned Hale Reservation, creating a contiguous wildlife refuge.

The trail network includes four main blazed trails and other unnamed paths. This hike begins at the trailhead parking lot on Powisset Street and combines portions of Peabody Loop, Caryl Loop, Noanet Peak Loop, and Larabee Trail. The walk to the ponds is relatively flat; the short climb to Noanet Peak is steep in spots.

From the parking lot, follow blue-blazed Peabody Loop, which leads north into the woods. After about 1,000 feet, cross a small footbridge and turn left at marker 25; turn right at the next intersection. Turn left at the fork and continue to marker 19; turn left again. At marker 18, turn right to head north. Pass scenic Sawmill Pond in about 500 feet on the right. Stay to the right at marker 34 and follow Peabody Loop for about 2,000 feet (Larabee Trail, which is the return part of the trip, is on the left at marker 35).

Near marker 36, Upper Mill Pond and Lower Mill Pond appear on the right. (You can make a short detour here on paths that circle the pond.) This was once the site of the Dover Union Iron Company, which operated from 1815 into the 1830s. The brook was too small to adequately power the mills, and the company eventually went out of business. The original dam was destroyed by flooding in 1876 but was reconstructed in 1954 by Amelia Peabody, who later bequeathed the land to The Trustees of Reservations. The holding ponds above the dam are a perfect place to sit and have lunch, serenaded by the sound of falling water and singing birds. Painted turtles, frogs, and bluegills inhabit the various ponds and wetlands. The large pines, oaks, maples, and beeches that surround the ponds complete the picturesque setting.

From marker 36, follow yellow-blazed Noanet Peak Loop about 2,000 feet (10 to 15 minutes of walking) to the summit (be sure to keep to the left at marker 47 to stay on the yellow-blazed trail). The top of the peak grants an excellent view of the Boston skyline and the hills to the east. Powisset Peak, part of the nearby Hale Reservation, is also visible. In fall, the hilltop is a good place to see migrating hawks flying south.

From Noanet Peak, head south to continue on Noanet Peak Loop, which travels along the ridge and slowly descends to marker 9, where you will begin following orange-blazed Larabee Trail. After a short 100 feet, stay to the left at the fork and head downslope on Larabee Trail until it rejoins Peabody Loop at marker 35. From here, bear right and retrace your steps to the trailhead by staying on blue-blazed Peabody Loop. You'll pass Sawmill Pond again, but this time on the left. Turn left at marker 18, right at marker 19 (very

The site of the former Dover Union Iron Company in Noanet Woodlands serves as a historical waypoint on this hike. *Photo by Mike Halsall, Creative Commons on Flickr.*

important to avoid reentering the trail network), and right at marker 25, across the footbridge, to complete your hike at the trailhead parking lot.

DID YOU KNOW?

Amelia Peabody was well known in Dover for her conservation efforts. She purchased a farm near the present Noanet Woodlands in 1923 and subsequently added hundreds of acres during the next six decades.

NEARBY

The historic Benjamin Caryl House, home of Dover's first minister, is at 107 Dedham Street in Dover. The house, which was added to the National Register of Historic Places in 2000 and is now owned by the Dover Historical Society (incorporated in 1900), was built in 1777 and includes eighteenth-century furnishings. Restaurants are in central Needham on Highland Avenue, Great Plain Avenue, and Chestnut Street.

MORE INFORMATION

Noanet Woodlands is open year-round, sunrise to sunset; no fee. Parking is free for members of The Trustees of Reservations; the charge for nonmembers is $6 per car. Dogs are allowed but must be leashed. Mountain biking requires a permit (free).

40 ROCKY WOODS RESERVATION

This expansive reservation offers a choice of walks exploring ponds, rocky outcroppings, and boulders, with opportunities to fish, picnic, and cross-country ski.

Features 👣 🐕 💧 🍂 ⛷ 💲 🎣

Location Medfield, MA

Rating Easy to Moderate

Distance 3.5-mile loop, southern section; 3.1-mile loop, northern section

Elevation Gain Southern section, 180 feet; northern section, 360 feet

Estimated Time Southern section, 1.5 hours; northern section, 1.75 hours

Maps USGS Medfield; The Trustees of Reservations: thetrustees.org/wp-content/uploads/2020/07/Rocky-Woods-Fork-Factory-Brook-Trail-Map.pdf

GPS coordinates 42° 12.386′ N, 71° 16.601′ W

Contact The Trustees of Reservations: thetrustees.org/place/rocky-woods, 508-785-0339

DIRECTIONS
From I-95 take Exit 31B for MA 109 west. Follow MA 109 5.5 miles through Westwood to Hartford Street in Medfield. Turn sharply right onto Hartford Street. Follow it 0.6 mile to the reservation entrance and parking lot on the left (38 Hartford Street).

TRAIL DESCRIPTION
Rocky Woods is one of the largest properties owned by The Trustees of Reservations, and it offers a wide variety of year-round recreational activities. The name Rocky Woods is appropriate; the land is a series of uneven ridges with many rocky outcroppings, including Whale Rock, which resembles the back of a whale rising from the forest floor. The reservation is rich in wildlife, and early-morning hikers are often treated to the sight of a fox, a ruffed grouse, or a great blue heron wading in one of the ponds.

Described here are two hikes that explore this large property. These may be done separately or combined as a longer outing. Both start at the main entrance.

Southern Section
From the south end of the parking lot near the gatehouse, follow yellow-blazed Yellow Trail along a wide, well-maintained path for a short distance to Echo Pond Trail, at junction 1. Continue straight on Yellow Trail, which skirts the shallow waters of Echo Pond. Stop for a moment on the wooden footbridge (near where Yellow Trail and Echo Pond Trail

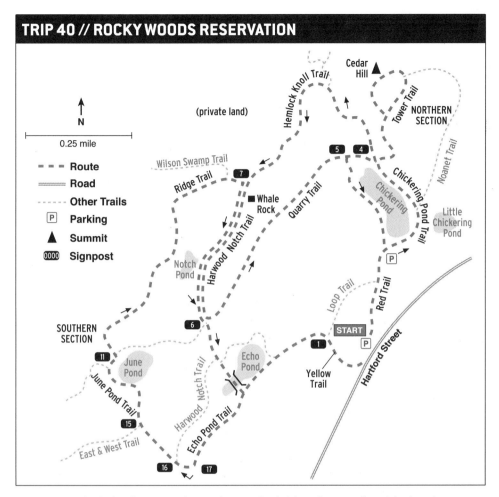

intersect) to look for frogs, turtles, and waterfowl. Then leave Yellow Trail and continue straight on Echo Pond Trail, heading in a southwesterly direction. This wide treadway is excellent for cross-country skiing, and the route has just enough slopes for excitement.

At the next intersection (junction 17), turn right; pass junction 16 and bear right at junction 15 onto June Pond Trail. This short path soon passes the west side of June Pond, which is often all but dry by midsummer. At the pond's northwest corner (junction 11), bear left onto 0.7-mile Ridge Trail. You will notice the trees and the terrain begin to change here. Beech and birch appear, and granite boulders—dropped during the retreat of the glaciers—fill the woods. This section of the hike makes clear the origin of the name Rocky Woods.

Walk along Ridge Trail to junction 7, where Harwood Notch Trail is on the right. Follow Harwood Notch Trail, rejoining the Yellow Trail loop, and soon you will see giant Whale Rock, stretching out like a beached whale on your left.

Continue on Harwood Notch Trail, keeping watch for a path that goes to the left beneath a sign that reads "Lookout Point." (The lookout is a narrow view that can be reached after a 4- or 5-minute walk.) Staying on Harwood Notch Trail, pass tiny Notch Pond on your right and then cross the intersection with Quarry Trail. About 400 feet after this intersection, you can either take the path on the left along the north end of Echo Pond or continue straight to the footbridge. From either route, turn left onto Echo Pond Trail/ Yellow Trail to return to the parking area.

Northern Section: Cedar Hill–Hemlock Knoll and Whale Rock Loop

This pleasant walk passes several attractions, including Chickering Pond and a scenic vista at the summit of Cedar Hill. From the parking area, follow Red Trail along the entrance road for roughly 0.25 mile to the start of the loop at Chickering Pond. Bear right and continue on Red Trail along the eastern shore of the scenic 5-acre pond. There is catch-and-release fishing here during the warmer months. Picnic tables and grills, some of which are ADA accessible, are scattered about the shoreline. Watch for great blue herons hunting along the shallow edges of the pond. You can also see kingfishers; it's thrilling to watch one dive from its perch and pluck its prey from the water. Chickering Pond is a good spot to fish with children because sunfish are relatively easy to catch here with worms or other bait. You never know when a largemouth bass might be hungry, so bring some lures as well. Remember, all fish you catch must be released.

At junction 4, a four-way intersection, turn right onto Tower Trail and ascend moderately steep Cedar Hill on an old gravel road. After approximately 0.25 mile, reach the partially exposed ridge. There is nothing quite so peaceful as gazing over the valleys and hills from multiple viewpoints, with cool breezes whispering through the cedars.

After enjoying the scenery, retrace your steps downhill to junction 4. Bear right on yellow-blazed Ridge Trail, walk a short distance, and then turn right onto Hemlock Knoll Trail at the next junction (unnumbered). One of the most interesting features in this section is the mini-canyon: a narrow, rocky passage that was formed during the time of the glaciers, when a stream passed through here.

At the end of Hemlock Knoll Trail, turn right, back onto yellow-blazed Ridge Trail. Continue to marker 7 and turn left onto Harwood Notch Trail. This leads to massive Whale Rock, where children will enjoy climbing. From Whale Rock, follow Harwood Notch Trail (also blazed yellow) past a short side path to a vista and Notch Pond. At junction 6, turn left onto Quarry Trail. On your way back to the parking area, you'll pass the remains of a quarry. In the early 1900s, blocks of stone were cut here and hauled out by horses and oxen. Drill marks can still be seen in the rocks. At junction 5, turn right to rejoin Red Trail. Follow it along Chickering Pond's western shore to complete the loop, and then return to the parking area. Witch hazel, sassafras, shagbark hickory, and dogwood can all be seen in the final quarter-mile.

DID YOU KNOW?

Rocky Woods' trails and ponds are artifacts of logging that began during the nineteenth century. The ponds were created as water sources for controlling forest fires, and the roads were built to transport timber and, later, granite from the quarry sites.

NEARBY

Medfield buildings on the National Register of Historic Places include the Peak House at 347 Main Street, which was burned during King Philip's War in 1676 and rebuilt. It is now

Boulders, such as this erratic, dot the landscape of the appropriately named Rocky Woods Reservation.

owned by the Medfield Historical Society and is open for tours. The Dwight-Derby House at 7 Friary Street, built in 1651, is one of the ten oldest homes in the United States. Restaurants are on and off Main Street (MA 109) and North Street.

MORE INFORMATION

The reservation is open year-round, sunrise to sunset. Parking is free for members of The Trustees of Reservations; for nonmembers, a $6 fee is payable at a self-serve station. Restrooms, picnic tables, and a universally accessible fishing platform are available. Dogs are allowed; follow posted leash rules.

4 // SOUTH OF BOSTON/CAPE COD

The southeast region of Massachusetts stretches from Boston's southern suburbs west and south to the Rhode Island border and Narragansett Bay, and south and east to Buzzards Bay and Cape Cod. As in other areas of eastern Massachusetts, it is home to a wide variety of natural features, although the topography is somewhat more level, with only scattered low hills, such as Moose Hill in Sharon and the distinctive Granite Hills of Borderland State Park in North Easton.

Natural communities include oak-hickory woodlands with diverse layers of shrubs and wildflowers, which thrive in rich, hospitable soils characteristic of the interior region. On Cape Cod and adjacent coastal areas, the dominant forest species are pitch pine and scrub oak (also known as bear oak), which are well adapted to sandy, impoverished soils and harsh growing conditions. Wetlands include tidal rivers, streams, and creeks; salt and freshwater marshes; bogs; and an extensive network of swamps. Hundreds of kettle ponds here were formed by melting blocks of ice as glaciers retreated from the landscape more than 10,000 years ago. The major rivers drop only a few feet from headwaters to mouth due to the level topography.

Along the mainland coast, 14,000-acre Myles Standish State Forest protects one of New England's largest pitch-pine and scrub oak forests, as well as a series of small kettle ponds. Nearby Ellisville Harbor State Park has a rocky beach that is home to a large colony of harbor seals during the winter months. Farther north, Great Esker Park in Weymouth includes a prominent glacial ridge that rises above Weymouth Back River and its marshes. West Island and Allens Pond Wildlife Sanctuary feature diverse habitats on Buzzards Bay and the Westport River watershed.

Cape Cod, a long, sandy peninsula formed by glacial deposits, is the southeast region's best-known landmark. Natural highlights of the Upper Cape, the area closest to the mainland, include Sandy Neck Beach, a 6-mile barrier beach bordered by a 3,500-acre salt marsh on Cape Cod Bay in Barnstable. The nearby Lowell Holly Reservation in Mashpee

Facing page: Arguably one of the best hikes on Cape Cod, Great Island offers an array of diverse marine life from whales to Atlantic horseshoe crabs to quahogs.

encompasses a small peninsula between two scenic freshwater ponds. One of the best destinations for exploring inland habitats is Nickerson State Park in Brewster, where extensive woodlands surround a series of kettle ponds. Roughly 300 of these glacial ponds, which are replenished by rainfall and groundwater alone, exist throughout Cape Cod.

Outer (or Lower) Cape Cod, which stretches from Chatham to Provincetown, is a narrow, ever-changing landscape that has been continually reshaped by the ocean and storms. In response to increasing development in the mid-twentieth century, 45,000-acre Cape Cod National Seashore was established during the 1960s. In addition to the famous ocean beaches that draw millions of visitors annually, its other natural features include Atlantic white cedar and red maple swamps; marshes and tidal flats; coastal pitch-pine, scrub oak, and beech forests; cranberry bogs; dunes; and historical sites. Most of the park's land lies on the ocean side, but one exception is Great Island, which is actually a peninsula that juts into Wellfleet Bay. Across the bay from Great Island are the tidal flats, creeks, and heaths of Wellfleet Bay Wildlife Sanctuary, home to wildlife that includes crabs, shorebirds, songbirds, and turtles.

MOOSE HILL WILDLIFE SANCTUARY

Moose Hill Wildlife Sanctuary protects nearly 2,000 acres and features trails, forests, fields, a red maple swamp, and a secluded hilltop with long views.

Features

Location Sharon, MA

Rating Moderate

Distance 2.5 miles (The Bluffs); 1.75 miles (Ovenbird/Kettle trails)

Elevation Gain 130 feet (The Bluffs); 50 feet (Ovenbird/Kettle trails)

Estimated Time 1.5 to 2 hours (The Bluffs); 1 hour (Ovenbird/Kettle trails)

Maps USGS Brockton, USGS Norwood; Mass Audubon: massaudubon.org/content/download/8080/145429/file/moosehill_trails.pdf

GPS coordinates 42° 07.409' N, 71° 12.434' W

Contact Mass Audubon: massaudubon.org/moosehill, 781-784-5691

DIRECTIONS

From I-95, take Exit 1 for US 1 north. Turn right onto MA 27, follow it 0.5 mile, and turn right onto Moose Hill Street. In 1.3 miles, turn left onto Moose Hill Parkway. The parking lot is immediately on your left.

By public transportation, take the Providence/Stoughton line of the MBTA Commuter Rail to the Sharon station. Walk to Depot Street, follow it north for two blocks, and turn left onto Moose Hill Parkway. Walk about a mile and bear left at Upland Road to stay on Moose Hill Parkway. Continue to the top of the hill; the visitor center is on the right.

TRAIL DESCRIPTION

The Bluffs

Moose Hill Wildlife Sanctuary features varied topography. As in many areas of New England, the forests here were cleared for agriculture in Colonial times but have grown back. The sanctuary offers 25 miles of walking trails, and one of the most popular leads to the Bluffs, offering one of the best views in eastern Massachusetts. Stunted cedar trees and sheer rock walls give the illusion that this is a hilltop in Maine, New Hampshire, or Vermont. And for scenery this impressive, the trip to the top is surprisingly gentle.

From the sanctuary entrance, follow Moose Hill Parkway and cross Moose Hill Street, watching for light traffic. Look for the stone pillars that mark the entrance to Billings Loop Trail. The trail follows a wide gravel road that's easy on the legs. Stone walls and large sugar

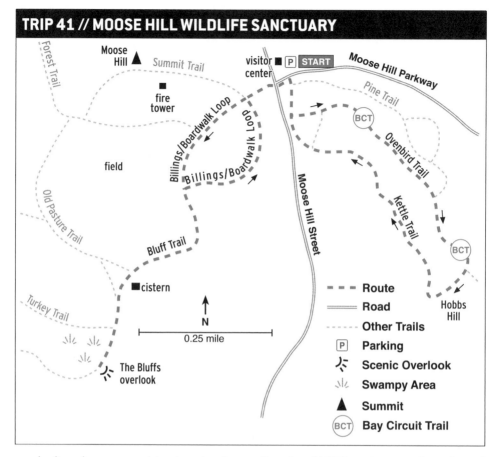

maples line the route, making it a visual treat. Pass the old Billings barn on the right and two enormous maples on the left. A short way from the maples, enter a circular opening in the woods and continue on Billings Loop Trail. Soon you will enter another open area, with low-lying plants and bushes. More than 400 species of wildflowers grow here, as well as 27 species of ferns, and thanks to the high elevations in the sanctuary, yellow and white birches add to the feeling of being in the New Hampshire North Country. Spring is the best time to see the woodland wildflowers bloom. Numerous nest boxes in the fields provide homes for tree swallows, black-capped chickadees, and bluebirds.

At a marked junction in a field, bear right onto Bluff Trail and follow it into the woods. (Those looking for a shorter hike can continue to the left on Billings Loop Trail through a red maple swamp on a boardwalk.) The exposed roots seem to grab at your boots, but the grades are gentle. A maple, oak, and pine forest surrounds the trail. On the left at about 0.7 mile, pass a huge, round cistern dug into the earth and lined with stones. Like the stone walls and old chimney remains scattered through these woods, it is an artifact of past land use. Cisterns are used to catch and store rainwater; they differ from wells in that they are lined with waterproof materials. Bluff Trail now becomes part of two thru-trails, Warner Trail and the Bay Circuit Trail. Just beyond the cistern is an impressive stand of beech trees on the left and a swampy area on the right. Stay straight (left) where Old Pasture and Turkey trails branch to the right.

Look for red and gray squirrels scrambling on the branches overhead. Other animals in the sanctuary include skunks, opossums, foxes, raccoons, fishers, coyotes, and deer. All are nocturnal, so your best chance to catch a glimpse of them is at dawn or dusk. The birdlife is varied and easier to see. It includes warblers, nuthatches, scarlet tanagers, northern orioles, bluebirds, woodpeckers, and a wide assortment of raptors, such as kestrels, red-tailed hawks, and broad-winged hawks.

The gradual climb to the Bluffs starts here. The designers of the trail knew what they were doing when they picked this route to the summit: It never gets steep and is a relatively easy walk to the top. As you begin your final steps to the summit, note the gnarled and windswept branches of the eastern red cedars that dot the hilltop. These trees can be distinguished from white cedars by their needlelike leaves with bluish-green berries. Birds eat these hard fruits.

At the 1-mile mark of your hike, the granite ledge at the 491-foot overlook offers sweeping views to the south and west. Gillette Stadium, home of the New England Patriots, is visible a few miles off. This is one of the nicest hilltops in eastern Massachusetts; it's the perfect place to sit, gaze off into the distance, and let your mind wander. You'll hear little more than the breeze as it whispers through the trees. Various outcroppings along this ridge offer vista changes. Use caution along the edge, as the dropoff is steep. In fall, you might see a hawk riding a thermal—a column of warm, rising air—on its migration.

When you are ready to head home, retrace your steps to the parking lot. If you are feeling ambitious, try Forest Trail, which adds about 1.2 miles to your trek with its long loop at the northern end of the property (see map).

Ovenbird/Kettle Trails

On another visit, you may want to hike the less traveled eastern end of the property. Coyotes have been seen here, and it may be only a matter of time before more are spotted in this secluded area. The trails are reached via the white-blazed Bay Circuit Trail and Warner Trail, which enters the woods across the road from the parking area. This trail soon turns left to follow Ovenbird Trail, which descends gradually through an oak-pine woodland, passing a junction with Pine Trail. After about a 10-minute walk, the combined Ovenbird/Warner/BCT path follows a bubbling brook. Swamp maples soon mix in with the other trees as the trail veers to the southeast. Woodland wildflowers abound here: pink lady's slipper, jack-in-the-pulpit, and maple-leaf viburnum, to name just a few. It's impressive to see plants with such dazzling displays of color in a natural setting.

At about 0.6 mile, reach a T junction where Ovenbird Trail meets Kettle Trail. For a longer hike, take the path on the left that leads to Hobbs Hill Loop, which makes a mile-long circuit around 342-foot Hobbs Hill near the sanctuary boundary, or continue straight on Kettle Trail. This trail got its name from the many kettle holes formed by huge blocks of ice left by the glaciers roughly 10,000 years ago. It is rugged in spots, hugging the ridges, called eskers. The eskers formed when streams, flowing beneath the glacial ice sheets, deposited sediments along the streambed, which became the thin ridgeline. The basin along Kettle Trail was once home to beautiful groves of rhododendrons and mountain

Northern green frogs are found in wetlands throughout eastern Massachusetts, but it pays to look closely or they may be missed.

laurels, but these were largely eaten by deer. Kettle Trail loops through the forest back toward the Bay Circuit and Warner trails and the trailhead, leading through a stand of hemlocks and then past a lush green field on the left. Backtrack across Moose Hill Parkway to the visitor center.

DID YOU KNOW?

The hill that the sanctuary now stewards was named long ago, and there are several theories behind the name. *Moose* is an Algonkin word, so the name may predate Colonial settlement. The hill is said to be shaped like a moose's hump, which would have been more easily visualized after settlers had cleared the forests for agricultural use. Historical records of early Sharon tell of a man having a startling encounter with a moose.

NEARBY

Sharon's historical district is on both sides of North Main Street, from Post Office Square to School Street. Among the old homes are the houses of patriots Job Swift and Deborah Sampson Gannett. Several restaurants are on North Main and South Main streets, not far from the sanctuary. The sanctuary is a short drive from Borderland State Park and Lake Massapoag (see Trip 42).

MORE INFORMATION

The visitor center is open Wednesday through Sunday, 9 A.M. to 4 P.M., and trails are open seven days a week, dawn to dusk. Pets are not allowed. Admission is free for Mass Audubon members and Sharon residents; otherwise, it's $4 for adults, $3 for children and seniors. The sanctuary offers programs for children, families, adults, and groups, as well as events including the Maple Sugaring Festival in March and the Halloween Prowl in October. Vernal Pool Trail is a great place to look for frogs and other wetland creatures. The sanctuary offers Quest Packs for Vernal Pool and Kettle trails (similar to a geocache) that are available at the visitor center and on its website. In addition, there is an on-site community-supported agriculture (subscription) organic farm.

 **BORDERLAND STATE PARK**

The level walking trails at Borderland State Park lead to close-up views of ponds, fields, and forests.

Features 🚶 🐕 💧 ⚲ 🎿 ⛺ 💲 🏇 🚲

Location North Easton, MA

Rating Moderate

Distance 3.5-mile loop

Elevation Gain 50 feet

Estimated Time 1.75 hours

Maps USGS Brockton; Massachusetts Department of Conservation and Recreation: mass.gov/doc/borderland-state-park-trail-map/download

GPS coordinates 42° 03.641′ N, 71° 10.023′ W

Contact Massachusetts Department of Conservation and Recreation: mass.gov/locations/borderland-state-park, 508-238-6566

DIRECTIONS

From I-95, take Exit 17 and follow South Main Street 3.3 miles to Sharon Center. Turn right onto Billings Street at the traffic signal and then immediately right again onto Pond Street. Stay south on Pond Street for 0.9 mile to a small rotary and then continue on Massapoag Avenue. Drive 3.6 miles on Massapoag Avenue to the park entrance on the left.

TRAIL DESCRIPTION

Borderland was opened as a state park in 1971. Before that, the property served as the country estate of the Ames family, who named it Borderland because it is on the border of Sharon and Easton. The family constructed the stone mansion in 1910, and the house is open year-round for regularly scheduled guided tours.

Hiking alongside water always makes an outing more interesting, and Borderland State Park features six ponds to explore. Add to that the flat hayfields and the option to test your legs on hilly, rocky terrain, and Borderland has something for everyone. The park can be a popular place, but with 1,843 acres it's easy to find the quiet and solitude that make hiking appealing to many people. Small, rocky hills cover the northern acres, while flatter land lies to the south.

You can make either a 3-mile circle around Leach Pond via Pond Walk Trail or a 3.5-mile walk by continuing around Upper Leach Pond. An excellent map is posted near the visitor center. This hike begins next to the visitor center, at a fork in the trail; bear left to start your walk on a portion of the white-blazed Bay Circuit Trail on the north side of the ponds.

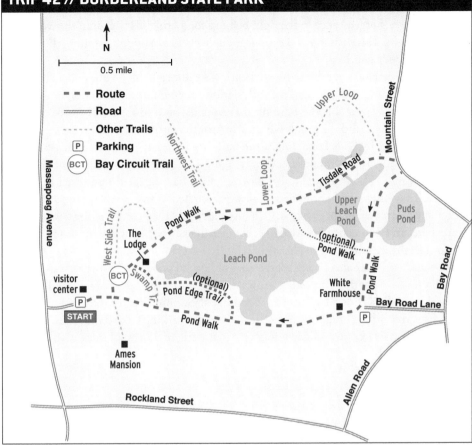

(Follow the sign to Leach Pond.) The trail leads down to the water's edge, where a stone building called the Lodge is located. The pondside trails are wide, flat, and well maintained—excellent for cross-country skiing. This is also a good spot for viewing waterfowl.

Continue to follow the route straight at a junction with West Side Trail, where the Bay Circuit Trail leaves to the left. (The route is unmarked from this point but easy to follow.) At various intervals, benches offer scenic views of the islands near Leach Pond's center. Near the junction with Northwest Trail, you will see a wetland and fields to the right that deer are said to frequent. Farther up the pondside trail on the left is a little stone cave that was probably a farmer's root cellar but could make a good home for the Virginia opossums that have been seen in the park in recent years.

Separating Leach Pond from Upper Leach Pond is Long Dam, built by the Ames family to create Leach Pond in 1939. If you wish to limit your walk to 3 miles, turn right here, cross the wooden footbridge over the stream, follow the path to its end, and go right to reach the parking lot. To complete the 3.5-mile loop, continue following the pondside trail (now Tisdale Road) to the northeast. You may wish to detour to the left on one of the Granite Hills trails, which explore open fields and lead to views of two secluded ponds. The main pondside trail, Tisdale Road, takes you around Upper Leach Pond and eventually to the old Tisdale cellar hole, near Mountain Street, where there is a beautiful vista of Upper Leach Pond. The trail intersects with Mountain Street, and you must follow this paved town road for a short distance to the right before a footpath leads back into the woods at a gate on the right. This path soon takes you through a field to a bridge spanning the outflow stream from Puds Pond.

Some of Borderland's ponds are covered with waterlilies and blue-flowered pickerelweed in summer. All the ponds are shallow, with significant amounts of vegetation growing. As the vegetation dies and fills the bottom of the ponds, swamp shrubs begin to encroach along the shorelines, and the ponds will slowly turn to marsh.

After the bridge by Puds Pond, follow the trail through a large restored agricultural field all the way to a white farmhouse and bear right. The fields and wooden fence here are especially scenic. Watch for red-tailed hawks, which have adapted fairly well to human presence. They often can be seen near highways, perched in trees and keeping a sharp eye out for any movement in the grassy strips along the roads. They are one of the few birds that winter here, and Thoreau acknowledged their hardiness when he wrote of "the hawk with warrior-like firmness abiding the blasts of winter."

The wide, level trail next passes a large cove of Leach Pond, a good spot to watch waterfowl. A few rare Atlantic white cedars grow adjacent to the cove, and Pond Edge Trail is on the right. Take Pond Edge Trail, Quiet Woods Trail, Swamp Trail, or the main trail (Pond Walk) back toward the Lodge, bearing left to the main parking lot and the Ames mansion. Pond Edge Trail is recommended, as it is a pleasant walk off the main route with attractive views of the pond.

DID YOU KNOW?

Before the Ames family owned the property, the ponds and streams powered multiple facilities at various times during the eighteenth and early nineteenth centuries, including a sawmill, a nail factory, a cotton mill, and an ironworks. The nearby land was cleared for farming, and stone walls can still be seen crisscrossing the woodlands.

NEARBY

On the way to Borderland, you'll pass 353-acre Lake Massapoag. The lake is the headwater of the Canoe River and is a summer resort area that includes a large town beach. It is also popular with sailors and sailboarders. Restaurants in Sharon are on North Main and South Main streets. For day-trippers, Borderland can be combined with a visit to nearby Moose Hill Wildlife Sanctuary (Trip 41).

MORE INFORMATION

The park offers organized hikes and educational programs. Challenging mountain-bike trails are very popular as well, mostly on the northern side. Parking fees ($5 for Massachusetts-registered vehicles, $20 for out-of-state vehicles) are charged at the main entrance parking lots.

A day-hiker takes a break at Borderland State Park, which offers hikes for all ability levels, families, and dogs. *Photo by Ryan Smith/Rooted in Light Media.*

AMES NOWELL STATE PARK

This hike offers a variety of wildlife and terrain, from woods to water.

Features

Location Abington, MA

Rating Easy

Distance 2-mile loop

Elevation Gain Minimal

Estimated Time 1 hour

Maps USGS Abington; Massachusetts Department of Conservation and Recreation: mass.gov/doc/ames-nowell-state-park-trail-map/download

GPS coordinates 42° 06.895′ N, 70° 58.570′ W

Contact Massachusetts Department of Conservation and Recreation: mass.gov/locations/ames-nowell-state-park, 781-857-1336

DIRECTIONS
From MA 3 south, take Exit 38 for MA 18 south. (If traveling north on MA 3, take Exit 38 for MA 18 south and turn left at the end of the exit ramp.) Follow MA 18 for 6.2 miles to the center of Abington and the intersection with MA 123. Turn right and take the next right onto Rockland Street. After 0.7 mile, bear left to remain on Rockland Street. At the end of Rockland Street, turn right onto Linwood Street and follow it to its end.

TRAIL DESCRIPTION
This scenic property features an 88-acre pond, a waterfall, brooks, boardwalks, and approximately 7 miles of hiking trails. Due to its proximity to Brockton and other densely populated towns, you might want to arrive early in the morning to have the trails to yourself and to improve your chances of seeing wildlife.

Go to the front of the information kiosk after you park. Locate the road about 50 feet ahead of you and take it downhill toward the pond. Follow this road about 200 feet and bear left toward the water, ignoring paths on your right.

You will soon reach the dam at the southern end of Cleveland Pond, also known as Ames Pond. The artificial pond was formed in 1920 when Beaver Brook was dammed. At the time, the Holmes family owned the land. On a concrete marker near where the water flows over the dam, look for an etching with "1920" and the words "Semloh Pond"—"Semloh" is Holmes spelled backward.

No matter the name, it's an attractive body of water that supports a range of warmwater fish, such as largemouth bass, pickerel, crappie, and sunfish. (The boat launch is open June

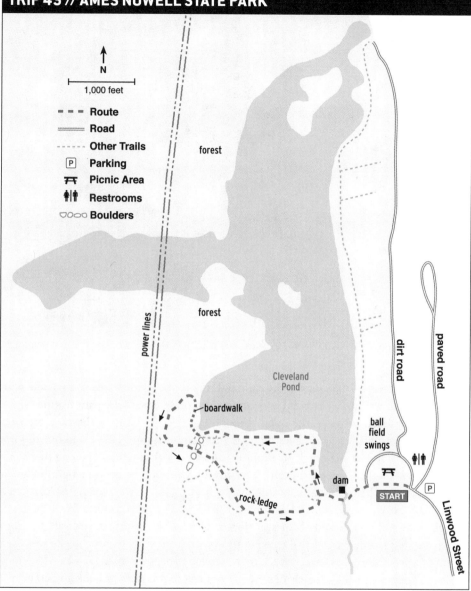

through September for canoes or kayaks; motorized boats are not allowed.) White and yellow waterlilies and purple pickerelweed grace the pond with color in the warm-weather months. The elegant flowers of the pickerelweed are funnel-shaped and bloom from June until fall. Its heart-shaped leaves taper to a point. Along the edge of the pond you will find blueberries, huckleberries, raspberries, and sweet pepperbush, with its pleasant summertime scent. In winter, you may see animal tracks in the snow.

A footbridge spans the brook that tumbles from a dam spillway at the pond. There is a pleasant picnic area on the other side, along the banks of the brook. Cross the footbridge,

Dragonflies are among the wildlife—frogs, snakes, raccoons, butterflies, birds, deer, turkey—you might spot at Ames Nowell State Park.

continue across the earthen dam to its end, and stay to the right to follow a narrow path that hugs the shoreline of the pond and enters the woods. The rocky path features small hills and occasional views of the pond through the foliage. Most of the trees are oak, although a few small American chestnut trees grow from stumps. Pass a trail on your left but continue to follow the pond. At about 0.5 mile, walk through an opening in a stone wall and pass another trail on the left. A boardwalk will soon be on your right; follow it over the wetlands. In autumn, the swamp maples here are ablaze with color. Also called red maples, they thrive in wet soil and are among the first trees to turn color in New England, sometimes as early as the end of August. Be sure to look beneath the boardwalk for frogs and snakes hidden in the grass. Raccoons also prowl both the swamp and the shoreline looking for freshwater mussels, crayfish, frogs, salamanders, fish, snakes, and a wide range of plants. They use their extremely dexterous front feet to probe every nook and cranny.

On the other side of the boardwalk the trail splits. Before continuing to the right along the pond's edge, take time to go left on the trail for a few feet. After you reach the power-line clearing, walk to the right a few more feet and climb a rock overlooking a portion of the park. The clearing beneath the power lines is a good place to see butterflies and birds, such as the kestrel, which hunts insects and small rodents. If you are here early, you might also see a white-tailed deer, a red fox, or a wild turkey.

Raccoons, pheasants, and quail live in the park, and muskrats live along the banks of the pond. Sightings of nesting marsh hawks and several other species of hawks, including red-tailed and sharp-shinned, are possible near the picnic area by the pond. A fully mature sharp-shinned hawk is about 10 inches long with a wingspan of 21 inches, and it is fairly common along the edges of the woods. It has a brown-and-tan pattern on its underside and a long, narrow tail. Sharp-shinned hawks often fly above the treetops in the early morning and soar higher at midday. Small birds are their preferred prey.

Retrace your steps to the pond and continue northward. Soon you will pass a clearing with a large rock by the edge of the pond, which makes a good rest stop. Scan the water for wading birds, such as great blue herons; you might also spot a belted kingfisher, which does not wade but scouts from branches along the water's edge. Both birds feed primarily on small fish. Ospreys are also seen here during brief periods in spring and fall, when they're migrating. The pondside path continues north for another quarter-mile before ending at the water's edge.

To return to the parking area, retrace your steps to the boardwalk. Once you cross the boardwalk, you can take a different trail back. Follow the unnamed trail to the right and make a quick left onto another unnamed trail that leads eastward. This trail is fairly level, passing small oaks and gray birches. Ignore the side paths on your left that connect back with the pondside trail.

About five minutes down this unnamed trail, a rock ledge on your right makes a good resting spot in the sun. From here it's only another five minutes back to the dam and parking area.

DID YOU KNOW?

Visitors who thoroughly explore the park may be rewarded by finding the gravestone of a veteran of the French and Indian War and the American Revolution. Joseph Richards Jr., who died in 1785, is buried at the northeast corner of Cleveland Pond, near a brook.

NEARBY

Fuller Craft Museum, off Oak Street in Brockton, is an interesting oasis of modern handcrafts, about 4 miles from Ames Nowell State Park. Children's classes are offered, as well as entertainment and an array of demonstrations. See fullercraft.org for more information.

Many restaurants and businesses are in central Abington, near the intersections of MA 18 and MA 123.

MORE INFORMATION

The park is open year-round, sunrise to sunset; no fee. Restrooms have not been available recently; portable toilet facilities may be in place. Dogs are allowed but must be leashed.

44 GREAT ESKER PARK

Easy trails exploring a glacial esker lead to views of Weymouth Back River and a salt marsh.

Features

Location Weymouth, MA

Rating Easy

Distance 1.5-mile loop

Elevation Gain 285 feet

Estimated Time 1 hour

Maps USGS Weymouth

GPS coordinates 42° 14.178′ N, 70° 55.905′ W

Contact Weymouth Recreation Department: weymouth.ma.us/recreation, 781-682-6124

DIRECTIONS

From MA 3, take Exit 38B for MA 18 south. (If traveling north on MA 3, take Exit 38 for MA 18 south and turn left at the end of the exit ramp.) At the first traffic light, turn left onto Middle Street. At the end of Middle Street, in 2.9 miles, bear left onto Commercial Street and proceed 0.4 mile to the first traffic light. Turn right onto Green Street and go 0.6 mile to the triangular divider. Bear right onto Elva Road and go uphill 0.2 mile to the road's end and park in the large lot adjacent to a playground.

By public transportation, take the MBTA Red Line to Quincy Center and transfer to the number 220 bus. Ride it to Riverway Plaza on Bridge Street (MA 3A). Walk west for a short distance along Bridge Street to Great Esker Park.

TRAIL DESCRIPTION

With a little imagination, a walk on top of the glacial esker at Great Esker Park is like walking on the back of a giant snake. Created by glacial deposits during the last ice age about 12,000 years ago, the 1.25-mile-long esker rises above the woodlands and the marsh, reaching a height of 90 feet. Eskers were formed when rivers within retreating glaciers filled with debris as the ice melted. The walk described here leads to fine views of Weymouth Back River (also called Back River) and its associated salt marshes.

For the Reversing Falls loop, follow the paved road (closed to vehicles) that begins to the right of the maintenance buildings in the parking area. Within five minutes you'll reach the top of the esker, at an intersection with an unnamed paved path that follows the contours of the esker. Turn left and walk along the top of the esker in a northerly direction,

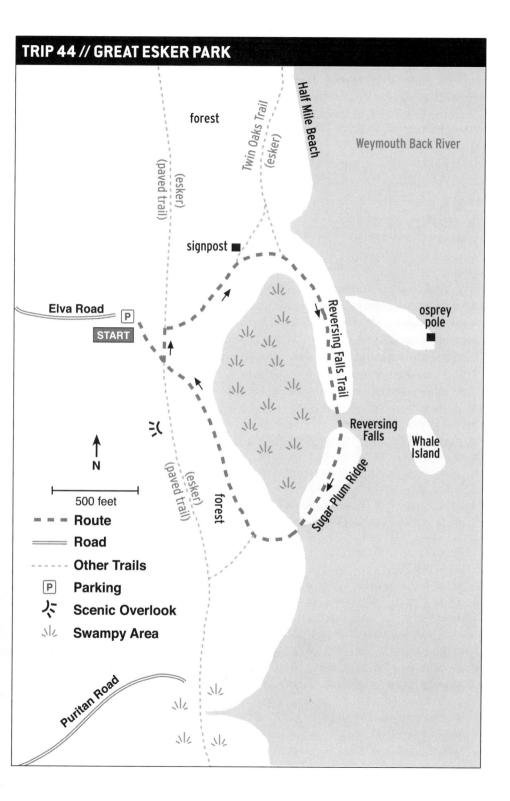

forest

Twin Oaks Trail

(esker)

Half Mile Beach

Weymouth Back River

(esker)
(paved trail)

signpost ■

Elva Road

P

START

Reversing Falls Trail

osprey
pole
■

N

500 feet

Reversing
Falls

Whale
Island

Sugar Plum Ridge

- - - Route

===== Road

- - - - Other Trails

P Parking

人 Scenic Overlook

心 Swampy Area

(esker)
(paved trail)

forest

Puritan Road

passing beneath oaks (red oaks have bristle-tipped lobes; white oaks have rounded lobes) and maples. In the understory are gray birch and staghorn sumac. Staghorn sumac gets its name from the velvet covering its stems that looks like the velvet on a stag's antlers. It is nonpoisonous and especially colorful in autumn, when the leaves are dark crimson.

In roughly 200 feet, at a sign for Reversing Falls, turn right (Twin Oaks Trail is to the left) and follow an unnamed dirt path downhill toward a salt marsh in the basin below. At the next intersection, bear right and continue toward Reversing Falls, keeping the marsh on your right. The path follows the edge of the marsh; look through the trees to spot birds feeding in the grass. Watch for wood ducks, snowy egrets, great egrets, and even an occasional little blue heron in the marsh. In winter, look for bald eagles, which are fairly new to the area, in the tops of trees.

The trail climbs a smaller esker and turns right at the top of the ridge. Good views of the marsh are on both sides; to your left, near Reversing Falls, you will see a pole that ospreys use as a nesting platform. These magnificent birds have successfully bred here since 1992. They enjoy an abundance of fish in Weymouth Back River and nearby Whitman's Pond, and they generally return to the area at the time of the herring run in spring.

After a quarter-mile, the trail reaches Reversing Falls, where there are scenic views across Weymouth Back River and the adjacent salt marsh. The "falls" are not a waterfall but instead a narrow passageway between two sections of the marsh, where water rushes in at high tide and exits at low tide.

The salt marsh and estuary at Great Esker are quite large. More than 30 species of fish can be found here, including flounder, bluefish, striped bass, eel, herring, and smelt. Many

The salt marsh and estuary of the Weymouth Back River offer habitat for fish and other intertidal marine life.

young fish and invertebrates grow up here, finding shelter in the dense grasses. Beneath the water's surface, a variety of creatures, such as soft-shell clams, shrimp, and worms, live and feed on top of or beneath the mud. Crabs use the tides to their advantage, burrowing in the mud at low tide for protection and scavenging along the bottom at high tide. Each spring, there is a herring run up Weymouth Back River to Whitman's Pond, where the fish spawn in the freshwater.

At low tide, you can use stepping-stones to traverse the passage. At high tide, remove your shoes and carefully wade across.

On the other side of the passage, follow the unnamed, narrow trail that crosses Sugar Plum Ridge, offering attractive views of Weymouth Back River and Whale Island. Look for mute swans on the water. Lowbush blueberries are scattered about the woods beneath the oaks. At the end of Sugar Plum Ridge, traverse another low-lying area (remove your shoes at high tide) and follow the trail straight into the woods, bypassing a side path on your left. In a couple of minutes, bear to the right, walking beneath a power line. At the next fork, stay to the right. (Going straight leads directly to the paved trail on top of the esker.) After passing through a grove of beech trees with smooth gray trunks, walk beneath the power line again, with the esker on your left.

After about three-quarters of a mile, the trail swings left and climbs to the top of the esker, where it intersects the paved road. From here, return to the parking area.

DID YOU KNOW?

Weymouth was once a hub for shipbuilding. In 1884, one of the largest schooners ever built was launched from Keen's Shipyard into the Fore River in Weymouth. According to historical accounts, 1,000 people were aboard the four-masted, 209-foot *Haroldine* when it was launched.

NEARBY

Webb Memorial State Park on River Street offers walking, picnicking, fishing, and views of Boston from a peninsula that juts into Hingham Bay. Boats to the Boston Harbor Islands depart from neighboring Hewitt's Cove. Wompatuck State Park, off Free Street in nearby Hingham, features hiking trails, 12 miles of paved bicycling trails, and more than 260 campsites. Restaurants are along and off Washington Street in Weymouth.

MORE INFORMATION

The park is open year-round, sunrise to sunset; no fee; no restrooms. Dogs are allowed but must be leashed. In season, the town of Weymouth offers kayaking and other outdoor recreation classes and opportunities.

CLIMATE CHANGE IN NEW ENGLAND

When you stroll along a riverside path or climb a mountain in New England, you might imagine you're seeing the same landscape enjoyed by Longfellow, Thoreau, and Metacomet. Due to climate change, however, you're not. The forests and their inhabitants are changing rapidly in ways our forefathers never could have predicted.

Flowers in New England bloom 2.3 days earlier for each temperature increase of 1 degree Fahrenheit. Most visibly, maple trees, hemlocks, and spruces are likely to die off as a result of higher temperatures and invasive pests. In the future, pockets of these trees may survive on colder, north-facing folds of northern mountains, but unless fossil fuel emissions are significantly reduced, future generations of hikers and nature lovers in central and southern New England won't know the landscapes we admire today.

Most scientists predict that in the next 75 years, New England's currently diverse flora could closely resemble North Carolina's pine and oak forests, with fewer evergreens, less boreal forest, and disappearing wildlife—consequences of modern civilization that were unforeseen just a few decades ago. Changes are expected to hit New England especially hard, affecting weather patterns and animal habitat from the ocean to the mountains.

Scientists have documented steady increases in temperatures across the Northeast—an average of 2 degrees Fahrenheit since 1970—and predict as much as a 10-degree increase in the next 85 years. These increases have allowed invasive species of plants and insects to flourish and to kill native flora. Changes in temperature can weaken native species and make them more susceptible to disease and invasive pests.

Animals have been affected as well. For example, the moose population has plummeted as the tick population has increased. Scientists have documented so many blood-draining ticks on moose that the animals become anemic and weak. Young moose can die before they are old enough to reproduce. Shorter winters are taking a toll, too, forcing cold-weather animals to adapt to warmer temperatures, and leading moose to rest on hot days instead of foraging for food. Migration patterns for various species are changing as well.

Watchful and concerned scientists from local observatories, universities, and conservation groups are studying and quantifying the creeping effects of climate change in New England and are putting in place plans to slow these repercussions. Their efforts include the Regional Greenhouse Gas Initiative, which caps the amount of carbon dioxide a power plant can emit. The Appalachian Mountain Club's Mountain Watch program encourages citizen scientists to monitor alpine flowers, tracking climate change's impact. Learn more at outdoors.org/conservation/priorities/land-and-trails/community-science and outdoors .org/conservation/action-center.

WORLD'S END RESERVATION

Tremendous views, rolling fields leading to the ocean's edge, and an impressive assortment of flora and fauna make for a beautiful walk.

Features 👣 🐕 💧 🔍 ⛷ ✳ 🚌 💲

Location Hingham, MA

Rating Moderate

Distance 4.5-mile loop

Elevation Gain 300 feet

Estimated Time 3 hours

Maps USGS Hull; The Trustees of Reservations: thetrustees.org/wp-content/uploads/2020/07/Worlds-End-Trail-Map.pdf

GPS coordinates 42° 15.490′ N, 70° 52.412′ W

Contact The Trustees of Reservations: thetrustees.org/place/worlds-end-hingham, 781-740-7233

DIRECTIONS

From MA 3, take Exit 35 to MA 228 north. Drive 6.5 miles to MA 3A and turn left. Proceed on MA 3A for 1.2 miles; then turn right onto Summer Street and proceed 0.5 mile. Turn left onto Martin's Lane at the light and continue 0.7 mile to the entrance and parking area.

By public transportation, from the MBTA Quincy Center Red Line station, take the number 220 bus (Hingham Depot) and exit at the intersection of North Street and Otis Street. From here, it is a 1-mile walk to World's End Reservation (walk northeast; Otis Street joins with Summer Street).

TRAIL DESCRIPTION

World's End, a peninsula jutting out from the mainland that separates Hingham Harbor from the mouth of Weir River, provides magnificent views in every direction. The rolling, open terrain will make you feel like you're on the landscaped grounds of an English estate. World's End has escaped development a many times; the property has been considered for projects ranging from a nuclear generator to public housing—even as a possible site for the United Nations. In 1967, local residents raised the money for The Trustees of Reservations to purchase the property.

Every season is a good one at World's End. In summer, there are cool ocean breezes; in fall, the foliage is alive with color; in winter, the cross-country skiing is superb when there's enough snow to cover the gentle slopes; and in spring, flowering trees, such as the

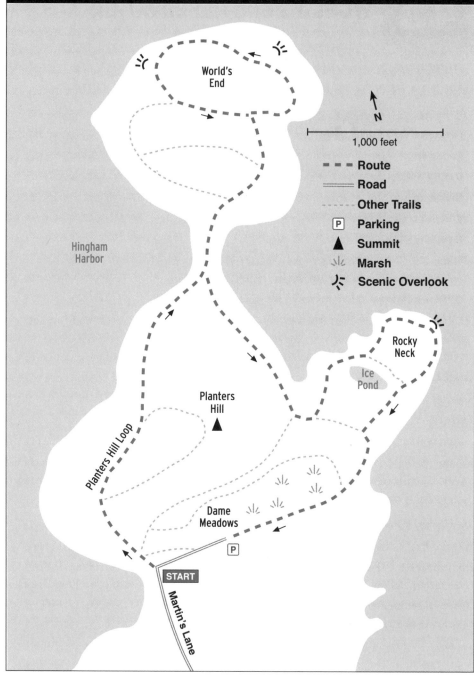

World's
End

N

1,000 feet

- - - Route
——— Road
- - - Other Trails
P Parking
▲ Summit
⸕ Marsh
⅄ Scenic Overlook

Hingham
Harbor

Rocky
Neck

Ice
Pond

Planters
Hill
▲

Planters Hill Loop

Dame
Meadows

P

START

Martin's Lane

sweet-smelling apple tree, show off their blooms. World's End is also a prime spot for viewing migratory birds, including wintering sea ducks.

After entering the reservation, take Planters Hill Loop to the left, which leads to two smooth hills. The trails here include roughly 4 miles of carriage roads that were designed by Frederick Law Olmsted during the 1890s as part of a proposed subdivision that was never built. Just a short way up the path is a sweeping vista of Boston Harbor, with the city's skyline rising in the distance. At about 0.5 mile, the trail climbs 120-foot Planters Hill, which is the highest point on the reservation. Along the way, benches are placed at some of the more strategic points for capturing the views.

From Planters Hill, the trail descends to the sandbar that links the Planters Hill drumlin to the main World's End drumlin. Early settlers built this causeway, known as "the bar," to allow travel between the two drumlins during high tide. Crossing the causeway allows easy access to the rocky beach. It's a perfect spot for children to explore. As you climb the outer hill at about 0.7 mile, look back toward Planters Hill and admire the topography. The outer drumlin has two connecting roads that loop around this island's two highest mounds.

Clumps of woodlands, primarily composed of eastern red cedar and tall hardwoods, such as maple and oak, provide habitat for a variety of small animals hunted by hawks. Lichen-covered stone walls are visible in some spots, remnants of the area's former agricultural days. Also visible along the woods and in the meadows is poison ivy. Learn to recognize the plant's three-leaf stems and give it a wide berth.

Walking in World's End Reservation feels like stepping back in time; the rolling hills and landscaped grounds are reminiscent of an English estate. *Photo by Liz West, Creative Commons on Flickr.*

Familiar small mammals of New England here include the red fox, an extremely human-shy animal that relies on its strong sense of smell to avoid interaction. Foxes have learned to live in close proximity to us by making nocturnal forays to hunt for mice, moles, and other rodents. The cottontail rabbit, a significant prey species for foxes and coyotes, also thrives in this combination of fields, shrubs, and patches of woods. Cottontails were once much more common in New England, when farmlands, rather than forests and development, dominated the region.

After exploring this area, cross the sandy causeway again and bear left onto an unnamed road that leads to Rocky Neck. Through the trees on the left, you can see the jagged cliffs of Rocky Neck standing in contrast to the smooth hills you have just traveled. Bear left at the next fork in the trail, and take the first left after that. As you enter Rocky Neck, the open landscape transitions to a more intimate woods, where the trail is often shaded. You will soon come to the edge of a cliff that rises 50 feet above the water.

Ice Pond, built by farmers in 1909 as a wintertime source of ice, adds to the enchanting character of Rocky Neck and attracts wildlife. Mallards, wide-ranging ducks that often form flocks with shyer black ducks, are common. They are surface feeders that eat aquatic vegetation and an occasional insect or mollusk. The males have green heads, white neck bands, and rust-colored breasts. Females are a mottled brown. Both sexes have a distinctive blue rectangle at the hind area of their wings. When you surprise a mallard, it may let out a loud quack and take off nearly vertically.

After following the perimeter of Rocky Neck, the trail soon intersects with another trail. Turn left onto the unnamed trail and follow it past the northeastern end of a marshy area. Just as you reach a section of hemlock trees on a knoll, about a quarter-mile down the trail, there is a cart path through a field on the right. This leads to the boardwalk that passes through tall cattails and marsh grass. (You can hear the birds in the reeds, but it's often impossible to see them.) Just ahead, a rock ledge offers a sweeping vista of the marsh. The ledge can easily be climbed from the rear, and it's a great place to sit and watch a few minutes of marsh life unfold.

From the ledge, it's only a short walk to the parking lot by continuing on this foot trail or by returning to the cart path near the hemlocks and going right.

DID YOU KNOW?

In pre-Colonial times, World's End was an island when tides were high. Then colonists dammed the adjacent salt marsh for the purpose of growing hay.

NEARBY

Restaurants are along and off North Street near the center of Hingham. Wompatuck State Park, off Free Street, offers hiking trails, paved bicycling trails, and more than 260 campsites (140 have electricity). The Whitney and Thayer Woods property (see Trip 46) is a short drive from World's End.

MORE INFORMATION

World's End is open year-round, 8 A.M. to sunset on weekdays and 7 A.M. to sunset on weekends. Admission is free for members of The Trustees of Reservations; nonmembers pay $10 per vehicle on weekdays and $15 per vehicle on weekends. Parking passes for specific arrival times are sold online at thetrustees.org—they are not sold at the reservation.

Visitors are welcome to bring their own food and drink for consumption on-site, but alcoholic beverages are prohibited. World's End has a carry-in/carry-out trash policy. Dogs are allowed but must be leashed. Swimming is prohibited. Horseback riding is by permit only. Portable restrooms are available.

46 WHITNEY AND THAYER WOODS

Depending on the season, these peaceful, well-maintained woodland trails offer easy hiking, cross-country skiing, or views of colorful rhododendrons.

Features

Location Hingham and Cohasset, MA

Rating Easy

Distance 3-mile loop

Elevation Gain 200 feet

Estimated Time 1.75 hours

Maps USGS Cohasset; The Trustees of Reservations: thetrustees.org/wp-content/uploads/2020/07/Weir-River-Farm-Whitney-Thayer-Trail-Map.pdf

GPS coordinates 42° 14.046' N, 70° 49.443' W

Contact The Trustees of Reservations: thetrustees.org/place/whitney-thayer-woods, 781-740-7233

DIRECTIONS

From MA 3, take Exit 35 to MA 228 north. Follow MA 228 north for 6.5 miles and turn right (southeast) onto MA 3A. Follow MA 3A for 2.0 miles and turn right onto Howes Lane. Continue on Howes Lane to the road's end at the parking area.

TRAIL DESCRIPTION

Quiet woodland trails—and plenty of them—are the primary feature of this reservation that straddles the towns of Cohasset and Hingham, adjoining other Trustees of Reservations lands. A large stand of giant rhododendrons and azaleas on the southern border of the property provides an attractive contrast to the thickly forested hills and glacial boulders that characterize the bulk of the reservation. This ramble makes a loop of the eastern portion of the site, including a stroll through the tunnel of rhododendrons and azaleas.

Before starting the walk, take a moment to scan the small open area adjacent to the parking lot for birds and insects, such as red-spotted purple and monarch butterflies. The wide gravel trail begins to the left of the information sign, where maps are available. Follow this path through pines and hardwoods for about five minutes; turn right onto the first trail you come to, at a green gate. This is Boulder Lane, marked in blue on the map, appropriately named because it passes many large erratics that were deposited by retreating glaciers.

This is a good section of trail for viewing the American holly tree's shiny green foliage in the understory of the larger oaks, pines, and maples. The native holly found here might be the northernmost stand in the United States. The hollies are easiest to see during winter

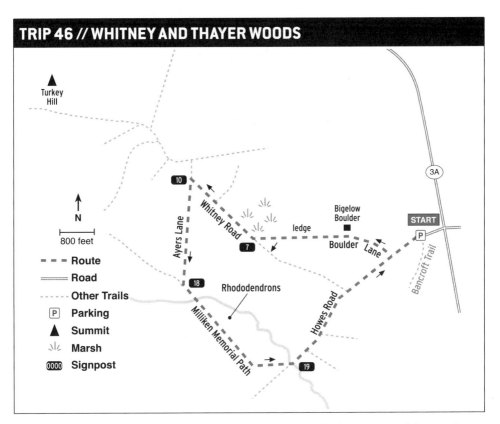

because their prickly evergreen leaves are still on the tree. The distinctive red fruit is also on the tree in winter if it hasn't been consumed by migratory songbirds, wild turkeys, bobwhite quail, and other wildlife.

About three-quarters of a mile into the walk, pass Bigelow Boulder, which weighs an estimated 200 tons, on your right. A bit farther down the trail is a pair of balanced boulders, with nooks and crannies in the jumble of rocks around them.

Boulder Lane passes beech trees that brighten the forest with their light-gray trunks. Even in winter they add a touch of color because the lower limbs' papery, golden-brown leaves often stay on until new growth pushes them off in spring. Large outcroppings of rock line Boulder Lane on the right and left before the trail crosses through a small swamp and arrives at the intersection with Whitney Road at marker 7, about 1.25 miles into your walk. Stay to the right at the intersection and continue another 0.5 mile to a junction at marker 10. Turn left onto signed Ayers Lane.

Along the trail, you may see coyote scat, especially at or near junctions along coyotes' hunting routes. It is uncommon to see these stealthy, nocturnal animals in the wild, however. They moved into the state in the 1950s, and their population has been slowly expanding. They are now present throughout Massachusetts, and their numbers continue to grow because their predator, the wolf, has been extirpated. Coyotes are very adaptable and have found a ready food source of mice, carrion, birds, rabbits, domestic animals (ducks, geese, and even cats), and berries.

Bright pink rhododendron grow along Milliken Memorial Path, a dazzling sight in spring and summer.

We often look straight ahead while hiking, but on this section of trail it's a good idea to look down to see what's growing on the forest floor. Watch for sarsaparilla, partridgeberry, and club mosses. Ayers Lane winds south to junction 18; bear left here onto Milliken Memorial Path, named by former local resident Arthur Milliken in honor of his wife, Mabel.

Rhododendrons and azaleas, planted during the 1920s, line this trail; hollies and hemlocks grow nearby. All this greenery gives the area a mysterious and enchanting feel, even in winter. (A storm caused extensive damage several years ago, but nature is repairing itself.) In late spring and early summer, the scene is truly magnificent, with the pinks and whites of thousands of azalea and rhododendron flowers brightening the woods. Rhododendrons grow up to 30 feet tall, and sometimes the branches from several trees interlace to form an impenetrable jungle. Their large, leathery evergreen leaves can reach a length of 10 inches. The flowers are often white or pink and grow in showy clusters. The bark is reddish brown; new twigs are green. Although rhododendrons flourish in southern New England, they are rare in the northern states.

Old stone walls crisscross these woods, indicating that the area was once used for pasture or farming—hard to believe, given the large white pines and other trees towering overhead. Settlers called their annual harvest of stones "New England potatoes" because the frost pushed up stones at such a great rate. If you look closely at the stone walls, they yield clues about the past. Walls with lots of little stones mixed with bigger ones indicate the adjacent land was probably cultivated, but if there are only large rocks in the walls, the land was probably used for grazing livestock or mowed for hay.

Milliken Memorial Path narrows in some spots, and the rhododendrons along the trail's edge give it the appearance of a tunnel. During wet periods, sections near swamps and streams may be flooded or muddy. After walking about a mile down the trail, you come to junction 19; bear left here onto Howes Road, which crosses a bridge over a stream. Follow the road straight past a solar panel on a pole and several junctions with other trails. You'll eventually come to a chain barrier near a private residence. Walk around it and follow Howes Road along the edge of the wetland opposite the house (please respect the private property). Reenter the woods on the other side of the clearing. The trail, which turns into a gravel road, leads 0.5 mile back to the parking lot.

If you are interested in a longer walk, on your next visit, explore Turkey Hill at the northwest end of the property (see map at kiosk). The summit offers a pleasant view of Cohasset Harbor. Adjacent to Turkey Hill is another Trustees property, Weir River Farm, which encompasses 75 acres of hayfields and woodlands. Both Turkey Hill and Weir River Farm can be reached from Turkey Hill Lane.

DID YOU KNOW?

The reservation is named in honor of Henry Whitney, who designed the property's original horse trails in the early 1900s, and Mrs. Ezra Ripley Thayer, who donated a significant parcel of land in 1943. A portion of the land was once part of the Bancroft Bird Sanctuary.

NEARBY

Wompatuck State Park, off Free Street, offers hiking trails, paved bicycling trails, and more than 260 campsites. World's End Reservation (Trip 45) is a short drive from Whitney and Thayer Woods. Restaurants are along and off North Street in Hingham.

MORE INFORMATION

The reservation is open year-round, dawn to dusk; no fee (donations accepted); no restrooms. Dogs are allowed but must be leashed.

CRANBERRIES IN NEW ENGLAND

Kettle holes and the rocky, wet soil that characterizes New England frustrated many early settlers. Sustenance farming was almost impossibly difficult, but a creative few looked past the usual practices. Some discovered bog iron buried in the sandy soil of what is now southeastern Massachusetts; others turned the poor soil into kiln-dried bricks for buildings.

Over time, cranberries—the small red berries that grew naturally in these wet areas— became more popular as a base for sauces that were spread on mutton and other meats. American Indians likely introduced settlers to this flavor, but the native groups prized the sour fruits for medicinal purposes as well.

Sometime in the mid-1800s, Cape Cod farmers began experimenting with the berries, seeking to grow enough to market them. Henry Hull, from Dennis, is credited with the first local cultivation of the fruit. Hull added sand to the low-growing vine's naturally acidic soil mix, prompting the plants to produce more fruit. By 1820, he was shipping barrels of cranberries to New York, and several more Cape Cod farmers soon followed his lead.

Cranberry cultivation turned out to be well suited for many of the bog iron–depleted areas and the naturally sandy, acidic soil in the region. By the end of the 1800s, cranberry farms were ubiquitous on the South Shore and Cape Cod, with 200 cranberry farms in Cape Cod alone by 1840. The vitamin-rich products were linked to the country's growing health food movement by 1900, when the berry juice was canned for export.

Many native residents have picked cranberries at one time or another, whether using scoops recreationally or wading in flooded bogs to help farmer friends. Most are proud of the area's cranberry traditions, even though other states, such as Michigan, have eclipsed Massachusetts in total output.

In general, commercial agriculture is not recognized as beneficial to the environment, but cranberry bogs have made the most of what the soil offers, and the open space they provide allows for significant wildlife corridors.

When strolling around cranberry bogs, it's not unusual to find otters or muskrats in the irrigation canals, great blue herons wading in the water, and fox dens in the sandy hills surrounding the bogs. In addition, the wide-open spaces offer wonderful views of the sky.

Some of the South Shore properties in this book that include cranberry bogs (currently cultivated or defunct) are Massasoit State Park (Trip 47), Burrage Pond (Trip 48), and Myles Standish State Forest (Trip 52).

MASSASOIT STATE PARK

This forested hike features glacial topography, waterfowl, and historical sites.

Features

Location East Taunton, MA

Rating Moderate

Distance 4-mile loop

Elevation Gain Minimal

Estimated Time 2.5 hours

Maps USGS Taunton; Massachusetts Department of Conservation and Recreation: mass.gov/eea/docs/dcr/parks/trails/massasoit.pdf

GPS coordinates 41° 53.062′ N, 70° 59.700′ W

Contact Massachusetts Department of Conservation and Recreation: mass.gov/locations/massasoit-state-park, 508-828-4231

DIRECTIONS
From I-495, take Exit 14 for MA 18 south, follow it for 0.6 mile, and then turn right onto Taunton Street, which becomes Middleboro Avenue. The entrance for Massasoit State Park is on the left in 2.2 miles.

TRAIL DESCRIPTION
This 1,500-acre state park serves the residents of many nearby towns who come to walk, bike, paddle, and ride horses, but it's large enough to make you feel like you're on an adventure of your own. Use this hike to familiarize yourself with the property, and then branch out to explore a variety of trails, waterfront vistas, historical sites, and glacial potholes deep in the park.

The campground reopened in 2018 with new water and electric, 94 campsites, 4 renovated comfort stations, and paved campground roads; it includes a new playground, gatehouse, and dam pavilion. The trails are regularly maintained, and new boardwalks have been built, in addition to a new kiosk and a brick fireplace. Several projects will be starting shortly, including the restoration of the Lake Rico parking lot and dam, Peter Adams Trail Boardwalk, trail improvements, and maintenance.

Park in the lot off Middleboro Avenue, where bright crimson cranberry bogs open the treeline to the left, curving out of sight. On the right, a ridge parallels the parking lot and paved road, with Lake Rico beyond it (near the park's headquarters). Following the paved road into the park from the ranger station, look for an unnamed path on the right side, at the first gate. Take the short path and continue straight at the first intersection. Turn right

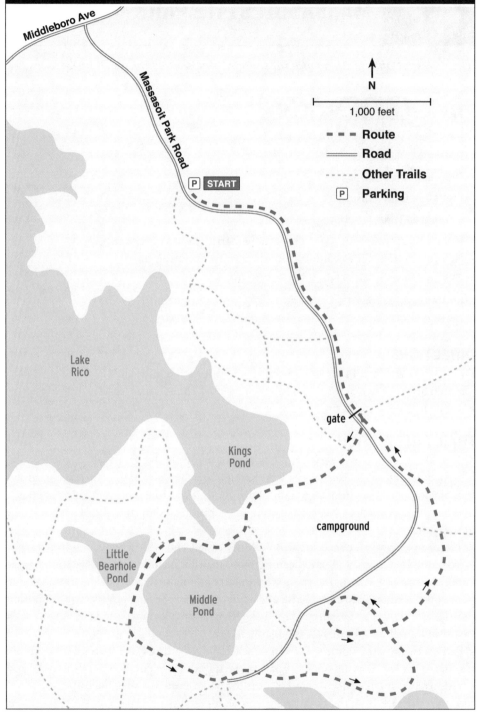

at the second intersection onto another unnamed path, which will take you toward the shore of the lake and some picturesque overlooks. You'll find opportunities to scan the waterfront for bird life, from migrating geese to kingfishers, which streak along the shoreline in search of small fish and frogs in shallow water.

Stay right at the next three trail intersections, walking parallel to the waterfront, and you will soon see the buildings of the former campground. At this point you are near the southern portion of Kings Pond, which is attached to Lake Rico. Here, near the former campground, you will find a couple of unusual glacial erratics. These rocks are called pudding stones, stand-alone boulders that look like hunks of concrete with fist-sized rocks mixed in. This conglomerate rock forms underwater and is the state rock of Massachusetts. Notice that the trees along the shore of the lake are generally pines, while those near the park entrance and along the cranberry bog are oaks and other hardwoods.

When you reach the former campground, stay on the path that skirts the perimeter of the sites, and look for the unnamed path that follows an isthmus between two bodies of water, Kings Pond and Middle Pond. If you're sure-footed, just after crossing the section where you can see both ponds, consider climbing the small hill to the right. It allows you to walk under a canopy of tall pines and out onto a long peninsula that juts into Kings Pond. Although it's a dead-end walk without a formal trail, the diversion offers lovely views of a marshy part of the lake that hosts many varieties of ducks and birds flitting among the cattails.

Returning to the unnamed main route, follow the contour of Middle Pond, on your left. Stay left when a horse trail branches off to the right, along Lake Rico. Middle Pond, Little Bearhole Pond, and Big Bearhole Pond are glacial potholes, created when the last glacier

The eastern box turtle may be found in meadows and ponds throughout Massachusetts. Watch for them crossing roads to nest in spring.

melted and left behind large puddles. On the far side of Middle Pond is a dam that separates it from Big Bearhole Pond, the site of Dean Cotton Mill in the 1800s. The city of Taunton once had 2,000 residents employed in similar industries.

Turtles thrive in the environment of these ponds and their sandy banks. Scan the shoreline closely for telltale lumps on rocks and logs at the water's edge, where you may see the dark shells of sun-loving painted turtles. They have smooth shells, yellow stripes on their heads, and distinctive yellow spots behind each eye. Box and Blanding's turtles are also residents of this park and may be seen foraging in the water or walking through the woods. It is difficult to distinguish between these two types of turtles, which are of similar size and have yellow markings on their necks. Snapping turtles, which grow to nearly 20 inches long, are also found here. Snappers and other turtles leave the ponds in early summer to bury nests of eggs in open, sandy areas. The eggs will stay there, at the mercy of raccoons and opossums looking for an easy meal, until they hatch in late summer.

In about a quarter-mile, cross the dam between the two ponds and turn left, following the paved road briefly. A short dirt bypass road, where anglers park their cars, intersects here; watch for the unnamed path through the trees on the right that departs from the paved road and runs along the shore of Big Bearhole Pond. Follow it through the woods, watching for the pale yellow leaves of beech trees growing under the pines. The contrast of the beech's heart-shaped, paper-thin leaves against the dark-green pine needles is dramatic, particularly when the ground is covered with a layer of fallen orange pine needles.

Near the campground's former dumping station, the path parallels the paved road. You can rejoin the road and walk back to the parking lot or explore cart paths in the woods between the road and the adjacent golf course.

DID YOU KNOW?

The hills of the park and the cranberry bog area were formed by the excavation and dumping of earth when iron was extracted and smelted here in the eighteenth century.

NEARBY

About 7 miles away in Middleboro is the Massachusetts Archaeological Society's Robbins Museum, with information on local history and artifacts, such as American Indian arrowheads. Hours are Wednesdays and Saturdays, 10 A.M. to 4 P.M. Check the society's website or call first: massarchaeology.org, 508-947-9005. Old Colony History Museum at 66 Church Green in Taunton has ever-changing exhibits, guest speakers, and an excellent research library. Hours are Tuesday through Saturday, 10 A.M. to 4 P.M. For more information, call 508-822-1622 or visit oldcolonyhistorymuseum.org.

MORE INFORMATION

The park is open year-round, dawn to dusk. Portable toilets are near the parking lot. Dogs are allowed but must be leashed.

48 BURRAGE POND

This hike combines wide-open views of a cranberry bog with forests, numerous freshwater ponds, and a white cedar swamp.

Features

Location Hanson and Halifax, MA

Rating Easy

Distance 3-mile loop

Elevation Gain 90 feet

Estimated Time 2 hours

Maps USGS Hanover, USGS Whitman; Massachusetts Division of Fisheries and Wildlife: halifax-ma.org/sites/g/files/vyhlif4496/f/uploads/burragepondmapdescription.pdf

GPS coordinates 42° 01.866′ N, 70° 51.766′ W

Contact Massachusetts Division of Fisheries and Wildlife: mass.gov/masswildlife, 508-759-3406

DIRECTIONS

From I-93, take Exit 7 for MA 3 south about 3.8 miles to Exit 38 for MA 18 toward Abington. In another 3.0 miles, turn left onto MA 58 south. In 4.5 miles take the second exit from the rotary for Raynot Avenue. In 0.7 mile turn left onto MA 27 south and follow it for 5.0 miles. In quick succession turn right on Reed Street, right on Pleasant Street, and right on Hawks Avenue. On the left is a large dirt parking area with map kiosk.

TRAIL DESCRIPTION

The Burrage Pond Wildlife Management Area, a 2,000-acre property straddling the Hanson–Halifax town line, includes many miles of trails among its cranberry bogs, woods, and ponds. The Massachusetts Division of Fisheries and Wildlife acquired it in 2002, and it is on the Bay Circuit Trail. About 100 acres are still actively farmed for cranberries.

Hikers, casual mountain bikers, snowshoers, anglers, and bird-watchers find Burrage Pond a treasure. The flat landscape, near the Taunton River in the coastal plain area of southeastern Massachusetts, is crisscrossed by numerous cart paths and causeways, creating myriad opportunities for access and long-distance views. The wildlife management area provides habitat to bird and wildlife species by linking parcels of open space throughout the property. State wildlife officials have released rehabilitated species here as part of their repopulation efforts.

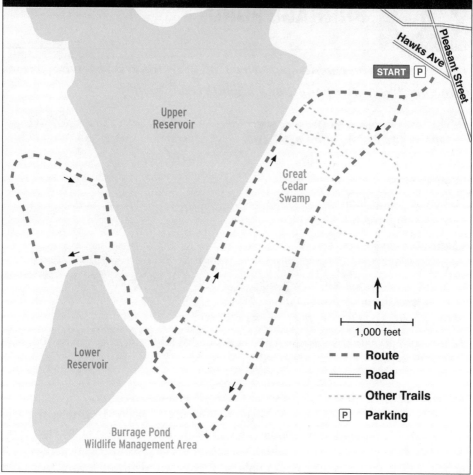

Upper
Reservoir

Great
Cedar
Swamp

START P

Hawks Ave

Pleasant Street

N

1,000 feet

- - - **Route**
===== **Road**
······· **Other Trails**
P **Parking**

Lower
Reservoir

Burrage Pond
Wildlife Management Area

This approximately 3-mile walk features broad vistas with a short passage through wooded paths. It's easy to follow, but trails are unmarked. No facilities are available on-site. If you follow these directions, it's easy to navigate by line of sight, but downloading and printing a map from the town's website is recommended.

Starting at the Hawks Avenue parking lot, proceed about 0.25 mile into the property, staying left at the fork. Here, the land opens up from pine woods to a wide sea of waving grass. Continue straight on what looks like an endless road toward the distant treeline; watch for great blue herons feeding in the irrigation canals and red-tailed hawks perched in trees at the perimeter. Follow this route about 0.6 mile, keeping track of the number of paths intersecting from the right. At the seventh path, turn right and traverse the water on a narrow isthmus between the upper and lower reservoirs (the lower reservoir is named Burrage Pond on some maps). Stay straight (right) at the next intersection and continue, with Upper Reservoir on your right.

Make a large loop of the wooded land between the reservoirs by staying left at the next four trail intersections. The route goes from the edge of Upper Reservoir to the edge of irrigation ponds and back to the traverse between Upper and Lower reservoirs. This portion of the hike is best done in dry weather because the trails often flood in this part of the property. Also note that many maps show trails that loop all the way around Lower Reservoir (a.k.a. Burrage Pond), but some of the land is posted private property.

On the fringes of the wildlife management area, particularly at dawn or dusk, deer, raccoons, and other wildlife may venture out, so it's advisable to stop and scan the edge of the woods. The truly adventurous may want to hike up to another crossing of Upper Reservoir to the north, which is called the Indian Crossway and is part of the Bay Circuit Trail. Many believe the name may be handed down from early settlers in the area. The path's location provided a logical place for a dam to control water when cranberry operations were active. Also to the north there may still be remnants of Great Cedar Swamp, an area of white cedar trees that were prized by American Indians for their rot-resistant wood and vitamin-infused berries.

All the ponds here are shallow—anglers say they're less than 10 feet deep—but still hold perch, largemouth bass, crappies, turtles, and water snakes. Fishing is generally catch-and-release.

Near the reservoirs, watch for animals in the water and birds atop poles, particularly ospreys in their nests. Depending on the time of year, you may witness a mature osprey returning to the nest with a fish in its talons to feed its young. Ospreys are hawklike birds of prey with brown wings and white undersides. Their call is a piercing screech. If you're fortunate, you may have an opportunity to see an osprey fishing. It circles high above the water, slows and practically hovers, and then dives straight in for its prey, usually emerging with a fish in its grasp.

Wide, flat walking paths typify Burrage Pond, where there are some 80 bird species.

Burrage Pond is a wonderland for bird-watchers, and its inhabitants vary from season to season. In spring, red-winged blackbirds swarm the marshes, one of the first signs of warmer weather to come. Summertime may be dominated by hundreds of fast-flying swallows that zip along inches above the water. If you're fortunate enough to see one land on a branch, you'll enjoy the glossy teal color of its plumage, which is not quite visible when the bird is flying at top speeds. Other summer birds may include cedar waxwings, which have dark markings, similar to those of blue jays, around their eyes but a distinctive line of yellow at the bottom of their tails; blue kingbirds, skirting the edges of ponds, hunting for frogs; and gray catbirds, whose song often sounds like a cat's meow. In late fall, many varieties of ducks stop here on their long migrations: mallards, wood ducks, mergansers, and buffleheads. You can identify mergansers and buffleheads by the distinctive white swoop of plumage on the sides of their heads. (On buffleheads, the white goes all the way around the back of the head.) Most interesting to birders is the presence of a nesting pair of sandhill cranes discovered by an Audubon bird survey.

When you return from the optional loop near Upper Reservoir, turn left immediately after crossing the bridge. Walking along the edge of Upper Reservoir on your way back, watch for painted turtles near the shore, witness frogs leaping into the water, or observe a heron fishing. By keeping the cell tower on the horizon in view you'll have no trouble returning to the parking lot on Hawks Avenue.

Whether you visit in summer and enjoy the shade of the young trees on the edges of the irrigation ponds or arrive in winter, when snow creates a glittering tunnel of bowed limbs, Burrage Pond has a magical feel. One special treat is seeing evidence of otters: smooth snow or mudslides that end near the water's edge, clear proof that a small animal has shimmied along.

DID YOU KNOW?

Great Cedar Swamp was not valued for its wildlife habitat or healthy watershed contributions until recently. Before cranberry businesses took possession, there was a long history of local residents harvesting cedar for shingles, using the swamp for munitions development (including lobbing mines across the property), filling in the ponds for cattle grazing, and dumping manure. But by 2003, a survey showed 81 species of birds using the area, and since then, local birders have reported a total of 224 species sightings.

NEARBY

Old Colony History Museum in Taunton describes the history of this area. It's open Tuesday through Saturday, 10 A.M. to 4 P.M. For more information, call 508-822-1622 or visit oldcolonyhistorymuseum.org.

MORE INFORMATION

Burrage Pond is maintained by the Massachusetts Division of Fisheries and Wildlife, which allows hunting on the property at certain times of year. The North and South Rivers Watershed Association (nsrwa.org/listing/burrage-pond-wildlife-management-area) notes Burrage Pond's importance to the Taunton River watershed.

NORTH HILL MARSH WILDLIFE SANCTUARY

Well-marked trails offer views of a wildlife-rich freshwater pond, its surrounding forests, and a small cranberry bog.

Features 🚶 🐕 📍 🏃

Location Duxbury, MA

Rating Moderate

Distance 3.3-mile loop

Elevation Gain 110 feet

Estimated Time 2 hours

Maps USGS Duxbury; Mass Audubon: massaudubon.org/content/download/8090/145521/file/northhill_trails.pdf

GPS coordinates 42° 02.143′ N, 70° 42.733′ W

Contact Mass Audubon: massaudubon.org/get-outdoors/wildlife-sanctuaries/north-hill-marsh, 781-837-9400; Duxbury Conservation Department: town.duxbury.ma.us/conservation, 781-934-1100, ext. 5471

DIRECTIONS

From MA 3, take Exit 22 (Congress Street) and head east toward Duxbury. About 100 feet from the exit, take the first right onto Lincoln Street. Follow Lincoln Street for 0.8 mile and bear left onto Mayflower Street. Follow Mayflower Street for 0.3 mile and bear left where the road forks to stay on Mayflower. The parking lot is about 0.5 mile down Mayflower Street, on the left.

From MA 3A in Duxbury, drive south past the town hall, turn west onto Mayflower Street, and continue 1.3 miles to the parking lot on the right.

TRAIL DESCRIPTION

North Hill Marsh, jointly owned and managed by Mass Audubon and the town of Duxbury, is an 823-acre tract of wetlands and forests within the town's Eastern Greenbelt. The sanctuary, which is centered on a 90-acre freshwater pond, includes several miles of nature trails that are split between the east and west sides of the pond. The main routes are color-blazed, but other paths are unmarked and potentially confusing for first-time visitors. A detailed trail map and brochure are available at the entrance.

This 3.3-mile excursion along the south and east sides of the pond follows a series of blazed trails that make a wide loop. The first part of the outing hugs the pond's shoreline, and the return portion passes through a pine-oak forest and then goes to a scenic cranberry

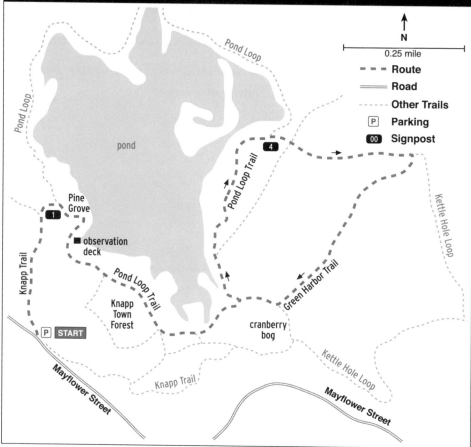

bog. The walking is mostly easy, with a few ups and downs over rolling terrain. If you are with young children, you have the option of walking a shorter loop to the south shore of the pond before doubling back.

Starting from the signboard at the parking lot, follow yellow-blazed Knapp Trail north to marker 1 and bear right on a short path that soon joins blue-blazed Pond Loop Trail. Turn right onto Pond Loop Trail, which quickly leads to a pine grove with pleasant views across the water. A short distance farther is an observation platform that overlooks a small cove. Continue on Pond Loop Trail along the south shore, passing several other trails that branch to the left and right.

The pond and its surrounding wetlands and forests are a magnet for birdlife. Species to watch for include ring-necked and black ducks, mute swans, buffleheads, hooded mergansers, herons, kingfishers, and egrets. Depending on the time of year, tree swallows may be zipping around; dozens of nest boxes were erected for them around the pond. Wood ducks find this a good place to nest due to the dead timber standing in the water, which offers a bit of protection from predators, such as raccoons; nest boxes were built for the ducks as well. (Nest boxes with small holes are for tree swallows, and those with larger holes are for

This cranberry bog is part of the diverse habitats of North Hill Marsh Wildlife Sanctuary.

wood ducks.) There have been several recent sightings of ospreys near the pond, and a nesting platform has been erected to entice these birds of prey, which have recovered nicely from mid-twentieth-century losses caused by DDT.

The dead timber in the pond also provides excellent cover for warmwater fish species, such as pickerel and largemouth bass. Several species of turtles inhabit these waters, too. Snapping and painted turtles are fairly common, but spotted and box turtles are rare.

Near the pond's southeast corner, Pond Loop Trail turns sharply left (north) at a junction where a red-blazed trail, part of this hike's return leg, continues straight. Pond Loop Trail curves downhill and then leads north along the pond's eastern shore. The route snakes to the right to bypass a closed section of trail and then zigzags up a small hill.

As you walk through the woods, keep an eye out for great horned owls. They do their hunting at night, but people have spotted them perched on limbs of the tall white pines during the day. They swoop into their nests, bringing mice, squirrels, rabbits, and skunks to their young.

After you have walked 45 minutes or so from the parking area (about 1.75 miles), the trail passes two posts, the second of which is marker 4. Bear right (straight) off Pond Loop Trail at marker 4 and follow the unnamed, red-blazed connector path east through the woods, crossing a four-way junction. After a little more than a quarter-mile on this path, turn right on white-blazed Green Harbor Trail, which leads south through both mature and sapling pines, with glimpses of the pond valley through the trees on the right. This portion of the route was once part of the 1623 Green Harbor Trail, a historical route that linked Marshfield and Plymouth.

After a half-mile of easy walking, Green Harbor Trail descends to a sign marking Duxbury town conservation land and soon reaches the cranberry bog. Bear right here off the white-blazed trail and follow the red-blazed connector path along the edge of the bog.

To conclude the walk from the bog, follow the red-blazed path for a short distance to a junction where it rejoins blue-blazed Pond Loop Trail. Turn left onto Pond Loop Trail and retrace your steps along the south shore of the pond, making sure to keep the water on your right. You can save a few minutes of walking by bearing left onto the red-blazed path near the observation platform and following it back to yellow-blazed Knapp Trail, or you can continue to the pine grove viewing area and the first connecting path near marker 1. Either way, turn left onto Knapp Trail and make the short, easy walk back to the parking area on Mayflower Street.

DID YOU KNOW?

The sanctuary land on the west side of the pond is home to 140-foot Waiting Hill, the second-highest point in Duxbury. It is so named because the wives of fishermen and merchants would stand on the hill and scan the ocean for returning ships. Today, trees obstruct the views.

NEARBY

The Myles Standish Burial Ground, at the intersection of Chestnut Street and Pilgrim Byway, is the burial site of Captain Myles Standish and several prominent Pilgrims from the 1620 voyage. It is the oldest maintained cemetery in the United States. Several restaurants are in South Duxbury near the meeting of Bay, Chestnut, Washington, and Depot streets.

MORE INFORMATION

The sanctuary is open daily, dawn to dusk; no restrooms. Boating, hunting, and trapping are prohibited. Dogs must be under control at all times and are not allowed in the pond.

50 ALLENS POND WILDLIFE SANCTUARY

On the shores of Buzzards Bay, Allens Pond Wildlife Sanctuary features diverse coastal habitats, including tidal ponds and a rocky barrier beach, with scenic views and excellent bird-watching and wildlife-viewing opportunities.

Features

Location Dartmouth, MA

Rating Easy to Moderate

Distance 5.9 miles round trip

Elevation Gain 130 feet

Estimated Time 3.25 hours

Maps USGS Head of Westport; Mass Audubon: massaudubon.org/content/download/1776/18663/file/MA_AllensPondmap_color.pdf

GPS coordinates 42° 02.143′ N, 70° 42.733′ W

Contact Mass Audubon: massaudubon.org/get-outdoors/wildlife-sanctuaries/allens-pond, 508-636-2437

DIRECTIONS

From I-195, take Exit 16 (formerly Exit 10) and follow MA 88 south for 11.4 miles. Bear left on John Reed Road and continue for 1.8 miles past Horseneck Beach State Reservation. Turn left and follow East Beach Road for 0.8 mile to another left turn, where the road becomes Horseneck Road. Continue 0.1 mile to the sanctuary entrance on the right (1280 Horseneck Road).

TRAIL DESCRIPTION

Allens Pond Wildlife Sanctuary, a Mass Audubon property, lies within a 5,000-acre mosaic of estuaries, marshes, and barrier beaches in the Westport River watershed. A 7-mile trail network and three entrances offer a variety of options for visitors. This walk, starting from the Field Station entrance on Horseneck Road, leads to diverse habitats and scenic viewpoints in the south-central portion of the sanctuary. Trails and junctions are well marked with color blazes and posts. The route passes several privately owned properties; please respect all posted areas.

From the welcome sign, follow the right branch of orange-blazed Beach Loop Trail south along a field-marsh edge to Buzzards Bay. Such open areas are ideal habitat for killdeers, shorebirds that emit loud calls and feign broken wings to lure potential predators away

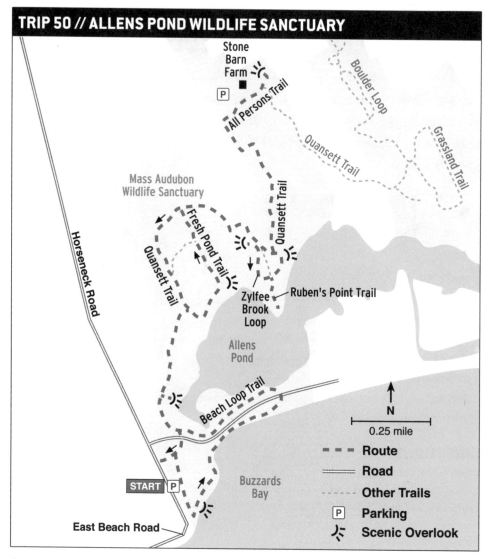

from their nests. Turn left to follow Beach Loop Trail along a rocky barrier beach that buffers Allens Pond and adjacent salt marshes and provides crucial breeding habitat for piping plovers and least terns. Blooms of Queen Anne's lace, goldenrods, beach roses, and other flowers color the path edge in summer. Traverse a rocky knob with a fine overview of the crescent-shaped beach and Buzzards Bay. Pass the junction with a short crossover path at an interpretive sign and continue northeast along the beach, a strip of round stones shaped by the ocean over thousands of years.

At 0.7 mile, make a 180-degree turn at the sanctuary boundary and follow Beach Loop Trail south along a dirt road on the east side of Allens Pond, an expansive tidal wetland bordered by a salt marsh. Pass the aforementioned crossover path at another interpretive sign and cross a small bridge at the pond's southeastern tip. In summer, look for black swallowtails, monarchs, and other butterflies feeding in shrubby vegetation bordering the road.

A wide variety of wildlife, including more than 300 bird species, benefits from the sanctuary's diverse habitats. One of the most rare and elusive visitors is the short-eared owl, which migrates south from northern breeding grounds to New England from fall through early spring. Snowy owls also periodically overwinter on the south coast, especially during years when lemmings, their primary prey, are scarce in their native Arctic range. Both species of owls favor open areas, such as salt marshes, meadows, and grasslands. Large flocks of migrating tree swallows make a striking spectacle in fall. Look for eiders, ruddy ducks, buffleheads, and other waterfowl in the ocean and wetlands. Protected salt marshes provide critical habitat for diamondback terrapin turtles, which are listed as threatened in Massachusetts because of coastal development and increasing predator populations.

At 1.2 miles, Beach Loop Trail branches left off the dirt road to return to the trailhead (an option for a shorter walk). To continue on blue-blazed Quansett Trail, turn right at the next intersection at a stone wall and walk along a field edge lined with thickets. Eastern cottontail rabbits and gray catbirds are familiar sights on the grassy path and among the low shrubs. A lookout at a stone bench provides views to Allens Pond's southern end. Pass Quansett Farm (private property), cross a boardwalk with another observation area, and continue to follow Quansett Trail through more thickets and a brushy field. Joe-pye weed, a key food source for butterflies, bees, and other pollinating insects, blooms in middle to late summer.

At 0.5 mile from Beach Loop Trail (1.7 miles overall), begin the first of two short detours off Quansett Trail by turning right on purple-blazed Fresh Pond Trail, which passes between diminutive Fresh Pond on the left and the marshy west side of Allens Pond to the right. Bear left at a stone wall and pass a side path to Poison Ivy Rock on the right. Enter oak-hardwood forest and follow Fresh Pond Trail past the junction with Tree Top Trail (a short connecting path to Quansett Trail) and through a gap in a stone wall.

Turn right at the next junction to rejoin Quansett Trail at 2.1 miles. This portion of the sanctuary is densely wooded now, but numerous stone walls offer evidence of the past when the land was cleared for agriculture. Although Carolina wrens are often hard to see, their cheerful *teakettle-teakettle-teakettle* song is a familiar sound in bottomland forests such as this.

After passing a tall oak arcing over a glacial boulder, cross narrow Zylfee Brook, one of Allens Pond's sources. Pass another stone wall and bear left at a view of the brook's marshy edge. Turn right at a marker for Reuben's Point and continue to follow Quansett Trail along a grassy woods road to the intersection with Zylfee Brook Loop Trail at 2.4 miles.

Begin the second detour by turning right on Zylfee Brook Loop Trail, marked with light-purple blazes. A short detour to the right at a marker post leads to a viewpoint overlooking wetlands near Zylfee Brook's confluence with Allens Pond. Follow Zylfee Brook Loop Trail along the wooded marsh edge to a four-way intersection. Turn right on Reuben's Point Trail and take a short out-and-back path across a brushy field to an open view at the northern edge of Allens Pond. Scan the marshes and water for great and snowy egrets, flocks of double-crested cormorants, and other waterfowl and wading birds. Nonvenomous eastern milk snakes, which inhabit field and forest edges, are sometimes mistaken for copperheads because of their similar coloration.

Coastal habitats at Allens Pond Wildlife Sanctuary, including tidal marshes and ponds, support a wide variety of wildlife.

Backtrack to the four-way intersection and turn right to stay on red-blazed Reuben's Point Trail, which leads up to a rocky lookout with a scenic, elevated perspective across Allens Pond. At 2.9 miles, turn right to rejoin Quansett Trail at a field edge and continue north, walking through thickets, a field near a private residence, and another hardwood forest grove. Enter a grassy field and follow Quansett Trail left and then right along a wooden fence at the sanctuary boundary.

Cross a dirt road at the sanctuary's Stone Barn Farm entrance, where parking, a picnic area, and restrooms are available. (The road is closed to public access south of the entrance.) Continue on Quansett Trail past nest boxes in a field adjacent to the barn. Turn left at the forest edge and reach an intersection where Quansett Trail merges with All Person's Trail, a universally accessible path.

Turn right and follow both trails on a boardwalk through a red maple swamp on Margaret's Brook. At the boardwalk's end, bear left on All Person's Trail to reach a nearby viewing area at the wetland edge, the end of this hike's outbound segment, at 3.6 miles. (The upper portion of Quansett Trail, which branches to the right after the boardwalk, connects with the Allens Neck Trail System in the northeastern portion of the sanctuary.)

To return, retrace your steps south on Quansett Trail to the intersection with Reuben's Point Trail. Turn right and follow Quansett Trail along the field edge and into the woods to bypass the side trip to Reuben's Point. At the northern junction with Fresh Pond Trail at 4.8 miles, turn right again to stay on Quansett Trail, which leads to a large boulder neatly capped by a small glacial erratic. From the lower junction with Fresh Pond Trail, follow Quansett Trail back to its southern terminus near the Field Station entrance. Turn left on the dirt road, and then bear right to follow Beach Loop Trail across a field and past a stone wall to return to the parking area.

DID YOU KNOW?

In April 2003, an oil spill affected roughly 100 miles of shoreline in Buzzards Bay. Mass Audubon is using funds from a natural resources damage settlement to expand and improve the Allens Pond Wildlife Sanctuary trail network. Volunteer trail maintainers are welcome; call the sanctuary (508-636-2437) for details.

NEARBY

Horseneck Beach State Reservation, on John Reed Road in Westport, protects a 2-mile-long barrier beach and salt marsh and has a 100-site campground. A parking fee ($13 for Massachusetts residents, $40 for nonresidents) is charged from May 15 through November. Visit mass.gov/locations/horseneck-beach-state-reservation for more information. Bayside Restaurant, open seasonally, is across the street from the sanctuary's Field Station entrance (see thebaysiderestaurant.com for hours and menu). Other places to eat are along and near MA 6.

MORE INFORMATION

Open year-round, dawn to dusk; no fee. Pets, biking, and hunting are prohibited. Swimming, sunbathing, and picnicking are prohibited on the beach, which is a conservation research and shorebird nesting area. The Allens Neck Trail System, with access via a trailhead on Allens Neck Road, features 3 miles of trails and a 55-acre grassland.

51 WEST ISLAND

Explore the sights and sounds of an oceanfront hike with views to the horizon.

Features

Location Fairhaven, MA

Rating Easy

Distance 1.75-mile loop

Elevation Gain Minimal

Estimated Time 1 to 1.5 hours

Maps USGS New Bedford; Buzzards Bay Coalition: savebuzzardsbay.org/places-to-go/west-island-town-beach

GPS coordinates 41° 35.076′ N, 70° 49.428′ W

Contact Buzzards Bay Coalition: savebuzzardsbay.org/places-to-go/west-island-state-reservation, 508-866-2580

DIRECTIONS

From US 93 south near Braintree take Exit 4 to MA 24 south toward Brockton for 22.0 miles. Take Exit 17 for MA 140 south toward New Bedford and continue 18.5 miles. Take Exit 2A to I-195 and follow I-195 for about 3 miles; then take Exit 29 for MA 240 south toward Fairhaven. Go straight through the intersection of MA 6 where MA 240 becomes Sconticut Neck Road. In 3.7 miles, turn left for Causeway Road/Goulart Memorial Drive. The trailhead for the northeast section of the island is on Fir Street, the sixth left turn once you arrive on the island. To get to the parking lot in the southern section near the beach, take the first right, Alder Street, and follow it to the end (where it becomes Balsam Street), then a left onto Bass Creek Road and a right on Fir Street to your destination.

TRAIL DESCRIPTION

West Island is that rare waterfront location with a million-dollar view but no mansions lining the beach. Explore a variety of trails on this 338-acre preserve, from woodland to waterfront, marshes, and tidal lagoons.

West Island has two distinct areas: the northeast corner and the southern tip near the beach. Hiking is primarily done in the northeast, where the trailhead is easily found on the side of Fir Street. On-street parking is plentiful. Enter by the kiosk and follow the trail into the woods. It's flat and wide, shady, well worn, and easily traveled.

At about 0.3 mile there are raised concrete structures that handle wastewater from residents on the western side of the island. Beyond this reminder of human impact on the

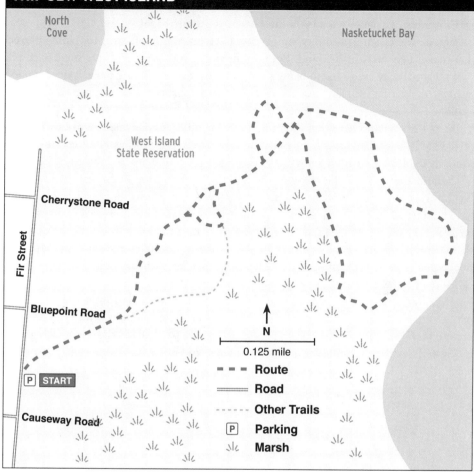

North Cove

Nasketucket Bay

West Island
State Reservation

Cherrystone Road

Fir Street

Bluepoint Road

N

0.125 mile

- - - **Route**
=== **Road**
----- **Other Trails**
P **Parking**
⊻ **Marsh**

P START

Causeway Road

environment, the trail continues east toward the water. Several side paths around and just after the main trail loops allow for a turnaround near the 0.5-mile mark. Just beyond the turnaround, trees thin out as the trail approaches the bay. Turn right here and cross the marsh grass, heading southeast toward the water on a well-worn treadway (no markers or blazes; hike by line of sight).

Observe how the terrain changes as you approach the beach: grasses are thick and hardy; the sand on this part of the island is up above the high-water mark, while rocks generally cover the beach to the waterline. Move toward the water while staying on the footpath in the sand. Soon the route turns east, and the trees of the island are behind you on a small hill above the water. This habitat provides optimal shelter for land-dwelling creatures that roam the beach for food, such as crabs and fish.

Along the waterfront, moving south to north around the outer edge of the island, notice the rocky lagoon giving way to a crescent-shaped beach about a quarter-mile long. Here, the view to the east on a clear day can include the Cape Cod Canal railroad bridge some 8 miles away.

Enjoy plenty of opportunities to examine remnants of sea life among the rocks, including mussels in the seagrass, shells of horseshoe crabs, and perhaps fiddler crabs—the ones with an oversized claw—moving in unison across a marshy spot.

High on the beach in summer, rangers are likely to cordon off areas for piping plovers that make their nests in the sand. Because the nests and young birds are small and well camouflaged, they are prone to being stepped on by visitors. Piping plovers, once hunted nearly to extinction, also have lost much of their natural habitat to development and coastal erosion.

The plover and another ground-nesting bird, the killdeer, may fake a broken wing and pretend to be injured in order to lure intruders away from their young. Killdeers are colored similarly to plovers, with brown wings and banded necks, but are slightly larger.

The bird species here change with the seasons, as migrating ducks commonly make Nasketucket Bay a stop in their travels. Common winter ducks include buffleheads, which have a large, white patch on the back of their heads, and mergansers, which have white breasts and reddish-orange heads with a distinctive raised crown. Summer is heralded by the return of ospreys to their nests at the tops of the tallest trees and on docks and telephone poles. These birds of prey are easily recognized by their high-pitched, whistle-like call and are frequently seen carrying fish in their talons.

After crossing the sandy crescent beach, head northwest back toward the treeline. Many paths through the seagrass allow you to return to the main trail, but before you go, look around for human activity: people standing in a lagoon, particularly the north-facing shallow water, are likely digging for quahogs, scallops, and other shellfish. Fishing boats just

A beach walk at West Island may reveal mussels, crab shells, and piping plover birds.

offshore could be bottom fishing for scup, flounder, tautog, or black bass, or they could be bait fishing for striped bass and bluefish.

Return to the trailhead on the same route you came in on. The round-trip hike is about 1.75 miles.

DID YOU KNOW?

In the late 1980s, local residents waged a battle against the development of this 338-acre parcel. Through the grassroots organization Save West Island, they were able to involve conservation groups, which helped to eventually convince the Commonwealth of Massachusetts to fund the purchase of the land for wildlife preservation.

NEARBY

A seasonal bar and grill is at West Island Marina in the middle of the causeway. Other restaurants are on Sconticut Neck Road in Fairhaven and on MA 6 in Fairhaven and New Bedford.

MORE INFORMATION

A local bird-watching group, Nasketucket Bird Club, keeps tabs on the species migrating through Nasketucket Bay through regular walks in the area and programs. Check the schedule on nbcbirdclub.com. The Buzzards Bay Coalition is dedicated to the health of southeastern Massachusetts's coastal waters through educational programs, social events, and land preservation efforts aimed at raising awareness of the interconnectedness of natural resources. West Island's hiking trails are free to the public, but the beach at the south end of the island is owned by the town of Fairhaven and requires resident beach stickers. Check with town officials before planning a visit: fairhaven-ma.gov/home/news/2021 -beach-permits-now-available.

52 MYLES STANDISH STATE FOREST

At more than 14,000 acres, Myles Standish State Forest is one of the largest reservations in the state system and offers many recreational opportunities.

Features

Location Plymouth and Carver, MA

Rating Moderate to Strenuous

Distance 3-mile loop (East Head Reservoir Trail); 4.5-mile loop (Bentley Loop); 7.5-mile loop (combined loop)

Elevation Gain 50 feet

Estimated Time 2 to 4 hours

Maps USGS Wareham; Massachusetts Department of Conservation and Recreation: mass.gov/doc/myles-standish-trail-map/download

GPS coordinates 41° 50.343' N, 70° 41.453' W

Contact Massachusetts Department of Conservation and Recreation: mass.gov/locations/myles-standish-state-forest, 508-866-2526

DIRECTIONS

To reach the state forest from MA 3, take Exit 7 for Clark Road. Turn right onto Long Pond Road and travel about 3 miles to the park entrance on the left, which is Alden Road. The hike begins at the state forest headquarters, which is on Cranberry Road at the opposite end of the park. To reach the headquarters from Alden Road, follow Alden Road south to a four-way intersection and turn left onto Upper College Pond Road. Follow Upper College Pond Road to its intersection with Halfway Pond Road; turn right onto Halfway Pond Road. When Halfway Pond Road curves sharply left and forks, take the left fork to follow Lower College Pond Road. This road intersects with Cranberry Road at the state forest headquarters.

From I-495, take Exit 2 (South Carver) to MA 58 north. When MA 58 turns left, continue straight on Tremont Street, and proceed a little less than a mile to Cranberry Road on the right. Follow Cranberry Road through the park gates to the state forest headquarters, where the hike begins.

TRAIL DESCRIPTION

Myles Standish State Forest is home to one of the largest forests of pitch pines and scrub oaks in New England. The forest is also well known for its numerous kettle ponds, which

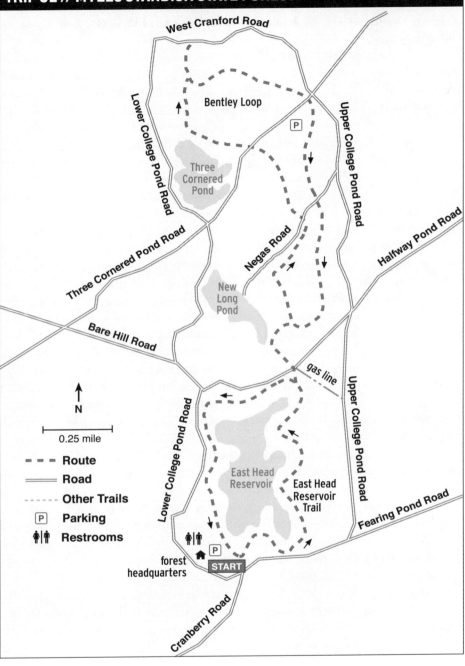

were created as huge chunks of glacial ice became partially embedded in the ground and then melted when the last ice age ended. Many fragile natural areas exist in the forest, including the shores of the kettle ponds, and these are marked with signs. Please stay on the trail in these areas.

This hike encompasses two of the forest's hiking loop trails, both of which are well blazed and maintained. East Head Reservoir Trail is an easy, level, 3-mile circuit, well suited for families. The 4.5-mile Bentley Loop, which begins at the northern end of East Head Reservoir Trail, is somewhat more rugged and winds through forests, meadows, and ponds. The two routes may be walked individually or combined as a 7.5-mile outing.

From the state forest headquarters and parking lot at the end of Cranberry Road, walk to the right (east) and cross a small bridge on Fearing Pond Road. At a sign, East Head Reservoir Trail enters the woods on the left and follows East Head Reservoir's southeastern shores. At marker 1, enjoy an attractive view from the waterside. The narrow trail curves to follow a promontory with more pleasant views and then turns north along the eastern side of the reservoir. Pitch pines rise high above the treadway; shadbush, withered viburnum, inkberry, red maple, and scrub oak are among the shrubs and saplings that grow along its margins. In summer, eastern pondhawk and blue dasher dragonflies are common.

After about 1.4 miles, East Head Reservoir Trail reaches the northern tip of the reservoir and turns left onto a well-used bridle path that follows a gas pipeline. Here, you can turn left to follow East Head Reservoir Trail on its return to the starting point via the western side of the reservoir, or you can extend the hike by walking to the start of Bentley Loop.

To reach Bentley Loop from the junction of East Head Reservoir Trail and the bridle path, continue straight past a metal gate, and then turn right onto a paved road (watch for light traffic). On the paved road, turn left onto the first dirt road on the left (junction B-2, with a metal gate numbered 75). The route continues along this dirt road and then turns right onto a woods road. At the end of the woods road, just before a meadow, is the trail junction where Bentley Loop begins.

This hike continues to the left, making a clockwise circuit. Bentley Loop is well marked with blue blazes, but watch carefully because many unmarked paths cross the trail in this section. If you don't see a trail marker after a short distance, retrace your steps to the last intersection. Bentley Loop leads north through the forests on the eastern shores of New Long Pond, bears right above another small pond, and briefly follows grassy, unpaved Negas Road. It bears left (north) off the road and crosses Three Cornered Pond Road. (You can detour left here for a short walk to the edge of Three Cornered Pond.)

After passing views of the pond, Bentley Loop traverses a series of meadows. This mix of fields, forest, and water is ideal wildlife habitat; watch for a variety of species, including coyotes, deer, foxes, butterflies, dragonflies, frogs, and turtles. The trail crosses the first meadow and turns left just before a second meadow, heading north toward College Pond. In summer, common mulleins, wildflowers that are part of the snapdragon family and can grow as tall as 7 feet, rise high above the grasses.

Bentley Loop turns left at another meadow and continues some distance along its left edge. The trail turns left into the woods at a marker and quickly reaches its northernmost

Along with mixed-use trails, such as Bentley Loop, Myles Standish State Park offers many dirt roads to explore by bike, horse, or foot.

point at a junction. The path heading north leads to the College Pond parking area. Follow Bentley Loop, which turns right and proceeds south.

After about 50 yards, Bentley Loop turns left and descends, turns right sharply, and comes to a meadow (the first since turning south). Traverse the meadow and exit left at the far end. Soon, Lower College Pond Road is visible on the left. The trail enters a parking lot, briefly follows its edge, and then turns right into the woods at the kiosk. After crossing another meadow, Bentley Loop reenters the woods before traveling straight across another large meadow at the bottom of a hill. From here, Bentley Loop follows a winding course back to its starting point (watch carefully for the blue blazes at junctions).

After completing Bentley Loop, backtrack to East Head Reservoir Trail by walking down the woods road, turning left onto the dirt road, and continuing to gate 75. Turn right onto the paved road and walk back to the junction with East Head Reservoir Trail. Bear right to follow East Head Reservoir Trail, which continues another 1.5 miles along the reservoir's western shores as it returns to the state forest headquarters and trailhead. After crossing two boardwalks, you are rewarded with a vista across the northern portion of the reservoir. East Head Reservoir Trail jogs right, briefly follows Lower College Pond Road, and then reenters the woods. It continues along the reservoir's southwestern shores, with more views across the water, and returns to the parking area behind the state forest headquarters.

DID YOU KNOW?

Myles Standish State Forest is one of the largest pine barrens in the Northeast, and along with its unusual topography and plants are frost pockets, which are depressions that hold cold air.

NEARBY

Restaurants are on Main Street (Route 58) in Carver, west of the state forest.

MORE INFORMATION

The state forest offers universally accessible restrooms, five camping areas, and sixteen ponds. A portion of land near Charge Pond is set aside for equestrian camping. The entire property provides 15 miles of paved and single-track cycling trails, 35 miles of equestrian trails, and 13 miles of hiking trails that venture deep into the woods. A group called Friends of Myles Standish State Forest (friendsmssf.com) offers guided hikes and other events.

 **ELLISVILLE HARBOR STATE PARK**

This compact property's diverse habitats include large, open meadows and a rocky ocean beach, where seals gather in winter.

Features 🚶 🐕 💧 ☘ ⚶ ⛩

Location Plymouth, MA

Rating Easy

Distance 2 miles round trip

Elevation Gain 75 feet

Estimated Time 1.5 hours

Maps USGS Sagamore

GPS coordinates 41° 50.717' N, 70° 32.474' W

Contact Massachusetts Department of Conservation and Recreation: mass.gov/locations/ellisville-harbor-state-park, 508-866-2526

DIRECTIONS
From MA 3 in Plymouth, take Exit 3 (formerly Exit 2) and follow MA 3A north for 2.4 miles to the state park entrance on the right.

TRAIL DESCRIPTION
Ellisville Harbor State Park is one of the lesser-known coastal preserves in Massachusetts, but if you love beachcombing and watching seals and other wildlife, it will soon become one of your favorites. Located at the southern end of the town of Plymouth, the park spans 101 acres of meadow, woodland, salt marsh, and rocky shoreline. This combination of habitats attracts seals, a variety of birds, and other wildlife, so bring your binoculars.

At the parking area, a lookout offers views across a large tidal marsh and mudflats associated with Salt Pond. Scan the flats carefully for sandpipers and other shorebirds, especially during the height of migration in August and September. An information sign includes a map and a history of the property. From a Healthy Heart Trail marker, begin an easy walk to the beach on an unblazed but obvious, well-maintained path into the woods and along the edge of fields adjacent to the entrance. The forest, characteristic of coastal southeastern Massachusetts, includes groves of scrub pine and oak, while staghorn sumac grows among the cedars and other evergreens in the meadows. Cedar and sumac are both opportunistic trees, among the first species to colonize abandoned fields.

If you have time, detour left off the main trail and explore the meadows, which offer opportunities for wildlife and wildflower viewing. Scan the fields for kestrels, which hunt in open areas for insects and small rodents. Sometimes they can be seen perched at the tops

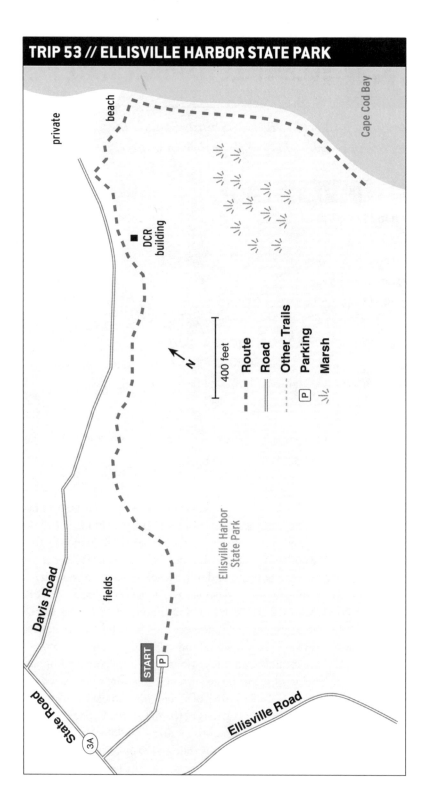

of cedar trees. Other animals that favor open and edge habitats include white-tailed deer, red foxes, and cottontail rabbits. Another familiar resident is the woodchuck (also known as the groundhog), which will make a beeline for its burrow when it senses danger.

Continue past a picnic table and a lookout on the right, with a partially open view across the marsh to Cape Cod Bay. Bright blue chicory wildflowers bloom along edges of a small clearing in summer. Cross a paved road with a Massachusetts Department of Conservation and Recreation building on the right and private property on the left, and continue straight at another Healthy Heart Trail marker. The path bends right and leads down to the edge of the beach at 0.5 mile.

Turn right and walk south along the shore (the land abutting the park to the left is privately owned). Enjoy views of the ocean to the left and the adjacent salt marsh to the right. Watch for ospreys at a nesting platform in the marsh; great blue herons, egrets, and other wading birds stalk the grasses and shallow water. In autumn, the marsh is tinted with hues of gold, rust, yellow, and brown. Pesky greenhead flies, which have sharp bites, can be a nuisance in July.

Carefully scan the ocean and exposed rocks for gray and harbor seals, which are often seen here. (In spring and fall, you may be able to observe distant whales by using binoculars or a spotting scope.) Harbor seals migrate each winter from Canada and Maine to Massachusetts. They arrive in October and leave in early spring. During low tide, they sun themselves on rocks, safely away from humans on the beach. Sometimes known as dog-faced seals because of their pug noses and canine-like appearance, they can grow to 5 or 6 feet in length and weigh as much as 250 pounds. The best viewing time is low tide, when more

Ellisville Beach is a great spot for watching seals and other aquatic wildlife.

rocks are exposed. If you see seals on the beach, do not approach them. Lone immature seals may appear to be abandoned, but it is a normal part of the maturation process.

During the late nineteenth century and much of the twentieth, there was a bounty on seals, and people would often kill them, fearing they were eating too many fish. However, humans were the ones depleting the fish stocks. Seals were feeding primarily on the sand lance, a small fish that has virtually no commercial value but is an important prey species for seals and many other marine creatures. The legal killing of seals ended in 1972 with the passage of the Marine Mammal Protection Act.

Beyond the breakers, you may see common loons, double-crested cormorants, and buffleheads bobbing in the water. In winter, many loons head to the south coast, including the Cape Cod Canal, when inland lakes freeze. Their distinctive summertime black-and-white coloring changes to brownish gray. These birds' underwater feeding feats are legendary, but their flight is equally impressive. Loons are surprisingly fast for such large, heavy birds. Walk the beach for approximately 0.5 mile to the mouth of a tidal creek that both drains and fills the marsh at Salt Pond's outlet (an area known as Ellisville Harbor, the park's namesake).

During low tide, the creek carries small fish out to the ocean, and birds and seals often station themselves along the water's edge to feed. Scan the water for cormorants and ducks diving beneath the surface as they hunt for fish. To the south is a view of shoreline extending to the Cape Cod Canal, roughly 5 miles away. You may hear the horns of trains passing along the canal. To return to the parking lot, retrace your steps along the beach and trail.

DID YOU KNOW?

A Christmas tree farm once operated on these grounds, and holdover planted trees, such as Colorado blue spruce and balsam fir, are still visible around the old fields.

NEARBY

Scusset Beach State Reservation, off MA 3 at Sagamore Bridge, includes 1.5 miles of frontage along the historic Cape Cod Canal, where visitors can watch for loons, seals, ducks, and other wildlife and enjoy a popular, paved recreational trail with scenic views. Restaurants are along and off MA 3A near the reservation and along US 6 near the canal.

MORE INFORMATION

The park is open year-round, sunrise to sunset; no fee; no restrooms. Dogs are not allowed on the beach from April 1 to September 15. Seasonal hunting is allowed.

 **LOWELL HOLLY RESERVATION**

A pleasant woodland trail winds through groves of beech and American holly and around a peninsula between two scenic ponds.

Features 🚶 🐕 💧 🎈 🎿 ☀️ 🏊 ⛺ 🎣

Location Mashpee and Sandwich, MA

Rating Easy to Moderate

Distance 3.1 miles round trip

Elevation Gain 100 feet

Estimated Time 1.5 hours

Maps USGS Sandwich; The Trustees of Reservations: thetrustees.org/wp-content/uploads/2022/02/lowell-holly-trail-map.pdf

GPS coordinates 41° 39.668′ N, 70° 28.468′ W

Contact The Trustees of Reservations: thetrustees.org/place/lowell-holly, 508-636-4693

DIRECTIONS
Take US 6 to Exit 59 (formerly Exit 2) and follow MA 130 south for 1.6 miles. Turn left onto Cotuit Road. After 3.4 miles, turn right onto South Sandwich Road and continue 0.6 mile to the year-round parking area on the right. (The road to the seasonal entrance is just beyond the lot.)

TRAIL DESCRIPTION
Abbott Lawrence Lowell, a former president of Harvard College, donated Lowell Holly to The Trustees of Reservations in 1934. With the exception of the cart paths that Lowell constructed, the reservation has been left primarily in its wild state for the past 200 years. It's a special place, where cool breezes coming off Wakeby and Mashpee ponds drift through the large stand of massive beech trees that shade this peninsula. Small pockets of white beaches, more than 300 native American holly trees, and several varieties of colorful rhododendrons are just a few of the numerous natural attractions.

This hike begins at the reservation's year-round parking area off South Sandwich Road. It follows a pleasant woodland path to Wakeby and Mashpee ponds and then travels a series of trails that explore the peninsula between the ponds. The trail names correspond with color blazes. The easy walk along mildly rolling terrain features scenic views of the trees, shrubs, and ponds; it also offers access to beaches. From the entrance, follow Red Trail northwest through a mixed forest of oak, beech, and pine toward the ponds. The winding path curves right at a junction and then rises easily through a beech grove. Holly trees, which are near the northern limit of their range on Cape Cod, are scattered about the

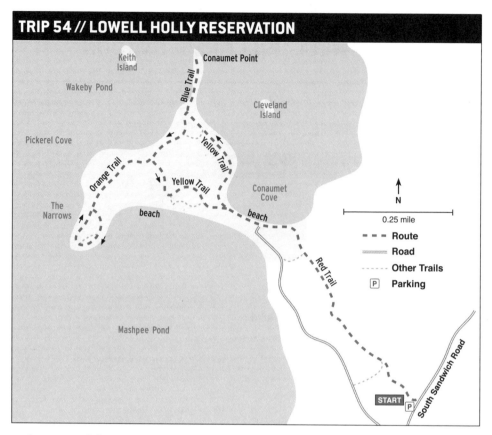

understory and thrive quite well in the shade of the beech trees. In addition to the numerous native trees, 50 more were planted by Wilfrid Wheeler, the reservation's first chairperson. In spring, the pink and white flowers of rhododendrons and mountain laurels are especially lovely.

The large beech trees are quite different from the typical oaks and pines in forest communities that cover so much of Cape Cod. Their smooth, gray trunks stand out, as if they are sentinels guarding the peninsula. In winter, the lower branches of the beech often retain their dried yellow-brown leaves, making a beautiful contrast with the snow. Other tree species here include pitch and white pines (the former is distinguished by its ball-shaped needle bundles), black birch, and red maple, which adds a splash of bright color in autumn. Watch for glimpses of Wakeby Pond's deep-blue water through the trees.

At 0.7 mile, reach the narrow neck between Wakeby and Mashpee ponds, where Red Trail ends. Bear left to cross the neck at the narrow swimming beach, where the resident flock of mallards may greet you. A picnic table at the water's edge makes an ideal stop for a break and a snack—now or after exploring the adjacent peninsula. Follow the route, now Yellow Trail, past the seasonal parking area to the west side of the neck, where the Yellow Trail loop begins.

To make a counterclockwise circuit, turn right and follow Yellow Trail north over gently rolling terrain along the eastern shores of the peninsula. A bench offers a rest stop with

Pleasant woodland paths wind through groves of American holly, rhododendrons, beech, and other species at Lowell Holly Reservation.

views across Wakeby Pond. After crossing a small knoll, reach a three-way intersection at 1.1 miles. Turn right on Blue Trail, a short out-and-back path that leads through a dense tunnel of trees and shrubs to the tip of Conaumet Point, a narrow sliver of land that extends into Wakeby Pond. Limited views appear through the vegetation. The pond's three small islands lie just beyond the point.

After exploring the point, backtrack to the junction and bear right to rejoin Yellow Trail, which continues southwest to another fork. Turn right onto Orange Trail, which leads southwest toward the southern end of the peninsula. (To shorten the hike by 0.6 mile, bypass this section by continuing to follow Yellow Trail.) This area usually has fewer visitors than the rest of the property, so chances are you will have these woods to yourself.

From the junction, Orange Trail follows gently rolling terrain as it negotiates a series of low hills and then forks into a short loop that winds around the peninsula's southwest corner. Follow either branch of the loop to 60-foot knolls, where there are fine views through the trees to the south across Mashpee Pond.

Both Mashpee and Wakeby ponds are well known for excellent fishing. Trout are stocked in both spring and fall, and warmwater species include largemouth and smallmouth bass, pickerel, and bluegill. The ponds also attract a variety of birdlife, including great blue herons, ducks, Canada geese, and osprey, which make speedy dives to catch fish. Raccoons and foxes often stalk wetland edges, especially in the early morning or evening.

After completing the Orange Trail loop, backtrack to the junction with Yellow Trail and turn right to resume the Yellow Trail circuit. Some very large holly trees grow on this side of the peninsula. A short side path on the right leads to a small, sandy beach on the north shores of Mashpee Pond, where a pleasant view across the water awaits. Yellow Trail turns to the left, away from the shore, and then to the right as it follows the base of another low hill. Complete the Yellow Trail circuit at the western edge of the neck, and bear right to retrace your steps past the beach and seasonal parking area at 2.4 miles. Backtrack along Red Trail to return to the trailhead.

DID YOU KNOW?

The reservation was once known as Conaumet, which was derived from *Kuwunut*, a Wampanoag term meaning "beach."

NEARBY

The town of Mashpee is known for its rural character and abundant protected land, which includes Quashnet Woods State Reservation on MA 28; Mashpee River Woodlands, just east of the junction of MA 151 and MA 28; and South Cape Beach State Park, at the end of Great Oak Road off MA 28. Restaurants are on MA 28 in Mashpee, at Mashpee Commons at the junction of MA 28 and MA 151, and in Falmouth and Hyannis.

MORE INFORMATION

The reservation is open year-round, sunrise to sunset; no fee. Mountain biking is allowed only on designated trails. Hunting is prohibited. The main entrance parking lot is open year-round.

55 SANDY NECK CIRCUIT

Loop trails offer excellent views of a long barrier beach's diverse habitats, including a salt marsh, dunes, and Cape Cod Bay.

Features 🐕 💧 🔍 🏃 ✨ 🏊 $

Location Barnstable, MA

Rating Moderate

Distance 4.7-mile loop

Elevation Gain Minimal

Estimated Time 2 to 3 hours

Maps USGS Hyannis, USGS Sandwich; online: town.barnstable.ma.us/
SandyNeckPark/fileuploads/snmap.pdf

GPS coordinates 41° 44.121′ N, 70° 23.100′ W

Contact Barnstable Marine and Environmental Affairs Department:
town.barnstable.ma.us/sandyneckpark, 508-790-6272 or 508-362-8300 (gatehouse)

DIRECTIONS
From US 6 in Barnstable, take Exit 65 (formerly Exit 5) and follow MA 149 north to the junction with MA 6A. Turn left, follow MA 6A west for 2.5 miles, and then turn right onto Sandy Neck Road and continue to a hiker parking area at the gatehouse.

TRAIL DESCRIPTION
Sandy Neck is a 6-mile-long, 1,390-acre barrier beach with associated marshes that borders Cape Cod Bay. Due to its unique and varied natural communities, the site was designated as a state Area of Critical Environmental Concern in 1978, and it is also recognized as a Cultural Historic District for its dune cottages and the Sandy Neck Lighthouse.

Marsh Trail, several numbered crossover paths that traverse the dunes, and the beach itself offer a variety of hiking options, ranging from a 1.6-mile nature walk to an ambitious outing of more than 13 miles along the protected marsh and 100-foot-tall dunes to the open waters of Cape Cod Bay. This guide describes a 4.7-mile loop that uses crossover path number 2. During exceptionally high tides, low-lying areas on Sandy Neck's marsh side, such as the start of Marsh Trail, may be temporarily flooded. (*Note*: Hikers are not allowed to enter private property or marked erosion control areas, and they must stay off the dunes, crossing only on designated trails.)

From a signed trailhead near the gatehouse parking area, begin the outbound portion of the circuit on Marsh Trail, which initially passes through an area of red pine and scrub oak. It then follows the edge of Great Marsh, an expansive 3,500-acre marsh that borders

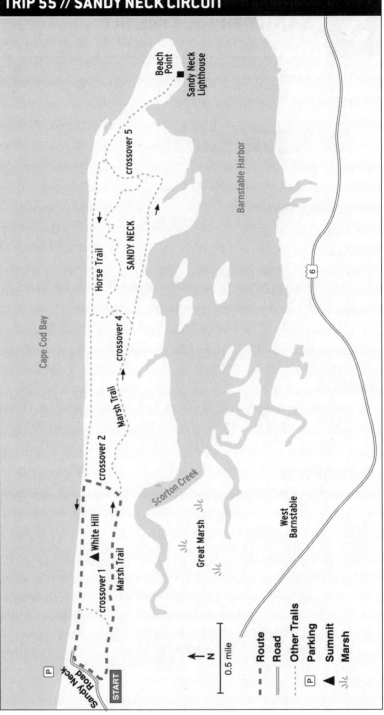

Beach Point

Sandy Neck Lighthouse

Barnstable Harbor

crossover 5

Horse Trail

SANDY NECK

Cape Cod Bay

crossover 4

Marsh Trail

6

crossover 2

Scorton Creek

West Barnstable

Great Marsh

crossover 1 ▲ White Hill

Marsh Trail

P

Sandy Neck Road

START

N

0.5 mile

- - - Route
——— Road
········· Other Trails
P Parking
▲ Summit
Marsh

Historic Sandy Neck Lighthouse, established in 1826, marks the entrance to Barnstable Harbor. *Photo by William DeSousa-Mauk, Creative Commons on Flickr.*

Scorton Creek and its vast maze of short tributaries. The blue trap boxes at the marsh edge are used to control greenhead flies, which are most active during hot, sunny periods from mid-July to early August. Greenheads have a nasty bite, and insect repellents are often ineffective at keeping them away.

To the left is an entirely different coastal habitat, a chain of tall dunes that obstructs the view of the ocean. Some are capped by trees, shrubs, cranberries, and wildflowers that grow when there's enough leaf litter to support seeds and roots. Stay on the sandy trail to avoid ticks and poison ivy and to keep from destroying the beach grass and other fragile dune plants.

At 0.5 mile from the trailhead, reach a bench at the signed junction with Trail 1, the first of the crossover paths, on the left. Although the hike described here continues straight on Marsh Trail, you can shorten the walk to 1.6 miles by taking this path and returning via the beach. Marsh Trail leads to the east; the terrain alternates between soft, sandy stretches and easier, more firmly packed sections. Continuous views of the open Great Marsh are on the right and rolling high dunes are to the left. Poverty grass displays its yellow blooms in early June, and pale purple patches of sea lavender grow prolifically along the trail. In late summer, look for golden asters, which have yellow petals and an orange center. A wide variety of wildlife is present throughout Sandy Neck, including river otters, white-tailed deer, coyotes, horseshoe crabs, and flocks of barn and tree swallows. The area also provides habitat for several endangered species, including piping plovers, diamondback terrapin turtles, and spadefoot toads.

Follow Marsh Trail as it winds past several private residences (please respect all posted areas) to the intersection with Trail 2 (crossover path) at 1.9 miles. Scorton Creek comes into view in the distance to the right as it meanders toward Barnstable Harbor and Cape Cod Bay.

The hike continues to the left on Trail 2, following a 4.7-mile loop. For a longer expedition, continue straight on Marsh Trail to Trail 4 (there is no Trail 3) for a 9-mile round trip via the beach or to Trail 5 for a 13-mile circuit. The historical cottages on Beach Point and the Sandy Neck Lighthouse come into view en route to the Trail 4 intersection. An optional out-and-back detour east along the beach, past private land to the lighthouse and the tip of Beach Point, adds approximately 2 miles to the Trail 5 round-trip. Another option is Horse Trail, which runs east–west for nearly 2 miles between Trails 4 and 5, traversing the neck's dunes and maritime forests.

Trail 2 winds north for approximately 0.4 mile across the dunes to the edge of Sandy Neck Beach, which extends along the southern shores of Cape Cod Bay. At this point, you are roughly 2 miles from the park entrance (to the left when facing the water) and 4.25 miles from Beach Point to the east. To continue the loop, turn left and walk west along the beach.

Visible across the bay to the left is the coastline near Plymouth; the Lower Cape's shoreline is on your right. Unlike other areas of Cape Cod, where substantial land has been lost to erosion, Sandy Neck Beach gains size annually from sands deposited from areas to the north, including Plymouth. In late autumn, migrating sea turtles, including Kemp's ridleys, loggerheads, leatherbacks, and green turtles, often wash up on Sandy Neck and other bay beaches after becoming hypothermic in the cold ocean waters. Most strandings at Sandy Neck Beach occur during or after days with north winds. Stranded turtles are taken to rehabilitation centers and transported to southern wintering grounds.

Sandy Neck is one of the most popular Lower Cape beaches, and during summer, recreational vehicles may be parked along the sands. The middle portion of the beach is rather rocky, but the shoreline offers easy walking along the tidal flats. As you near the entrance on your return, pass the signed Trail 1 crossover path on the left and then turn left on a short beach access path (created after stairs repeatedly washed out during winter storms) that leads to the beach parking lot. From the parking lot, follow the entrance road back to the gatehouse and the hiker parking area.

DID YOU KNOW?

During World War II, the U.S. Army used the Sandy Neck beach and dunes as a training ground for troops bound for the Sahara Desert.

NEARBY

Scenic Barnstable Harbor is the departure point for whale-watching cruises to Stellwagen Bank, a marine sanctuary near Provincetown (see whales.net for details). The Coast Guard Heritage Museum at 3353 Main Street (Route 6A) in Barnstable is dedicated to the history of the Coast Guard. Call 508-362-8521 or visit coastguardheritagemuseum.org for information. Restaurants are on and near Main Street in Barnstable; many more places to eat are in the nearby village of Hyannis.

MORE INFORMATION

Sandy Neck is open daily from 8 A.M. to 9 P.M. The gatehouse is open seasonally or by appointment. Limited free parking for hikers is available adjacent to the gatehouse; a seasonal fee ($25 weekends, $15 weekdays) is charged at the beach parking lot. Leashed dogs are allowed on Marsh Trail and the off-road vehicle portion of the beach year-round; they are prohibited from the bathing beach near the parking area from May 15 to September 15. Four-wheel drive vehicles are allowed in certain sections by permit, and hunting is allowed during designated seasons; visitors in late autumn should wear blaze-orange clothing. A primitive tent area is available on Trail 4.

56 NICKERSON STATE PARK

A scenic loop trail passes beaches and coastal forests on the shores of Cliff Pond, one of Cape Cod's largest kettle ponds.

Features 🚶🐕💧⛵🏊⛷️🔆⛺️⛴️🏕️💲🛶🚴

Location Brewster, MA

Rating Easy to Moderate

Distance 2.9-mile loop

Elevation Gain 50 feet

Estimated Time 1.75 hours

Maps USGS Orleans OEW; Massachusetts Department of Conservation and Recreation: mass.gov/doc/nickerson-state-park-trail-map/download

GPS coordinates 41° 45.618′ N, 70° 01.110′ W

Contact Massachusetts Department of Conservation and Recreation: mass.gov/locations/nickerson-state-park, 508-896-3491

DIRECTIONS

From US 6, take Exit 89 (formerly Exit 12) and follow MA 6A west toward Brewster for 1.5 miles to the well-marked park entrance on the south side of the highway. From the contact station, follow the park entrance road for 0.4 mile, turn left onto Flax Pond Road, and continue 1.2 miles to the parking area at the road's end.

TRAIL DESCRIPTION

Situated on the elbow of Cape Cod, Nickerson State Park protects nearly 2,000 acres of inland coastal habitats, including eight kettle ponds and a large, unbroken forest of pitch pines and scrub oaks. Numerous recreational amenities include hiking trails, boat launches, several campgrounds with more than 400 total sites, and a paved bicycle path that connects to the Cape Cod Rail Trail. The park was created in 1934 through the donation of a 1,700-acre private estate; it was subsequently upgraded through the efforts of the Civilian Conservation Corps.

This hike follows Cliff Pond Trail around the perimeter of Cliff Pond, which, at roughly 200 acres, is the largest of the park's kettle ponds. The yellow-blazed route is easy to follow, but it is narrow in places and has a number of unmarked junctions with other side trails. Along the way, you'll pass several sand beaches and boat launches that offer scenic views, swimming, or just places to rest and enjoy the sun. These areas may be crowded during summer, although the rest of the route offers plenty of solitude.

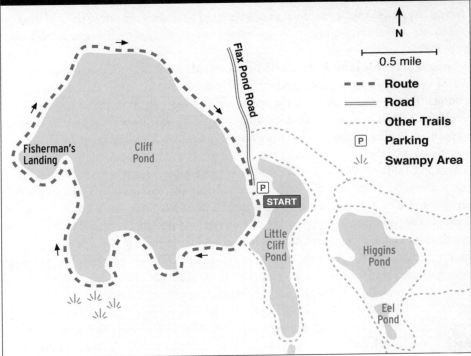

From the parking lot, walk past the sign reading "No Vehicles Beyond This Point" to the narrow neck of land between Cliff and Little Cliff ponds. (Little Cliff Pond Trail, a loop around Little Cliff Pond that rejoins Cliff Pond Trail south of the trailhead, begins on the east side of the parking lot. A circuit combining both trails is 3.8 miles.) Cliff Pond's swimming beach is on the right, and the Little Cliff Pond boat launch is to the left.

Begin a clockwise circuit by following Cliff Pond Trail away from the beach, along the water's edge, and beneath a steep slope on the left. After a few hundred feet, reach another beach and boat launch, where seasonal boat rentals are available from a private company (see "More Information" below). Continue straight past the southern junction with Little Cliff Pond Trail on the left.

Cliff Pond and the park's other kettle ponds, which include Flax, Little Cliff, and Higgins ponds, are among the roughly 300 kettle ponds of various sizes that dot Cape Cod. These ponds, which formed some 10,000 years ago as glaciers retreated, are not fed by any streams or brooks. They are dependent on precipitation and groundwater, which means water levels can vary annually.

Continue to a beach on the pond's southeast corner. Walk across the beach and follow the trail back into the woods, keeping close to the water on your right. A hill rises out of the shoreline to the left, and the slopes are covered with pitch pine. Note the almost complete lack of vegetation in the grassy understory. The park's extensive forests provide food and habitats for a variety of wildlife, including eastern coyotes, white-tailed deer, red foxes, raccoons, and striped skunks. All these creatures are highly adaptable and thrive in a variety of habitats, including areas close to humans. As with the other animals, skunks are most often encountered early or late in the day, when they make feeding forays as the light changes. As those unfortunate enough to be sprayed by skunks can attest, the critters often make their dens under buildings or near campgrounds, such as those found at Nickerson State Park.

Birds of prey that inhabit these woodlands include great horned, eastern screech, and barred owls; woodland warblers and other migratory songbirds are present in spring and summer. During spring and fall, the ponds serve as crucial rest stops for large flocks of waterfowl, such as ring-necked ducks, common goldeneyes, and common and red-breasted mergansers, as they migrate to and from northern summer breeding grounds. Bald eagles have frequented the pond in recent years.

Stay on Cliff Pond Trail as it curves to the left, following the first of several coves that jut out of the pond's southern and western shores. In another quarter-mile (1.0 mile overall), arrive at the second cove, where the trail turns sharply right and travels a narrow beach that separates the pond's southern tip from a shallow wetland known as Grassy Nook. Scan this marshy area for great blue herons, green herons, and other wading birds. At the next fork, bear right and continue along the pond edge. The trail rises gently as it traverses the mildly rolling terrain along the southwest corner and follows bluffs above the water. The swimming beach at the trailhead is visible through the trees, across the water to the northeast.

Cliff Pond Trail turns abruptly left again and leads to the last of the coves at the pond's west side, where views provide a good perspective of how large the pond is. At 1.8 miles, reach a boat launch and beach off Joe Long Road, an area known as Fisherman's Landing. A small, shallow pond will be on your left, just beyond the boat launch. Bear right here to follow Cliff Pond Trail along Cliff Pond's northwestern shores. (Be aware of other paths that lead up the slope to camping Area 4.) Continue below the campground past a series of small beaches, a large boulder, and another small shallow pond on the left.

From the small pond, continue on Cliff Pond Trail through pitch-pine groves along Cliff Pond's northeastern shores, past a private path that leads up the slopes on the left. (Please respect all posted areas.) After making a quick climb to follow the bluffs above the water, the trail curves to the left and returns to the parking area. The circuit ends opposite the trailhead for Little Cliff Pond Trail.

DID YOU KNOW?

Samuel Mayo Nickerson (1830–1914), a founding officer of the First National Bank of Chicago, built an estate on the grounds during the nineteenth century. The property became Massachusetts's first state park in 1934. The Department of Conservation and Recreation owns and manages more than 450,000 acres of land statewide.

NEARBY

Several Cape Cod Bay beaches in Brewster and Orleans are off MA 6A near the park. The Cape Cod Museum of Natural History, which includes walking trails to Wing's Island and Cape Cod Bay, is on US 6A (869 Main Street) in Brewster, near the Dennis town line. Call 508-896-3867 or visit ccmnh.org for details. Restaurants are on MA 6A in Brewster and along MA 6A and MA 28 in Orleans.

Cliff Pond Trail offers a scenic circuit past beaches and coastal pitch-pine forests on Cliff Pond's shores.

MORE INFORMATION

Nickerson State Park is open to day-use visitors year-round, sunrise to sunset. A parking fee ($8 for Massachusetts residents, $30 for nonresidents) is charged from Memorial Day through November. The park provides 8 miles of paved bike trails, as well as access to the 27.5-mile Cape Cod Rail Trail, which runs from Yarmouth to Wellfleet. As of 2021, Lea's Boat Rentals (leasboatrentals.com) provides canoes, kayaks, sailboats, and paddleboards at Cliff Pond and Flax Pond. The park offers numerous interpretive and recreational activities in season.

FORT HILL

This varied hike offers scenic views from open meadows and explores the heart of a large red maple swamp.

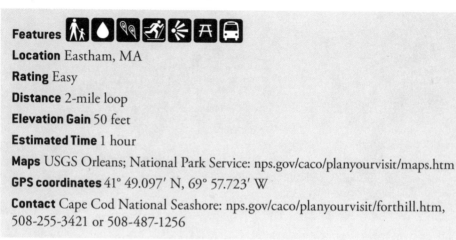

Features 🥾⚫🔍⛷️💥🏕️🚌

Location Eastham, MA

Rating Easy

Distance 2-mile loop

Elevation Gain 50 feet

Estimated Time 1 hour

Maps USGS Orleans; National Park Service: nps.gov/caco/planyourvisit/maps.htm

GPS coordinates 41° 49.097′ N, 69° 57.723′ W

Contact Cape Cod National Seashore: nps.gov/caco/planyourvisit/forthill.htm, 508-255-3421 or 508-487-1256

DIRECTIONS

From the rotary junction of US 6, MA 6A, and MA 28 at the Orleans–Eastham town line, drive north on US 6 for 1.3 miles. Following signs for the Fort Hill area, turn right onto Governor Prence Road, and after about a quarter-mile bear right onto Fort Hill Road. Continue past the lower parking lot on the left to the upper parking area at the road's end.

By public transportation, the Cape Cod Regional Transit Authority's Flex bus offers stops between Harwich and Provincetown. Riders may board at scheduled stops or make arrangements for other stops. The Flex bus also connects with other lines, including the Plymouth & Brockton service. A bike shuttle is provided to the National Seashore from several Outer Cape towns in summer. Visit capecodtransit.org for information.

TRAIL DESCRIPTION

The Fort Hill area encompasses low hills, meadows, and a coastal red maple swamp that borders Nauset Marsh and a long barrier beach. It is in the southern portion of the 44,000-acre, 40-mile-long Cape Cod National Seashore, which stretches from Chatham all the way to the tip of Cape Cod in Provincetown.

Attractions of this popular loop hike include panoramic coastal vistas from Fort Hill, wildlife-viewing opportunities in fields along Nauset Marsh, a long boardwalk that winds through the red maple swamp, and the historical Penniman House, once owned by the captain of a whaling ship. The combination of water, boardwalk, and expansive views makes this hike a favorite for families. The route is not blazed, but junctions are signed.

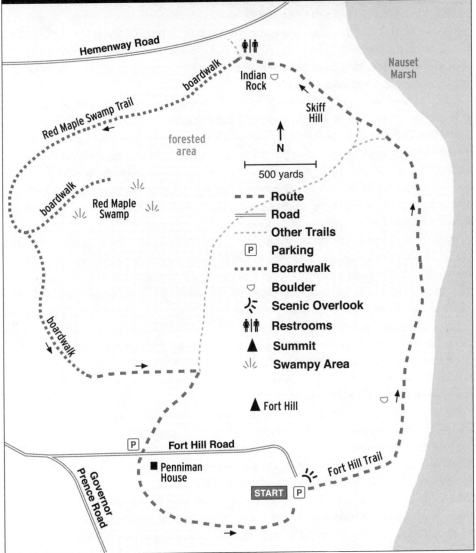

Begin at the upper parking lot at the top of Fort Hill, where there are outstanding views across meadows to Nauset Marsh and the Atlantic Ocean. The hill is a great spot to watch a colorful sunrise or to admire the moon over the water. The meadows, thickets, and marsh edges provide excellent bird-watching opportunities. You might see a snow bunting, which looks a bit like a sparrow until it reveals a belly that is almost pure white. This ground bird, about 6 inches long, favors open habitats, such as tundra, dunes, and fields. Monarch butterflies visit Fort Hill in summer, and eastern cottontail rabbits can be seen year-round. Familiar summer flowers include Queen Anne's lace, goldenrod, common evening primrose, chicory, and sweet pea—an escaped garden perennial distinguished by its pink and white petals. Colorful non-native lupines bloom in late spring.

Follow Fort Hill Trail along the edge of the meadows as it descends gently to the marsh and a huge boulder deposited by glaciers during the last ice age. Watch for northern harriers (hawks) hovering above the salt marsh; wading birds, such as great blue herons and green herons; and shorebirds, such as greater yellowlegs and semipalmated plovers, feeding in the mudflats. Bayberry, black cherry, honeysuckle, and salt-spray rose grow along the edge of the marsh. Autumnal tints here are subtle but pleasing to the eye, with golden marsh grass ringed by russet vegetation.

From the boulder, bear left in a northerly direction until you reach the woods, composed primarily of cedar trees. Bear right and continue to a pavilion atop Skiff Hill, from which there's another fine view, at 0.4 mile. The pavilion shelters Indian Rock, another glacial boulder used by the Nauset to sharpen fishhooks and tools (it was originally farther out in the marsh but was moved here for ease of viewing). The abrasive qualities of this fine-grained metamorphic rock were perfect for grinding and polishing implements. Let children run their fingers over the grooves in the rock as you explain how American Indians sharpened their tools in those same grooves.

From the pavilion, continue for roughly 300 yards to the signed upper junction with Red Maple Swamp Trail, opposite the restrooms near Hemenway Road at the property boundary. (A short detour to Hemenway Road leads to a boat landing with another scenic view of Nauset Marsh.) Turn left and follow Red Maple Swamp Trail down to the wetland edge, where the long boardwalk will keep your feet dry and will delight children. The contrast between this dark, shaded wetland and the sunny fields at the hike's start makes this walk special. Interpretive signs along the trail identify plants such as highbush blueberry, netted chain fern, and fox grapes. Other species include winterberry, a low plant with bright red berries that are a favorite food for birds, and sweet pepperbush, which gives off a fragrant aroma from its flowers in late summer.

The boardwalk winds past groves of red maples (also known as swamp maples), for which the trail is named, including several tall, twisted specimens. The standing water in the swamp is freshwater (not salt water), and the red maples can tolerate wet roots. Red maple is one of the Northeast's most common tree species because of its adaptability to a variety of habitats, including coastal wetlands and mountain forests. In autumn, its leaves turn bright crimson, although dry years may cause drabber brown hues.

At a junction at 0.8 mile, a short out-and-back segment of the boardwalk offers a quick 0.1-mile detour to the heart of the swamp. Return to the junction and turn left to continue on the main trail to the boardwalk's end; then make a gentle climb on a dirt-and-gravel path to the lower junction with Fort Hill Trail. Look for meadowlarks and bluebirds around meadow edges.

Turn right and follow Fort Hill Trail to the lower parking lot (the upper lot where you parked is visible up the hill to the left). Cross Fort Hill Road to view the distinctive Penniman House, where a large archway formed by the jawbones of a whale frames the front yard. Captain Edward Penniman first took to the sea in 1842 at age 11 and eventually circled the world seven times. His home became a local landmark. From the back of the house, follow Fort Hill Trail east through low-lying woods for about one-third of a mile back to Fort Hill. An easy ascent to the parking area completes the loop.

DID YOU KNOW?

Author Henry Beston wrote *The Outermost House* while living in a cottage on nearby Nauset Beach during the 1920s. The classic work helped inspire Cape Cod National Seashore's creation. The cottage, known as the Fo'castle, washed out to sea during the great blizzard of 1978.

NEARBY

The historic Nauset Lighthouse, adjacent to Nauset Light Beach on Ocean View Drive in Eastham, is one of Cape Cod's best-known landmarks. Originally built in Chatham, it was moved to Eastham in 1923 and then relocated farther inland in 1993 due to substantial erosion of the bluffs and beach. The Three Sisters, a trio of small lighthouses, are on Cable Road near the Nauset Light Beach entrance. Many restaurants are on US 6, MA 6A, and MA 28 in Eastham, Orleans, and Wellfleet.

MORE INFORMATION

The Fort Hill area is open year-round, dawn to dusk; no fee. Dogs are prohibited. The Red Maple Swamp Trail boardwalk is universally accessible.

Fort Hill offers some of the best and easiest to achieve scenic views at Cape Cod National Seashore.

GREAT WHITE SHARKS RETURN TO MASSACHUSETTS

The 1975 movie *Jaws*, about a fictional great white shark that terrorized a New England seaside community, drew record-breaking audiences. The real-life return of great whites to the coastal waters of Massachusetts has also attracted much attention in recent years.

As one of the ocean's apex predators, great white sharks are at the top of the marine food chain. They can weigh as much as 5,000 pounds and live more than 70 years. Relatively little is known about their historical presence in New England, which is at the northern limit of their Atlantic range. Before 2012, there were only four known attacks on humans by great white sharks in Massachusetts. The shark's western North Atlantic population declined late in the twentieth century, and sightings were sporadic. Since 2009, however, this trend has reversed, and great white sharks rapidly have become a well-established presence around Cape Cod and the adjacent mainland coast. They arrive during summer, when the ocean warms, and head south in fall, when the water temperature drops.

The return of great white sharks is due largely to the recovery of gray seals, one of the sharks' primary prey species. An adult seal can weigh as much as 700 pounds and can sustain an individual shark for a month or longer. After hunting led to significant declines, state and federal officials placed the gray seal on protected lists. With the seals shielded from hunters, their population in Massachusetts has grown from a low of an estimated 15 individuals in the mid-twentieth century to more than 15,000.

The surging shark population has led to increasingly frequent conflicts with humans. During summer, outer Cape Cod ocean beaches are often temporarily closed to swimming because of shark sightings. In September 2018, a surfer was killed by a shark off Newcomb Hollow Beach in Wellfleet. It was the first shark-related fatality in Massachusetts since 1936. In 2012, a shark seriously injured a man wading at Truro's Ballston Beach. Several paddlers have been pursued and even displaced from their boats, and an increasing number of shark attacks on seals have been witnessed close to beaches. Beach visitors should be alert for advisories and avoid swimming, wading, or paddling near seals, as sharks are drawn to them.

Great white sharks are indicators of healthy marine ecosystems; top-line predators such as sharks keep the food web in balance and maintain populations of prey species. An increasing number of people have come to appreciate the great white's role in nature, and tourism related to both sharks and seals now thrives on Cape Cod. Although great white shark sightings are unpredictable, gray seals are commonly seen at Cape Cod's outer beaches, from Chatham to Provincetown, and along the mainland coast, including Ellisville Harbor State Park and Plymouth's coastal waters.

58 WELLFLEET BAY WILDLIFE SANCTUARY

Enjoy the excellent bird-watching, diverse plant life, and scenic views along Silver Spring Brook, Goose Pond, and the marshes and mudflats near Try Island.

Features 👣 ♿ 💧 🔍 ❄ ⛺ 🚻 💲

Location South Wellfleet, MA

Rating Easy

Distance 2.3 miles round trip

Elevation Gain 50 feet

Estimated Time 1.5 hours

Maps USGS Wellfleet, USGS Wellfleet OOE; Mass Audubon: massaudubon.org/content/download/7939/144410/file/wellfleet_trails.pdf

GPS coordinates 41° 52.937′ N, 69° 59.638′ W

Contact Mass Audubon: massaudubon.org/get-outdoors/wildlife-sanctuaries/wellfleet-bay, 508-349-2615

DIRECTIONS

From the Eastham–Wellfleet town line, follow US 6 east (heading north) for 0.3 mile to signs marking the sanctuary on the left (west) side of the highway. Turn left and follow the sanctuary entrance road 0.4 mile to the nature center.

TRAIL DESCRIPTION

Abundant wildlife, scenic coastal views, and family-friendly trails make Wellfleet Bay Wildlife Sanctuary a popular destination for explorers of all ages. Diverse natural features, including Wellfleet Bay, tidal flats, salt marshes, forests, ponds, brooks, and meadows, provide habitats for nearly 300 bird species. This hike combines Goose Pond and Try Island trails as a 2.3-mile round trip that includes a boardwalk leading through a salt marsh to a small beach and tidal flats. Trail junctions are well signed. (*Note:* During some high tides, the boardwalk and marsh edges may be wet or temporarily flooded; check tide times at the nature center.)

Trail access is through the nature center during operating hours; follow signs at other times. At the center, be sure to check out the natural history exhibits, the aquariums, and the butterfly garden, where colorful planted flowers provide nourishment for butterflies and hummingbirds.

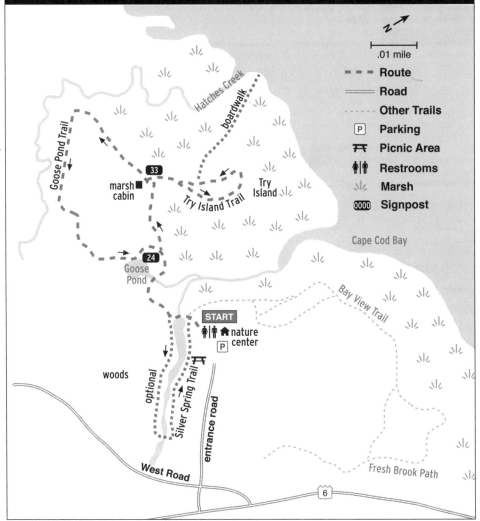

Following signs for Goose Pond Trail, walk past a playground and a solar panel. Bear right at the first junction with Silver Spring Trail and continue to a T junction near an overlook at the edge of a salt marsh. Watch for tree swallows—with glistening blue-black coats and white bellies—hunting insects above the fields and marshes. They favor nest boxes in open areas, such as the fields adjacent to the nature center, and often compete with bluebirds for choice spots. Turn left (Bay View Trail branches to the right) and follow Goose Pond Trail to a pond formed by a small dam on Silver Spring Brook. The shoreline on the left is surrounded by marsh fern, white poplar trees, swamp milkweed, and purple loosestrife—a nonindigenous plant with bright purple flowers that crowds out native vegetation. Painted turtles and frogs often bask on waterlilies in the pond during warm months.

Hatches Creek meets Wellfleet Bay at a picturesque area of sand beach and tidal flats favored by shorebirds.

Box turtles, distinguished by high-domed shells with yellow, orange, and black markings, inhabit brushy open areas, marsh edges, and low-elevation forests. They are now rare in Massachusetts because human development has led to a loss of suitable habitat throughout their range. Another uncommon reptile you may encounter is the black racer—a rather large, extremely quick, and nonpoisonous snake. It can grow to more than 5 feet in length and can be seen basking in the sun or hunting for small rodents.

Cross the dam and follow Goose Pond Trail past the second junction with Silver Spring Trail on the left. Continue through a forest of pines, including white, pitch, red, and Scotch varieties, which were planted here to stabilize the sandy soil. When the Pilgrims landed at Cape Cod, trees covered the peninsula, but by the time Henry David Thoreau made his four explorations of the Cape, he lamented that the land was literally blowing away because settlers had cut most of the trees. These forest groves provide habitat for white-tailed deer, eastern coyotes, and migratory songbirds. Pine warblers, distinguished by their trilling calls, are among the first songbirds to arrive in spring.

At Goose Pond, a small tidal wetland, a short side path on the left leads to an observation blind, where you can look for green herons, snowy egrets, kingfishers, and migratory shorebirds. Goose Pond Trail bends to the right and follows a short boardwalk between the pond and the marsh on the right. Red-winged blackbirds are present from March to October; the male is recognizable by its red shoulder patch, while females are dark brown. These birds build grass-and-weed nests in the wetlands, usually set in low bushes, and they feed on insects and marsh plants. Other pond dwellers include the snapping turtle, which has a ridged green-black shell, and the painted turtle, identifiable by its smooth, black shell and its head streaked with yellow markings.

Continue to follow Goose Pond Trail through another forest grove that borders the edge of the salt marsh. Watch for eastern cottontail rabbits feeding along the sandy path. Pass a signed junction where the circuit portion of Goose Pond Trail begins (the return route is on the left). Red cedars are scattered throughout the woods, and a small observation deck on the right offers views across the marsh. About 0.25 mile from Goose Pond (0.5 mile overall), reach a junction at marker 33 at the forest–marsh edge near a small cabin that once hosted sanctuary visitors (now closed). Turn right on Try Island Trail, which leads north along the marsh edge to Try Island, a small oasis of forest. Northern harriers, red-tailed hawks, and wading birds frequent in this open area.

At a signed fork on Try Island Trail, follow the right branch to a scenic vista of the bay and marsh. Turn right at the next junction and follow a boardwalk through the heart of the marsh. Enjoy close-up views of fiddler crabs scampering in and out of thousands of narrow holes in the mudflats. Well-adapted beach grass, once harvested by Colonial farmers for cattle feed, has a narrow profile that reduces the amount of evaporation caused by the constant coastal winds and an extensive root system that helps stabilize the sand on the dunes and beach.

At the boardwalk's end at 1.0 mile, reach an interface of marsh, tidal flats, and a barrier beach, where Hatches Creek empties into Wellfleet Bay. Great Island, actually a peninsula, is visible across the water to the west. Watch for shorebirds, such as the greater yellow-legs—a 14-inch-long wading bird with long yellow legs and grayish underparts—and flocks of sandpipers, terns, and gulls. Prime shorebird viewing is during spring and late summer migrations, when many species use Wellfleet Bay and other preserves along the Atlantic coast as resting areas. (*Note*: If you venture toward the edge of the flats, keep an eye on the tides.)

After exploring the beach and flats, retrace your steps on the boardwalk and Try Island Trail to the junction at the cabin. Turn right to resume the Goose Pond Trail loop, which leads along the edge of the salt marsh on the right and fields and woods on the left. Look for Virginia rose and salt-spray rose, both with curved thorns and pale pink blossoms, in early summer. Sea lavender, also called marsh rosemary, grows at the upper edge of the marsh, staying close to the ground to conserve moisture. Its tiny white flowers remain on the plant into fall.

About a quarter-mile from the cabin junction (1.5 miles overall), turn left at an arrow marker at the sanctuary boundary and continue on Goose Pond Trail, which leads through a rare open heath natural community. Beach plums, which have pink and white flowers in May before the leaves are fully out, grow in sheltered spots. In September, they yield deep purple fruit that is eaten by red foxes, raccoons, and birds. Other plants include oak, black locust, pokeweed, goldenrod, spindle tree, and golden aster. Oak trees often hold rust-colored leaves well into November, when other species have lost their foliage. Look closely for the tall, green, fernlike leaves of asparagus, the wild descendant of farming that took place here more than 60 years ago. Bear left at a trail sign and complete the circuit portion of Goose Pond Trail at the junction near Goose Pond. Turn right and retrace your steps to

Silver Spring Brook. For a short, optional extension, turn right and follow Silver Spring Trail along the east side of the brook then cross a wooden bridge and continue along the west bank to return to the nature center. For the most direct route, retrace your steps on Goose Pond Trail to the trailhead.

DID YOU KNOW?

Before Mass Audubon acquired the Wellfleet Bay property, it was the site of an asparagus farm and a bird-banding station.

NEARBY

The historical Wellfleet Drive-In Theatre, on US 6 at the Eastham–Wellfleet town line just south of the sanctuary, is open from late May to September. Call 508-349-7176 or visit wellfleetcinemas.com for schedules and other information. Many restaurants are along US 6 in Eastham and Wellfleet.

MORE INFORMATION

The trails are open year-round. Admission is free for Mass Audubon members; fees for nonmembers are $8 for adults, $5 for seniors, and $3 for children ages 2 through 12. Dogs are prohibited, and hunting is not allowed. The nature center, an award-winning, green-certified building, features restrooms, natural history exhibits, and a gift shop.

59 GREAT ISLAND

The combination of quiet pine woodlands, towering dunes, and scenic coastal views makes Great Island a special place to explore.

Features

Location Wellfleet, MA

Rating Moderate

Distance 4.0 miles round trip

Elevation Gain 120 feet

Estimated Time 2.5 hours

Maps USGS Wellfleet OEE; National Park Service: nps.gov/caco/planyourvisit/maps.htm

GPS coordinates 41° 56.008′ N, 70° 04.157′ W

Contact Cape Cod National Seashore: nps.gov/caco/planyourvisit/greatislandtrail.htm, 508-255-3421

DIRECTIONS

From US 6 in Wellfleet (5.1 miles north of the Wellfleet–Eastham town line), take the Wellfleet Town Center exit at a traffic light. After 0.2 mile, turn left onto East Commercial Street and continue 0.8 mile to Wellfleet Harbor and the town pier. Turn right onto Kendrick Avenue and follow it along the waterfront for 0.8 mile. Bear left onto Chequesset Neck Road and continue 1.7 miles to the Great Island parking lot on the left.

By public transportation, the Cape Cod Regional Transit Authority's Flex bus offers stops between Harwich and Provincetown. Riders may board at scheduled stops or make arrangements for other stops. The Flex bus also connects with other lines, including the Plymouth & Brockton service. A bike shuttle is provided to the National Seashore from several Outer Cape towns in summer. Visit capecodtransit.org for information.

TRAIL DESCRIPTION

The peninsula called Great Island, one of Cape Cod National Seashore's finest hiking destinations, is a knob of glacial debris connected to the mainland by a narrow hill of sand. Winds and tides have continually reshaped this area, which was an island until a storm linked it to the mainland during the early nineteenth century. Signed trails and a long section of undeveloped beach on Cape Cod Bay provide several hiking options, ranging from short walks to the beach and marsh to loops of 6 miles or longer, depending on how far one ventures to Jeremy Point at Great Island's southern tip. The trip described here offers a good sampling of the peninsula's diverse features, including a historical site where a tavern once stood.

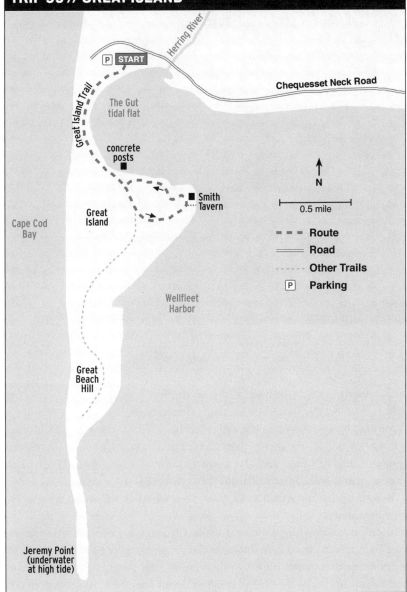

Herring River

P START

Chequesset Neck Road

Great Island Trail

The Gut
tidal flat

concrete
posts

■ Smith
Tavern

Great
Island

Cape Cod
Bay

N

0.5 mile

- - - Route

▬▬▬ Road

·········· Other Trails

P Parking

Wellfleet
Harbor

Great
Beach
Hill

Jeremy Point
(underwater
at high tide)

Because the peninsula is large and many visitors stay at the beach, you can often experience Great Island in relative solitude and enjoy listening to the lapping waves and birdcalls. Be sure to bring plenty of water, sunscreen, and a hat, as the trails traverse areas with soft sand and sun exposure.

From the information sign at the parking lot, follow Great Island Trail downhill through a stand of pitch pines that were planted during the late nineteenth century. Early settlers cut down most of the timber that once covered Cape Cod, and without diverse tree cover, the Cape was literally blowing away before planting efforts began to stabilize the soil.

The molted skins of Atlantic horseshoe crabs are a familiar sight along the estuarine tidal flats, which also offer rich habitat for marine life such as fiddler crabs, oysters, and quahogs.

At the base of the steps at the water's edge on the Wellfleet Harbor side of the peninsula, turn right and follow the shore in a southerly direction. A sign lists the mileage of Great Island's various hiking options. The estuarine tidal flats formed by the Herring River drainage are rich habitat for marine life, such as fiddler crabs, oysters, and quahogs. The latter (pronounced "KO-hog" and also known locally as a hard-shell clam) is a clam that can live as long as 20 to 25 years. The salt hay growing along the shore was used by early settlers as cattle feed. On a winter walk, you may see harbor seals swimming in the bay or sunning on the shore.

As you walk the shore, look for oyster shells. Oysters were important to the diet of the American Indians who lived here. Later, settlers commercially harvested oysters for food and used their shells to make lime. Overharvesting, and perhaps other unknown factors, led to the disappearance of the Wellfleet oyster. In an attempt to reestablish oysters in the bay, oyster stock from the southern United States has been introduced.

During high tide, this shoreline path may be wet or muddy, so wear boots or waterproof footwear during cold-weather months. At approximately 0.5 mile from the trailhead, reach the junction with a short crossover path on the right that leads past the dunes to the beach on Great Island's west side, where there are sweeping vistas across Cape Cod Bay to Provincetown. On clear days, distant Provincetown landmarks, such as the Pilgrim Monument and the Long Point and Wood End lighthouses, are visible across the water. You can detour to the beach now or at the end of the walk.

Great Island Trail continues along the tidal flat known as the Gut, curving to the left in front of a tall dune. (Please respect all posted signs and stay off the dunes; access is restricted to prevent erosion.) Watch for fiddler crabs burrowing into small holes in the sand and mudflats. The males have a large single claw they use during territorial duels during mating season.

Continue along the contour of the shore for about a half-mile to a marked junction near concrete posts at 1.1 miles, where the circuit portion of this hike begins. Turn right, away from the shore, onto the trail that leads to the peninsula's interior, following the sign for Great Beach Hill. On hot days, the pitch-pine groves provide welcome shade. Walking is easier on the woodland path's firm ground.

Continue for about a quarter-mile to another signed junction (approximately 1.4 miles from the trailhead). The hike continues left here along a narrow path that leads east across the peninsula. (The trail straight ahead leads south to Great Beach Hill and Jeremy Point.) Traverse a low hill and continue to a short, unmarked side path on the right that leads to fine views and a pleasant resting spot atop a small bluff. After about a half-mile of walking on the main path from the junction with the trail to Great Beach Hill, you will arrive at a sign for Smith Tavern, which in the late 1600s and early 1700s served as a meeting place for weary mariners, including ship and shore whalers. An excavation of the site by archaeologists revealed more than 24,000 artifacts, including wineglass stems, clay pipes, and even a lady's fan.

Bear left at the trail signs and continue to the tavern interpretive sign and an overlook with an impressive view across the sparkling blue water of Wellfleet Bay. In pre-Colonial times, American Indians were on the lookout for shore-stranded whales in this area; they ate whale meat. When the Pilgrims landed on the cape before settling in Plymouth, they came upon American Indians butchering a whale on a beach near Great Island. During one of his four mid-nineteenth-century visits to Cape Cod, Henry David Thoreau witnessed 30 pilot whales (also known as blackfish) stranded on the beach: "They were a smooth shining black, like India-rubber, and had remarkably simple and humplike forms for animated creatures, with blunt round snout or head, whale-like, and simple, stiff looking flippers."

Indeed, whales were once so plentiful in the bay and surrounding waters that lookouts were posted on Great Island's high ground. These spotters alerted the waterborne whalers, who pursued the great mammals in small boats equipped with harpoons and lances. Shore whalers stayed close to land, often driving the whales up on the sand where they could be killed and butchered. Whale houses (in which gear was stored) and try-works (used to boil the whale oil from the blubber) were built around the perimeter of the island. The height of whaling activity in New England came in the 1840s, when more than 700 American whaling vessels were at sea. After the discovery of petroleum oil in Pennsylvania, the demand for whale oil dropped. Today, whale-watching tours are a popular attraction for many visitors to Cape Cod. Conservation groups continue efforts to protect whales worldwide, as the animals are still killed by commercial whalers in some places.

Follow a footpath leading through woods above Great Island's eastern shore back to the Gut. (You also have the option of walking along the shore, reachable via a side path on the right.) At approximately 3 miles, complete the loop at the junction by the concrete posts. Bear right and retrace your steps along the marsh edge to the trailhead.

DID YOU KNOW?

A community called Billingsgate once existed south of Jeremy Point and was home to 30 families and a lighthouse. By 1935, it was abandoned and inundated by rising sea levels.

NEARBY

Wellfleet is home to several art galleries and shops along and off Main and Commercial streets. Mayo Beach, adjacent to Wellfleet Harbor, offers scenic views to Great Island. Several places to eat are near Wellfleet Harbor and in the town center.

MORE INFORMATION

The Great Island area is open year-round, 6 A.M. to midnight; no fee. Portable restrooms are available seasonally. Dogs are prohibited. Check tide times and watch water levels carefully when exploring Jeremy Point, which may be flooded at high tide.

60

CAPE COD NATIONAL SEASHORE: PILGRIM HEIGHTS

Two short loop trails lead to a former farm in a kettle hole, panoramic overlooks, and the Pilgrim Spring historic site.

Features

Location Truro, MA

Rating Easy

Distance 1.3 miles round trip

Elevation Gain 115 feet

Estimated Time 1 hour

Maps USGS North Truro; National Park Service: nps.gov/caco/planyourvisit/maps.htm

GPS coordinates 42° 03.317′ N, 70° 06.388′ W

Contact Cape Cod National Seashore: nps.gov/caco/planyourvisit/smallsswamp.htm (Small's Swamp Trail), nps.gov/caco/planyourvisit/pilgrimspring.htm (Pilgrim Spring Trail), 508-255-3421

DIRECTIONS

From US 6 on the Truro–Wellfleet town line, drive north for 7.5 miles to the Pilgrim Heights entrance, marked with a brown sign. Bear right and follow the access road 0.5 mile to the trailhead at an interpretive shelter on the west side of the parking area.

By public transportation, the Cape Cod Regional Transit Authority's Flex bus offers stops between Harwich and Provincetown. Riders may board at scheduled stops or make arrangements for other stops. The Flex bus connects with other lines, including the Plymouth & Brockton service. A bike shuttle is also provided to the National Seashore from several Outer Cape towns in summer. Visit capecodtransit.org for information.

TRAIL DESCRIPTION

Situated at the narrowest part of Cape Cod, between Highland Cliffs to the south and Pilgrim Lake and the Province Lands dunes to the north, the Pilgrim Heights area of Cape Cod National Seashore is a locale rich in both history and scenery. Artifacts indicate American Indians were present at least 7,000 years ago. This was one of the first sites visited by the Pilgrims when they landed on Cape Cod in 1620. During the late nineteenth and early twentieth centuries, a large farm operated in the base of a sheltered kettle hole.

This hike combines Small's Swamp Trail and Pilgrim Spring Trail, which are unblazed but obvious, to form a 1.3-mile outing that visits the historical sites and three scenic overlooks with panoramic coastal vistas. The route, which is ideal for young children, can be completed

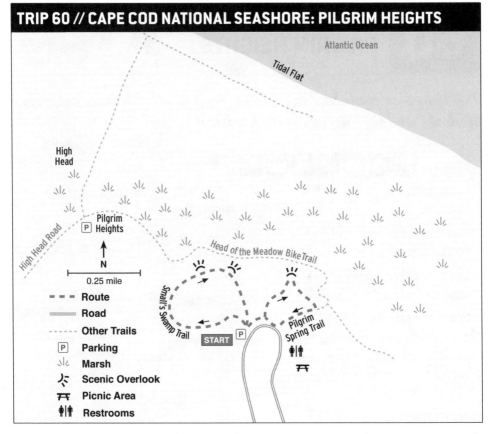

in an hour or so, although you'll want to allow extra time to enjoy the views. It is a mostly easy walk, with several short climbs and descents over gently rolling terrain. Both trails connect with Head of the Meadow Bike Trail, a 2-mile paved path that links Head of the Meadow Beach and a parking area on High Head Road west of Pilgrim Heights.

Begin at the shelter at the edge of the parking area, where an interpretive sign details the routes followed by the Pilgrims when they arrived in 1620. An overlook provides views of the kettle hole and swamp that you're about to explore. In autumn, foliage of red maples and understory shrubs makes a colorful sight. Follow Small's Swamp Trail into the woods to a junction where a 0.5-mile loop begins. To make a clockwise circuit, follow the left branch downhill through a grove of black oaks. The trail soon levels off at the base of the kettle hole, a large depression that formed more than 10,000 years ago, when a giant hunk of ice deposited by a retreating glacier melted. Other similar depressions that filled with water, called kettle ponds, are common throughout eastern Massachusetts.

In more recent times, the hollow was the site of Small Farm. The Small family cultivated the land from 1860 until the early 1920s, when the property was abandoned. Today, there is little visible evidence of the farm, although careful observers may spot apple, plum, and other fruit trees growing amid the vegetation. Interpretive posts identify many of the trees and shrubs, including swamp azalea, sweet pepperbush, bullbrier, and Virginia rose. All these species are well adapted to the harsh growing conditions of the coastal region.

Scenic overlooks and historical sites await visitors to Pilgrim Heights in the northern portion of Cape Cod National Seashore.

Follow a short boardwalk across a portion of the swamp and continue through a grove of aspen trees. At a wooden fence adjacent to Head of the Meadow Bike Trail, turn right and follow Small's Swamp Trail uphill out of the kettle hole to a small clearing of bearberry shrubs with a glimpse of the dunes and ocean.

A few hundred feet farther is the first of three open overlooks offering excellent panoramic perspectives of the various coastal habitats that make up this part of the National Seashore. The easterly views take in the marshes and a meandering creek in the valley below, backed by a chain of dunes and the ocean.

During spring, late summer, and early fall, these overlooks are ideal places to watch for migrating birds. Raptors often pass close above as they attempt to navigate this narrowest portion of Cape Cod. In some years, fortunate observers may see large swarms of dragonflies, including common green darners, which are among a handful of New England species that migrate at irregular intervals. These flights generally occur from late July to mid-October and are most likely in September. A swarm makes for a striking sight, as it may include thousands of individual dragonflies.

Continue to the nearby second overlook, where the creek makes a wide U-shaped turn below the dunes. Watch for ducks and wading birds along the marsh edge here. A portion of the bike trail is visible below, on the far right. From the overlook, make a short descent through the woods to the end of the loop, and then turn left and retrace your steps to the shelter.

The 0.7-mile Pilgrim Spring Trail loop begins adjacent to the shelter and leads through a grove of pitch pines and an open, shrubby area to the third overlook, which offers a similar easterly perspective to those on Small's Swamp Trail. Watch for white-capped waves on the horizon after passing storms.

From the overlook, follow Pilgrim Spring Trail downhill through thickets of winterberry. During the warm months, a familiar resident of these shrubby areas is the gray catbird, named for its catlike *me-ow* call. It is one of the most visible songbirds, and if you wait a few minutes, you'll likely get a good look at one hopping about the shrubs and thickets that make up its preferred habitat.

At 0.3 mile from the shelter, arrive at the base of the hill and the Pilgrim Spring historical site, marked with a plaque. The Pilgrims reputedly drank water from the spring after landing in the area in November 1620. Head of the Meadow Bike Trail passes by here (approximately 1.1 miles west of Head of the Meadow Beach). Watch for eastern cottontail rabbits feeding along trail edges early and late in the day, and osprey hunting over the adjacent salt marsh.

From the right-hand side of the spring (when facing the bike trail), resume the loop by following Pilgrim Spring Trail back up the hill through another pitch-pine grove. Blueberry shrubs, common in mixed habitats and along forest and trail edges, bear fruit in midsummer. After leveling off, the trail passes by restrooms at the east side of the parking area and access road. Cross the parking area, enter the woods at a posted Cape Cod National Seashore map, and continue for a few hundred feet to the end of the loop at the west side of the parking area.

If you have the time and energy for another walk, nearby Beech Forest Trail at Cape Cod National Seashore's Province Lands is an excellent option. This easy 1-mile loop leads to a shallow pond and a rare grove of mature coastal beech trees. To drive to the trailhead from Pilgrim Heights, follow US 6 north for 4.7 miles into Provincetown. Turn right on Race Point Road at a sign for Province Lands and continue 0.5 mile to the parking area on the left.

DID YOU KNOW?

The treacherous ocean waters and sandbars off Pilgrim Heights and the adjacent outer coast of Cape Cod have caused many shipwrecks. The steamer *Portland* was lost in 1898 with 192 fatalities.

NEARBY

The Highland Lighthouse and Highland House Museum, two well-known Truro landmarks, are on Highland Light Road off US 6. The lighthouse includes a gift shop and has a short path to an overlook with ocean views; tours are offered seasonally. For museum hours and information, call 508-487-3397 or visit trurohistoricalsociety.org/highlandhouse. Several places to eat are on US 6 in Truro, and more options are available in Provincetown.

MORE INFORMATION

The property is open year-round; no fee; restrooms are available at the parking area. The closest National Seashore visitor center is at Province Lands, on Race Point Road off US 6 in Provincetown.

THE BIRTH OF CAPE COD NATIONAL SEASHORE

Cape Cod National Seashore, stretching 40 miles from Nauset Beach in Chatham to Race Point in Provincetown, is one of America's most popular and beloved national parks. An estimated 5 to 6 million people visit annually to enjoy beaches, trails, and diverse natural and historical attractions.

When sitting in heavy weekend traffic or navigating beaches crowded with sunbathers and umbrellas, it's hard to imagine that Cape Cod was once considered an unfashionable, barren, and desolate wasteland. Most of the region's trees had been cut down by the mid-nineteenth century. But in the early twentieth century, when rail lines and increasingly popular automobiles facilitated access from Boston and other southern New England communities, the Cape began its transformation into one of the country's best-known vacation and weekend resort destinations.

In the midst of intensive developmental pressures during the post–World War II building boom, Francis Sargent of the Massachusetts Department of Natural Resources proposed a national park on Outer Cape Cod to Senator John F. Kennedy in 1957. The ambitious plan called for the protection of more than 40,000 acres of ocean beaches and associated habitats.

The timing of the proposal was crucial, occurring at the end of a period when real estate prices were still relatively low and development plans had already been drawn up for Fort Hill and other areas. Shortly after the seashore's designation, land prices skyrocketed to values that likely would have been unacceptable to Congress. Not surprisingly, given the amount of land involved in multiple towns, there was some strong and often emotional local opposition to the project. Longtime Cape Cod residents recall friendships and business relationships that abruptly and permanently ended during the debates.

Nevertheless, the proposal proved successful, as people recognized the value in protecting this fragile landscape. Senator Kennedy, a chief proponent of the project along with Senator Leverett Saltonstall, signed the act establishing Cape National Seashore in August 1961, and the park was officially dedicated in 1966.

In addition to ocean beaches, the National Seashore's varied natural habitats include a rare Atlantic white cedar swamp and coastal beech forest, salt marshes, tidal creeks, and the Great Island peninsula on Cape Cod Bay. Numerous historical sites include three lighthouses and a former Coast Guard lifesaving station in Provincetown; Pilgrim Spring and the Highland Lighthouse in Truro; the Nauset and Three Sisters lighthouses in Eastham; and the site of Guglielmo Marconi's wireless telegraph station in Wellfleet. For information, see nps.gov/caco.

APPENDIX A: CAMPING AND STATE PARKS

NORTH OF BOSTON

Harold Parker State Forest Lorraine Park Campground
133 Jenkins Road, Andover, MA 01810
978-686-3391; mass.gov/locations/harold-parker-state-forest
89 sites for tents, trailers, and RVs; on the Bay Circuit Trail corridor

Pearl Hill State Park
105 New Fitchburg Road, West Townsend, MA 01474
978-597-8802; mass.gov/locations/pearl-hill-state-park
50 sites; abuts Willard Brook State Forest

Salisbury Beach State Reservation
State Reservation Road, Salisbury, MA 01952
978-462-4481; mass.gov/locations/salisbury-beach-state-reservation
484 sites for tents, trailers, and RVs

Willard Brook State Forest
599 Main Street (MA 119), West Townsend, MA 01474
978-597-8802; mass.gov/locations/willard-brook-state-forest
21 sites at Damon Pond; abuts Pearl Hill State Park

Winter Island Maritime Park (town of Salem)
50 Winter Island Road, Salem, MA 01970
978-745-9430; salem.com/winter-island-park
22 tentsites and 28 RV sites on Salem Harbor waterfront

BOSTON AREA

AMC Ponkapoag Camp
P.O. Box 582, Randolph, MA 02368
ponkapoagcamp.org; outdoors.org/community/volunteer-led-camps-and-cabins/
massachusetts-and-new-hampshire/ponkapoag-camp
20 rustic cabins at Ponkapoag Pond in Blue Hills Reservation

Boston Harbor Islands National and State Park
Boston Harbor Islands Welcome Center, 191W Atlantic Avenue, Boston, MA 02110
617-223-8666; bostonharborislands.org
Tentsites and yurts on Peddocks Island; rustic sites on Lovells, Grape, and Bumpkin islands

Camp Nihan Education Center
131 Walnut Street, Saugus, MA 01906
781-233-0834 (Breakheart Reservation); mass.gov/locations/camp-nihan-education-center
Group cabin and tentsites near Breakheart Reservation

Wompatuck State Park
204 Union Street, Hingham, MA 02043
617-895-8245; mass.gov/locations/wompatuck-state-park
More than 260 sites for tents, trailers, and RVs; near Whitney and Thayer Woods

WEST OF BOSTON
Rocky Woods Reservation Campground
38 Hartford Street, Medfield, MA 02052
781-259-3676; thetrustees.org/program/rocky-woods-campground
15 walk-in tentsites; available weekends and holidays

SOUTH OF BOSTON/CAPE COD
Bourne Scenic Park
370 Scenic Highway, Bourne, MA 02532
508-759-7873; bournescenicpark.com
439 sites: tents, cabins, and lodges; on the Cape Cod Canal

Dunes' Edge Campground
386 US 6, Provincetown, MA 02657
508-487-9815; thetrustees.org/place/dunes-edge-campground
85 tentsites and 15 RV sites; managed by The Trustees of Reservations

Horseneck Beach State Reservation
5 John Reed Road, Westport, MA 02791
508-636-8816; mass.gov/locations/horseneck-beach-state-reservation
100 sites for tents, trailers, and RVs; by the ocean

Massasoit State Park
1361 Middleboro Avenue, East Taunton, MA 02718
508-828-4231; mass.gov/locations/massasoit-state-park
Tentsites and RV sites; universally accessible facilities

Myles Standish State Forest
194 Cranberry Road, Carver, MA 02330
508-886-2526; mass.gov/locations/myles-standish-state-forest
400 sites for tents, trailers, and RVs; at kettle ponds

Nickerson State Park
3488 Main Street, Brewster, MA 02631
508-896-3491; mass.gov/locations/nickerson-state-park
418 sites; near Cape Cod Bay and Cape Cod National Seashore

Scusset Beach State Reservation
20 Scusset Beach Road, Sagamore, MA 02562
508-888-0859; mass.gov/locations/scusset-beach-state-reservation
98 RV sites and 5 tentsites; at the Cape Cod Canal

Shawme-Crowell State Forest
42 Main Street, Sandwich, MA 02563
508-888-0351; mass.gov/locations/shawme-crowell-state-forest
285 sites; near the Cape Cod Canal and Cape Cod Bay

Waquoit Bay National Estuarine Research Reserve
131 Waquoit Highway, East Falmouth, MA 02536
508-457-0495; waquoitbayreserve.org/visit-the-reserve/camping
10 sites on Washburn Island (boat access only)

Wellfleet Bay Wildlife Sanctuary
291 State Highway, Route 6, South Wellfleet, MA 02663
508-349-2615; massaudubon.org/get-outdoors/wildlife-sanctuaries/wellfleet-bay
20 sites for Mass Audubon members

Wellfleet Hollow State Campground
180 Old King's Highway, Wellfleet, MA 02667
508-349-3007, mass.gov/locations/wellfleet-hollow-state-campground
108 tentsites; near beaches and the Cape Cod Rail Trail

STATE PARKS (WITHOUT CAMPGROUNDS)
Boston region
Alewife Brook Reservation
Alewife Station Access Road, Cambridge, MA 02140
617-727-9693; mass.gov/locations/alewife-brook-reservation

Beaver Brook Reservation
66 Mill Street, Belmont, MA 02478
617-727-5290; mass.gov/locations/beaver-brook-reservation

Belle Isle Marsh Reservation
1399 Bennington Street, East Boston, MA 02128
617-727-5350; mass.gov/locations/belle-isle-marsh-reservation

Brook Farm Historic Site
670 Baker Street, West Roxbury, MA 02132
617-698-1802; mass.gov/locations/brook-farm-historic-site

Charles River Reservation
1175A Soldiers Field Road, Boston, MA 02116
617-727-4708; mass.gov/locations/charles-river-reservation

Chestnut Hill Reservation
355 Chestnut Hill Avenue, Brighton, MA 02135
617-727-5290; mass.gov/locations/chestnut-hill-reservation

Hammond Pond Reservation
Hammond Pond Parkway, Newton, MA 02168
617-333-7404; mass.gov/locations/hammond-pond-reservation

Hemlock Gorge Reservation
Hamilton Place, Newton, MA 02464
617-333-7407; mass.gov/locations/hemlock-gorge-reservation

Neponset River Reservation
76 Hill Top Street, Boston, MA 02124
617-727-5290; mass.gov/locations/neponset-river-reservation

Pope John Paul II Park Reservation
Hallet Street, Boston, MA 02124
617-727-6034; mass.gov/locations/pope-john-paul-II-park-reservation

Quincy Quarries Reservation
Quincy Quarries, Quincy, MA 02169
617-727-4573; mass.gov/locations/quincy-quarries-reservation

Quincy Shores Reservation
Quincy Shore Drive, Quincy, MA 02170
617-727-5290; mass.gov/locations/quincy-shores-reservation

Southwest Corridor Park
38 New Heath Street (headquarters), Boston, MA 02130
617-727-0057; mass.gov/locations/southwest-corridor-park

North of Boston

Georgetown-Rowely State Forest
Route 97, Georgetown, MA 01833
978-887-5931; mass.gov/locations/georgetown-rowley-state-forest

Lowell-Dracut-Tyngsboro State Forest
Trotting Park Road, Lowell, MA 01850
978-369-6312; mass.gov/locations/lowell-dracut-tyngsboro-state-forest

Maudslay State Park
74 Curzon Mill Road, Newburyport, MA 01950
978-465-7223; mass.gov/locations/maudslay-state-park

Mystic Lakes State Park and Reservation
481 Mystic Valley Parkway, Medford, MA 02155
617-727-5290; mass.gov/locations/mystic-lakes-state-park

Rumney Marsh Reservation
Route 107, Saugus, MA 01906
617-727-5350; mass.gov/locations/rumney-marsh-reservation

Sandy Point State Reservation
Parker River Wildlife Refuge Road, Ipswich, MA 01938
978-462-4481; mass.gov/locations/sandy-point-state-reservation

Willowdale State Forest
252 Ipswich Road, Topsfield, MA 01983
978-877-5931; mass.gov/locations/willowdale-state-forest

Wilson Mountain Reservation
384 Common Street, Dedham, MA 02026
617-698-1802; mass.gov/locations/wilson-mountain-reservation

West of Boston

Ashland State Park
156 West Union Street, Ashland, MA 01721
508-881-4092; mass.gov/locations/ashland-state-park

Cochituate State Park
43 Commonwealth Road, Natick, MA 01760
508-653-9641; mass.gov/locations/cochituate-state-park

Cutler Park Reservation
84 Kendrick Street, Needham, MA 02494
617-698-1802; mass.gov/locations/cutler-park-reservation

Elm Bank Reservation
900 Washington Street, Wellesley, MA 02482
508-653-9641; mass.gov/locations/elm-bank-reservation

Farnham-Connolly State Park
705 Neponset Street, Canton, MA 02021
617-698-1802; mass.gov/locations/farnham-connolly-state-park

Hopkinton State Park
164 Cedar Street, Hopkinton, MA 01748
508-435-4303; mass.gov/locations/hopkinton-state-park

Leo J. Martin Ski Track
190 Park Road, Weston, MA 02493
781-894-4903; mass.gov/locations/leo-j-martin-ski-track

Upper Charles River Reservation
96 Forest Grove Road, Waltham, MA 02453
617-727-1058; mass.gov/locations/upper-charles-river-reservation

Whitehall State Park
300 Wood Street, Hopkinton, MA 01748
508-435-4303; mass.gov/locations/whitehall-state-park

South and Cape Cod

Bristol Blake State Reservation
108 North Street, Norfolk, MA 02056
508-528-3140; mass.gov/locations/bristol-blake-state-reservation

Demarest Lloyd State Park
115 Barneys Joy Road, Dartmouth, MA 02748
508-636-3298 (summer), 508-363-8816 (winter); mass.gov/locations/demarest-lloyd-state-park

Dighton Rock State Park
Third Avenue, Berkley, MA 02779
508-822-7537; mass.gov/locations/dighton-rock-state-park

F. Gilbert Hills State Forest
45 Mill Street, Foxborough, MA 02035
508-543-9084; mass.gov/locations/f-gilbert-hills-state-forest

Fort Phoenix State Reservation
Green Street, Fairhaven, MA 02719
508-992-4524; mass.gov/locations/fort-phoenix-state-reservation

Franklin State Forest
80 Forge Hill Road, Franklin, MA 02038
508-543-9084; mass.gov/locations/franklin-state-forest

Freetown–Fall River State Forest
110 Slab Bridge Road, Assonet, MA 02702
508-644-5522; mass.gov/locations/freetown-fall-river-state-forest

Manuel F. Correllus State Forest
Barnes Road, Edgartown, MA 02539
508-693-2540; mass.gov/locations/manuel-f-correllus-state-forest

Nasketucket Bay State Reservation
Branch Beach Road, Mattapoisett, MA 02739
508-992-4524; mass.gov/locations/nasketucket-bay-state-reservation

Rehoboth State Forest
90 Peck Street, Rehoboth, MA 02769
508-543-9084; mass.gov/locations/rehoboth-state-forest

South Cape Beach State Park
668 Great Oak Road, Mashpee, MA 02649
508-457-0495; mass.gov/locations/south-cape-beach-state-park

Stodder's Neck and Abigail Adams Park
457 Lincoln Street, Hingham, MA 02043
617-727-5293; mass.gov/locations/stodders-neck-abigail-adams-park

Watson Pond State Park
1644 Bay Street, Taunton, MA 02780
508-884-8280; mass.gov/locations/watson-pond-state-park

Webb Memorial State Park
371 River Street, North Weymouth, MA 02191
781-337-8624; mass.gov/locations/webb-memorial-state-park

Wrentham State Forest
690 Taunton Street, Wrentham, MA 02093
508-543-9084; mass.gov/locations/wrentham-state-forest

APPENDIX B: THE BAY CIRCUIT TRAIL

First envisioned nearly 100 years ago by the open-space pioneers Henry Channing, Charles W. Eliot II, and Benton MacKaye (the founder of the Appalachian Trail), the Bay Circuit Trail and Greenway is a permanent recreational trail that connects 37 towns, from Plum Island in Newburyport to Kingston Bay in Duxbury. Arcing through Boston's outer suburbs between Route 128 and Interstate 495, the Bay Circuit Trail (BCT) serves as a longer version of the Emerald Necklace, the chain of parks and open space in the greater Boston area.

The BCT network comprises more than 230 miles of multiuse, passive recreational trails. Connecting trails, such as Charles River Link from Newton to Medfield, branch off the main route and link more tracts of protected land and historical sites. These routes provide additional points to gain access to the BCT, extending its reach into more communities. Although the trail primarily winds through woods, wetlands, and fields, some sections follow scenic country roads, passing many points of historical interest; other sections follow sidewalks in villages.

The concept of walking in peaceful solitude through so large a portion of highly developed eastern Massachusetts is exciting. The Bay Circuit Trail not only provides urban and suburban dwellers with critical connections to green spaces but also draws nature lovers into the nation's past, when American Indians followed footpaths from one tribal land to another and from inland hunting grounds to the coast. As more people discover and explore the BCT, it has the potential to galvanize the public around protecting more of our open spaces before it's too late.

While the vision for the Bay Circuit Trail dates to 1929, it wasn't until the 1980s that the trail became a reality, when what is now called the Massachusetts Department of Conservation and Recreation funded trail planning and some very important land acquisitions. The greenway has been expanded by more than 4,000 acres since the 1980s. A key component was the connection across the Massachusetts Turnpike in Ashland. In the 1990s, the Bay Circuit Alliance, an entirely volunteer organization, was formed. Initially spearheaded by Alan French, who retired in 2012 after twenty years of leadership, the alliance is a dynamic partnership of towns, organizations, and dedicated individuals.

Since 2012, the Appalachian Mountain Club has led the Bay Circuit Alliance in the completion, enhancement, and long-term protection of the greenway. Ongoing projects include improving existing sections, moving the trail off-road wherever possible, and filling the few remaining gaps. In 2015, AMC published the *Bay Circuit Trail Map and Guide* (available at amcstore.outdoors.org/collections/trail-guides-maps/products/bay-circuit-trail-map -and-guide), which features three large sheet maps showing the trail and numerous conservation areas along the corridor. Also included are more than 30 multiuse trip suggestions, safety tips, and information about the natural and cultural history of the BCT corridor. For updated trail maps and details, including a virtual "story" map that highlights history, nature, indigenous experiences, and stewardship, visit baycircuit.org.

Volunteers are an integral part of the Bay Circuit Trail. Some of the many ways to participate include trail maintenance and improvement, leading walks, planning, and fundraising.

Massachusetts has a well-established network of long-distance trails. The Appalachian Trail runs through the Berkshires; the New England National Scenic Trail travels through the Connecticut River Valley; and the Midstate Trail winds through central Massachusetts. Thanks to the development of the Bay Circuit Trail, millions of residents in eastern Massachusetts now enjoy similar recreational opportunities close to home. To learn more, visit baycircuit.org.

The following hikes in this book are part of the Bay Circuit Trail:
- Trip 16: Ward Reservation
- Trip 17: Baker's Meadow
- Trip 18: Bald Hill Reservation
- Trip 20: Bradley Palmer State Park
- Trip 22: Old Town Hill
- Trip 30: Great Meadows National Wildlife Refuge
- Trip 31: Minute Man National Historical Park: Battle Road Trail
- Trip 32: Walden Pond
- Trip 33: Lincoln Conservation Land
- Trip 34: Nobscot Hill and Tippling Rock
- Trip 35: Callahan State Park
- Trip 36: Sudbury Reservoir
- Trip 38: Rocky Narrows Reservation and Sherborn Town Forest
- Trip 41: Moose Hill Wildlife Sanctuary
- Trip 42: Borderland State Park
- Trip 48: Burrage Pond

INDEX

A

Abington, trips near, xii–xiii, 198–201
Adams National Historical Park, 66
Addison Gallery of American Art, 78
Allens Pond Wildlife Sanctuary, xiv–xv, 229–233
Amelia Earhart residence, 7
Ames Nowell State Park, xii–xiii, 198–201
Andover, trips near, x–xi, 75–78, 80–83
Arnold Arboretum, viii–ix, 29–33
azaleas, 214

B

Bacon Free Library, 172
Baker's Meadow, x–xi, 80–83
Bald Hill Reservation, x–xi, 84–87
Barnstable, trips near, xiv–xv, 251–255
Barnstable Harbor, 254
Bay Circuit Trail (BCT), 83, 286–287
    in Metro West region, 155–158, 164–167,
        173–176
    in Northeastern Massachusetts, 75–78, 85,
        94–96, 102–104, 173–176
beaches. *See* ocean access
Bellevue Hill, 42
Benjamin Caryl House, 181
bicycling, recommended trips
    in Northeastern Massachusetts, 93–96
    in Southeastern Massachusetts/Cape Cod,
        194–196, 217–220, 221–224, 238–242,
        256–259, 275–278
birdwatching, recommended locations
    in Boston urban/inner suburban region, 5,
        22–23, 26, 32, 36, 42, 60
    Metro West region, 123, 135, 139–140, 144,
        169–171
    in Northeast Massachusetts, 84, 86, 95–96,
        97–101, 105, 106, 109, 117
    in Southeastern Massachusetts/Cape Cod, 204,
        223–224, 226, 229–231, 236–237, 243,
        246, 250, 261–262, 265–269, 277
Blue Hill Meteorological Observatory, 47–48

Blue Hills Reservation
    Great Blue Hill Green loop, viii–ix, 49–52
    history of, 48
    Houghton's Pond Yellow Dot loop, viii–ix,
        58–61
    Observation Tower loop, viii–ix, 44–47
    Ponkapoag Pond, viii–ix, 53–57
    Skyline Trail, viii–ix, 62–66
Blue Hills Trailside Museum, 52, 66
boat rentals, 15, 257, 259
bog environments, 79
    cranberry bogs, 216
Borderland State Park, xii–xiii, 194–196
Boston, hikes within city limits, viii–ix, 29–33,
    34–37, 39–43
Boston urban/inner suburban region
    easy hikes in, 25–28, 29–33, 34–37, 39–43,
        49–52, 53–57, 58–61
    moderate hikes in, 8–11, 21–24, 25–28, 29–33,
        44–47, 49–52
    region description, 1–2
    strenuous hikes in, 12–15, 62–66
Boxford, trips near, x–xi, 84–87
Boxford State Forest, 84–87
Bradley Palmer State Park, x–xi, 93–96
Breakheart Reservation, viii–ix, 21–24
Brewster, trips near, xiv–xv, 256–259
Broadmoor Wildlife Sanctuary, xii–xiii, 169–172
Burrage Pond, xii–xiii, 221–224

C

Callahan State Park, xii–xiii, 159–163
camping, 280–282
    in Boston urban/inner suburban region, 56, 66,
        280–281
    Leave No Trace principles, xxiv–xxv
    in Metro West region, 281
    in Northeast Massachusetts, 105, 280
    in Southeastern Massachusetts/Cape Cod, 205,
        217, 233, 242, 256, 281–282

Canton, trips near, viii–ix, 44–47, 49–52, 53–57, 62–66
Cape Ann, 115–118
Cape Cod. *See* Southeastern Massachusetts/Cape Cod
Cape Cod National Seashore, 279
    Great Island region, xiv–xv, 270–274
    Pilgrim Heights region, xiv–xv, 275–278
Cape Cod Rail Trail, 259
Carlisle, trips near, x–xi, 134–137
carnivorous plants, 79
Carver, trips near, 238–242
Castle Hill, 109
Charles W. Ward Reservation, x–xi, 75–78
chestnut trees, 38
children, recommended trips for
    in Boston urban/inner suburban region, 8–11, 25–28, 29–33, 34–37, 39–43, 44–47, 49–52, 53–57, 58–61
    in Metro West region, 121–124, 126–129, 130–133, 134–137, 138–141, 142–145, 146–149, 151–154, 155–158, 159–163, 164–168, 169–172, 173–176, 178–181, 182–185
    in Northeastern Massachusetts, 71–74, 80–83, 84–87, 88–92, 93–96, 97–101, 102–105, 115–118
    in Southeastern Massachusetts/Cape Cod, 189–193, 194–196, 198–201, 202–205, 207–211, 212–215, 217–220, 221–224, 225–228, 229–233, 234–237, 238–242, 243–246, 247–250, 256–259, 260–263, 265–269, 275–278
climate change, 206
Cohasset, trips near, xii–xiii, 212–215
common loons, 117, 123, 246
Concord, trips near, x–xi, xii–xiii, 138–141, 142–145, 146–149
coyotes, 107–108, 175, 213
cranberry bogs, 216, 227
Crane Beach, x–xi, 106–110
Crane Wildlife Refuge, 109
cross-country skiing, recommended trips
    in Boston urban/inner suburban region, 8–11, 16–20, 21–24, 25–28, 34–37, 39–43, 49–52, 53–57, 58–61
    in Metro West region, 130–133, 134–137, 138–141, 142–145, 146–149, 151–154, 164–168, 169–172, 173–176, 178–181, 182–185

    in Northeastern Massachusetts, 71–74, 75–78, 80–83, 84–87, 93–96, 106–110, 111–114
    in Southeastern Massachusetts/Cape Cod, 189–193, 194–196, 207–211, 212–215, 225–228, 238–242, 247–250, 251–255, 256–259, 260–263
cycling. *See* bicycling, recommended trips

D

Dartmouth, trips near, xiv–xv, 229–233
Dover, trips near, xii–xiii, 178–181
drinking water, xxi
Drumlin Farm, 153
Dungeon Rock, 27–28
Duxbury, trips near, xiv–xv, 225–228

E

eastern timber rattlesnake, 67
Eastham, trips near, 260–263
East Taunton, trips near, xii–xiii, 217–220
easy hikes
    in Boston urban/inner suburban region, 25–28, 29–33, 34–37, 39–43, 49–52, 53–57, 58–61
    in Metro West region, 121–124, 126–129, 130–133, 134–137, 138–141, 146–149, 164–168, 182–185
    in Northeastern Massachusetts, 75–78, 80–83, 84–87, 88–92, 93–96, 97–101, 102–105, 111–114, 115–118
    in Southeastern Massachusetts/Cape Cod, 198–201, 202–205, 212–215, 221–224, 229–233, 234–237, 243–246, 247–250, 256–259, 260–263, 265–269, 275–278
Ellisville Harbor State Park, xiv–xv, 243–246
emerald ash borer, 38

F

Fairhaven, trips near, xiv–xv, 234–237
Fern's Country Store, 136
fishing, recommended locations
    in Boston urban/inner suburban region, 42
    in Metro West region, 123–124, 164–168, 182–185
    in Northeastern Massachusetts, 58–61
    in Southeastern Massachusetts/Cape Cod, 198–201, 205, 223, 247–250
Flynn Ice Rink, 15
food, xxi
Forbes House Museum, 52
Fort Hill, 260–263
Fort Warren, 37

Framingham, trips near, xii–xiii, 155–158, 159–163, 164–168
Friends of the Middlesex Feels Reservation, 11
Fruitlands Museum, 133
Fuller Craft Museum, 201

G

Garden in the Woods, 163
gear, essential, xxi–xxii
Georges Island, 37
Gloucester, trips near, x–xi, 111–114
Gloucester Fisherman's Memorial, 114
Great Blue Hill, 48
Great Brook Farm State Park, x–xi, 134–137
Great Brook Ski Touring Center, 137
Great Cedar Swamp, 224
Great Esker Park, xii–xiii, 202–205
Great Island, xiv–xv, 270–274
Great Meadows National Wildlife Refuge, x–xi, 138–141
great white sharks, 264
Griffin Museum of Photography, 11

H

Halibut Point State Park and Reservation, x–xi, 115–118
Halifax, trips near, xii–xiii, 221–224
Hamilton, trips near, x–xi, 93–96
handicapped accessible trails. *See* universally accessible trails
Hanson, trips near, xii–xiii, 221–224
Harvard, trips near, x–xi, 130–133
hemlock trees, 38
hemlock woolly adelgid (HWA), 31, 38
herons, 23, 56, 139–140, 176
Highland House Museum, 278
Highland Lighthouse, 278
Hingham, trips near, xii–xiii, 207–211, 212–215
horseback riding, recommended locations
    in Southeastern Massachusetts/Cape Cod, 194–196, 217–220, 238–242
Horseneck Beach State Reservation, 233
Houghton's Pond, 58–61

I

ice skating, 13–15
insects, xxii–xxiii
climate change and, 206
invasive species, 38, 100, 206
Ipswich, trips near, x–xi, 106–110
Ipswich River, 92
Ipswich River Wildlife Sanctuary, x–xi, 88–92

J

John C. Phillips Wildlife Sanctuary, 84–87
Jonathan Wade House, 7

K

kettle-hole ponds, 79, 216, 276–277
King Philip's Overlook, 173–176
King Philip's War, 177

L

Lake Cochituate, 167
Lake Massapoag, 196
Leave No Trace principles, xxiv–xxv
Lexington, trips near, x–xi, 142–145
lighthouses, 118, 253, 263, 278
Lincoln, trips near, x–xi, xii–xiii, 142–145, 151–154
Lincoln Conservation Land, xii–xiii, 151–154
Little Brewster Island, 37
Longfellow's Wayside Inn, 158
lookout towers, trips featuring
    in Boston urban/inner suburban area, 5, 27–28, 44–47, 64
    in Metro West region, 139
    in Northeastern Massachusetts, 99
loons, 117, 123, 246
Lowell Holly Reservation, xiv–xv, 247–250
Lynn, trips near, viii–ix, 25–28
Lynn Museum and Historical Society, 28
Lynn Woods Reservation, viii–ix, 25–28

M

Malden, trips near, viii–ix, 12–15, 16–20
Mashpee, trips near, xiv–xv, 247–250
Massasoit State Park, xii–xiii, 217–220
Mass Audubon's Museum of American Bird Art, 57
Mass Audubon's Norman Smith Environmental Education Center, 66
Medfield, trips near, viii–ix, xii–xiii, 12–15, 16–20, 182–185
Medford, trips near, 3–7, 8–11
Melrose, trips near, viii–ix, 12–15, 16–20
Metro West region
    easy hikes in, 121–124, 126–129, 130–133, 134–137, 138–141, 146–149, 164–168, 182–185
    moderate hikes in, 142–145, 151–154, 155–158, 159–163, 169–172, 173–176, 178–181, 182–185
    region description, 119–120

Middlesex Fells
    Cross Fells Trail, viii–ix, 16–20
    Reservoir Trail, viii–ix, 8–11
    Rock Circuit Trail, viii–ix, 12–15
    Skyline Trail, viii–ix, 3–7
Milton, trips near, viii–ix, 44–47, 49–52, 58–61, 62–66
Minute Man National Historical Park, x–xi, 142–145
mockingbirds, 14
moderate hikes
    in Boston urban/inner suburban region, 8–11, 16–20, 21–24, 25–28, 29–33, 44–47, 49–52
    in Metro West region, 142–145, 151–154, 155–158, 159–163, 169–172, 173–176, 178–181, 182–185
    in Northeastern Massachusetts, 71–74, 75–78, 80–83, 84–87, 88–92, 102–105, 106–110, 111–114
    in Southeastern Massachusetts/Cape Cod, 189–193, 194–196, 207–211, 217–220, 225–228, 229–233, 238–242, 247–250, 251–255, 256–259, 270–274
Moose Hill Wildlife Sanctuary, xii–xiii, 189–193
Moseley Estate, 101
Motif No. 1, 118
mountain biking, 20, 114, 196. *See also* bicycling, recommended trips
Mount Pisgah Conservation Area, x–xi, 126–129
Myles Standish Burial Ground, 228
Myles Standish State Forest, 238–242

N

Nasketucket Bird Club, 237
Natick, trips near, xii–xiii, 169–172
Nauset Lighthouse, 263
Neponset River Reservation, 47
Newbury, trips near, x–xi, 102–105
Newburyport, trips near, x–xi, 97–101
Nickerson State Park, xiv–xv, 256–259
Noanet Woodlands, xii–xiii, 178–181
Nobscot Hill, xii–xiii, 155–158
Noon Hill Reservation, 177
Norman Smith Environmental Education Center, 47, 52
North Andover, trips near, x–xi, 71–74
North Andover Historical Society, 74
Northborough, trips near, x–xi, 126–129
Northeastern Massachusetts
    easy hikes in, 75–78, 80–83, 84–87, 88–92, 93–96, 97–101, 102–105, 111–114, 115–118

    moderate hikes in, 71–74, 75–78, 80–83, 84–87, 88–92, 102–105, 106–110, 111–114
    region description, 69–70
North Easton, trips near, xii–xiii, 194–196
North Hill Marsh Wildlife Sanctuary, xiv–xv, 225–228

O

ocean access, hikes including
    in Northeastern Massachusetts, 105, 106–110, 115–118
    in Southeastern Massachusetts/Cape Cod, 233, 234–237, 243–246, 251–255, 265–269, 270–274
Old Colony History Museum, 220, 224
Old Manse, 145
Old North Bridge, 145
Old Stone Church, 124
Old Town Hill, x–xi, 102–105
Oxbow National Wildlife Refuge, x–xi, 130–133
oysters, 273

P

Parker River National Wildlife Refuge, x–xi, 97–101
Peabody, Amelia, 181
Penny Bridge, 28
Plymouth, trips near, xiv–xv, 238–242, 243–246
poison ivy, xxii
Ponkapoag Camp, 57, 66
public transportation, trips accessible by
    in Boston urban/inner suburban region, 3–7, 8–11, 12–15, 16–20, 21–24, 25–28, 29–33, 34–37, 39–43, 44–47, 49–52, 53–57, 58–61, 62–66
    in Metro West region, 138–141, 142–145, 146–149, 151–154
    in Northeastern Massachusetts, 106–110, 115–118
    in Southeastern Massachusetts/Cape Cod, 189–193, 202–205, 207–211, 260–263, 270–274, 275–278

Q

Quabbin Reservoir, 125
Quashnet Woods State Reservation, 251
Quincy, trips near, viii–ix, 62–66

R

Randolph, trips near, viii–ix, 53–57
rattlesnakes, 67
Ravenswood Park, x–xi, 111–114

rhododendrons, 212–215
Robbins Museum, 220
The Rockery, 88–91
Rockport, trips near, x–xi, 115–118
Rocky Narrows Reservation, xii–xiii, 173–176
Rocky Woods Reservation, xii–xiii, 182–185

S

safety considerations, xxi–xxiii
Salisbury Beach State Reservation, 105
Sandwich, trips near, xiv–xv, 247–250
Sandy Neck, xiv–xv, 251–255
Saugus, trips near, viii–ix, 21–24
Saugus Iron Works National Historic Site, 24
seals, 116–117, 243–246, 265
sharks, 264
Sharon, trips near, xii–xiii, 189–193
Sherborn, trips near, xii–xiii, 169–172, 173–176
Sherborn Town Forest, xii–xiii, 173–176
snakes, 67, 231, 267
snapping turtles, 90
Solstice Stones, 75–77
Southborough, trips near, xii–xiii, 164–168
Southeastern Massachusetts/Cape Cod
    easy hikes in, 198–201, 202–205, 212–215,
        221–224, 229–233, 234–237, 243–246,
        247–250, 256–259, 260–263, 265–269,
        275–278
    moderate hikes in, 189–193, 194–196,
        207–211, 217–220, 225–228, 229–233,
        238–242, 247–250, 251–255, 256–259,
        270–274
    region description, 187–188
    strenuous hikes in, 238–242
South Wellfleet, trips near, xiv–xv, 265–269
Spectacle Island, viii–ix, 34–37
Spot Pond, 14–15
state park contact information, 280–285
Stellwagen Bank, 254
Stoneham, trips near, viii–ix, 3–7, 8–11, 16–20
Stone Zoo, 20
Stony Brook Reservation, viii–ix, 39–43
strenuous hikes
    in Boston urban/inner suburban region, 3–7,
        12–15, 16–20, 62–66
    in Southeastern Massachusetts/Cape Cod,
        238–242
Sudbury, trips near, xii–xiii, 155–158
Sudbury Reservoir, xii–xiii, 164–168
Sunset Beach Reservation, 246
swimming, recommended locations
    in Boston urban/inner suburban region, 24,
        58–61

    in Metro West region, 146–149
    in Northeastern Massachusetts, 106–110
    in Southeastern Massachusetts/Cape Cod,
        243–246, 247–250, 251–255, 256–259,
        270–274

T

Thoreau, Henry David, 119, 148–150, 267. *See also*
    Walden Pond
Thoreau Farm, 148
Three Sisters (lighthouses), 263
tide pools, 117–118
Tippling Rock, xii–xiii, 155–158
Topsfield, trips near, x–xi, 88–92, 93–96
Topsfield Fair, 92
Tougas Family Farm, 129
trip planning, xxi–xxiii
Truro, trips near, xiv–xv, 275–278
turtles, 51

U

Underground Railroad, 177
universally accessible trails
    in Boston urban/inner suburban region, 35
    in Metro West region, 149, 169–172, 184
    in Northeastern Massachusetts, 75–78, 97–101
    in Southeastern Massachusetts/Cape Cod,
        229–233, 263, 265–269

W

Wachusett Reservoir, x–xi
Wachusett Reservoir and Reservation, 121–125
Waiting Hill, 228
Walden Pond, xii–xiii, 146–149
Ward Reservation, 79
water supply reservoirs, 125
Webb Memorial State Park, 205
Weir Hill Reservation, x–xi, 71–74
Wellfleet, trips near, xiv–xv, 270–274
Wellfleet Bay Wildlife Sanctuary, xiv–xv, 265–269
Wellfleet Drive-In Theater, 269
West Boylston, trips near, x–xi, 121–124
West Island, xiv–xv, 234–237
West of Boston. See Metro West region
Weymouth, trips near, xii–xiii, 202–205
whale-watching, 245, 254, 273
Whitney and Thayer Woods, xii–xiii, 212–215
Willowdale State Forest, 96
Winchester, trips near, viii–ix, 3–7, 8–11
Witch Hollow Farm, 87
Wompatuck State Park, 205, 210, 215
World's End Reservation, xii–xiii, 207–211

ABOUT THE AUTHORS

Michael Tougias is a *New York Times* best-selling author and co-author of 25 books, including *The Finest Hours*. **John S. Burk** is a photographer, historian, and author of multiple books, including AMC's *Massachusetts Trail Guide*. **Alison O'Leary** is a longtime journalist, public speaker, and the author of several books, including *Inns and Adventures: A History* and *Explorer's Guide to Vermont, New Hampshire, and the Berkshires.*

ABOUT AMC IN MASSACHUSETTS

The Appalachian Mountain Club has four active chapters in Massachusetts: Boston, Southeastern Massachusetts, Worcester, and Western Massachusetts. Each offers a range of activities, from rock climbing and backpacking to local walks, skiing, paddling, and cycling. Each chapter also offers social and young member events. A complete listing of upcoming events is available on activities.outdoors.org.

Chapter volunteers are active in maintaining the state's long trails, including the Appalachian, New England, Midstate, and Bay Circuit trails. Volunteers also manage two self-service lodging options: Noble View Outdoor Center in the Pioneer Valley and Ponkapoag Camp in the Blue Hills Reservation near Boston.

AMC works closely with youth agencies in Boston and Worcester through its Educator Outdoors Program, offering leadership training, equipment, and support to agency staff. AMC also advocates on behalf of sound land conservation, energy, climate, and clean air policies in the Commonwealth.

AMC BOOK UPDATES

AMC Books strives to keep our guidebooks as up-to-date as possible to help you plan safe and enjoyable adventures. If we learn after publishing a book that relevant trails have been relocated or route or contact information has changed, we will post the updated information online. Before you hit the trail, visit outdoors.org/books-maps and click "Book Updates." While hiking, if you notice discrepancies with the trip descriptions or maps, or if you find any other errors in this book, please let us know by submitting them to amcbookupdates@outdoors.org or to Books Editor, c/o AMC, 10 City Square, Boston, MA 02129. We will verify all submissions and post key updates each month. AMC Books is dedicated to being a recognized leader in outdoor publishing. Thank you for your participation.

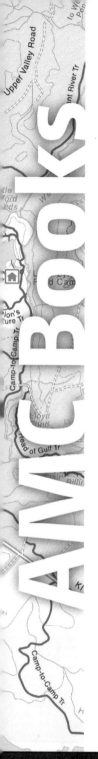